HELLROARING
The Life and Times of a Fire Bum

by

Peter M. Leschak

North Star Press of St. Cloud, Inc.

DEDICATION

For all my fellow fire bums, but especially for Minnesota DNR Smokechasers—the only contemporary Americans I know of who must work 106 hours in a two-week pay period before they earn overtime. Is it any wonder we love the BIG fires?

Credits:

Chapter One — A condensed version appeared in a September 1988 issue of *The Twin Cities Reader,* and in the March/April 1989 issue of *Minnesota Fire Chief.*

Chapter Two — A portion appeared in the September 1987 issue of *Minnesota Monthly,* and the September/October 1988 issue of *The Minnesota Volunteer.*

Chapter Four — A portion appeared in the July 1989 issue of *Harper's Magazine.*

Chapter Nine — A slightly different version appeared in the November 10, 1989 edition of *The Pioneer Press/Dispatch,* and the August 1994 issue of *Minneapolis/St. Paul Magazine.*

Chapter Ten — A portion appeared in the summer 1991 issue of *The Fireman's Journal,* and in the July/August 1991 issue of *Minnesota Fire Chief.*

Cover art and illustrations: Mark Coyle

921
LESCHAK
LES

Copyright © 1994 Peter M. Leschak

ISBN: 0-87839-087-1

Published by North Star Press of St. Cloud, Inc.
P.O. Box 451, St. Cloud, Minnesota 56302.

Contents

Introduction

I keep an empty turtle shell on the window sill. It's discolored and peeling, but not from decay. The shell was burned over by a wildfire in Minnesota during the crackling-dry season of 1988. Its occupant was completely incinerated along with several other turtles who couldn't escape a fast-moving blaze that ripped across normally soggy ground. The baked shell is pathetic but eloquent—a reminder of the hazards inherent to the fireground.

It can get ugly out there. I've been poisoned by carbon monoxide in Oregon, showered with burning embers in Wyoming, spiked out in a mud puddle in Idaho, threatened by grizzlies in Montana, and I've broken through swamp ice in Minnesota. I've been burned, bruised, scraped and lacerated. I've twisted my back, blistered my feet, torn cartilage in my knee. Though never seriously injured, I acknowledge that in some cases only luck eased me through. It's often said that we make our own luck, and maybe sometimes we do, but luck is also a free, unearned gift. Those turtles were extremely unlucky.

But the vacant shell on the sill doesn't speak to the joy, to the occasional moments when firefighters understand they're among the blessed of the earth, and that all other jobs are as ashes beneath their boots.

On a Minnesota April afternoon in 1991, for example, my engine crew and I were staked out on a hill, pre-positioned on a dry, windy day, scanning the horizons for smoke. We had battled one fire that morning—a small, but satisfying blaze that had primed us for more action. At about 3:00 PM Lonnie said, "Check that out!"

Due north and only a mile or two away was a column of dense smoke, perhaps on the outskirts of a nearby town. As we rolled downhill I got on the radio to report it, and was given a "go" to respond. We raced along the highway, the smoke plainly in sight, and, as we topped a rise, we saw long flames in tall grass pushed by wind and snapping for a garage and house.

By then another forestry engine and the local volunteer fire department were only moments behind, but we were first, and, as I swung into the yard between the fire and the buildings, we were delighted to be in precisely the right spot at exactly the right time. Dispatch asked if we needed a heli-

1

copter, and I was able to reply "Negative!" just before I hopped out of the truck to grab a pump can. This fire was ours, and we were a practiced team.

Lonnie spun out the passenger door and made two quick strides to the pump controls. Phil scrambled onto the truck, grasped the hose nozzle and vaulted over the reel. As Lonnie started the pump, Phil jumped off the other side of the truck, trotting as he hit the ground—water already spraying. He waded into fire and Lonnie and I backed him up with pump cans. In less than ninety seconds, the flames were knocked down, and what had looked like a swelling wave of ferocious fire was reduced to smoldering hummocks and dust devils of ash. The next engine in had little to do.

A couple of eight-year-old boys had rushed over to witness our assault from near the garage, and I heard one exclaim to his pal: "Gee, Jimmy, it was just like Desert Storm!"

We still laugh about that, but the smoke lingering in my nostrils supported a decidedly sweet aroma.

I'm writing this on a warm spring-like day in mid-March. But the snow is still deep, and it'll be at least a week or two before I'm called to resume the life of a traveling freelance firefighter—a "fire bum." I'll start with the Minnesota Department of Natural Resources and fight fires in the northwoods through April and into May. By mid-June I'll be with the U.S. Forest Service in Idaho, tracking the fire season west. In autumn it's back to Minnesota blazes, until snowfall blankets the forest and curtails the payroll. By then I'll probably be ready for winter, ready to rest like a tired old bear.

But here in March I'm consumed by anticipation for the annual initiation of the other half of my life. Fire season's just over the horizon, about to burgeon into a blaze of heat and light—a rising sun of opportunity, income, and adventure. Buddies will surface, unseen for six months. Paydays, lean and/or non-existent over winter, will put on weight. Soot-stained gear smelling faintly of woodsmoke and Nomex will be dragged out of closets, primped and inspected for worthiness, not unlike the tackle box of an avid angler eager for ice-out.

At age forty-one I'm uncertain how many seasons I have left; the fireground offers no quarter, and, like an aging ballplayer, I'll probably push it too far—until some critical body part finally gives way. But I am certain of this: I don't regret a single moment spent on a fire, and when my career is done I shall pine for fire season as for a lost love. To mumble wistfully of "an old flame" will carry special meaning.

A line from the poetry of Schiller resonates in my head: "Drunk with fire, toward Heaven advancing,/Goddess, to thy shrine we come."

Indeed. I'll show you the way.

"I have a smoke to report." — George Henley,
fire lookout, Yellowstone, June 23, 1988

A Night on
Shadow Mountain

It was the night Dave fell down the mountain. Ordinarily such trauma would have been reason enough for remembering a particular shift. Our fourteen-hour stints on the fireline—bracketed by a hasty breakfast, fitful daylight sleep (on the ground), and then dinner—easily merged into a single span of shadows and smoke. But that night, August 24-25, 1988, would've been memorable even if Dave hadn't nearly been killed.

We were traversing the flanks of Shadow Mountain, just across the Snake River from the Grand Tetons. It was the Hunter Fire, twenty miles south of Yellowstone National Park. The sunset was a fabulous revue of the spectrum. The sky melted from deep tangerine to feathery purplish-rose—sunlight filtered by dust and smoke. Waves of molded light silhouetted the peaks, shading mountains to violet. It was a post-card evening, the kind of Wyoming dusk Ansel Adams would have gladly waited a month to shoot. Our crew members who packed cameras snapped pictures, enduring wry cracks about being paid tourists. The comments were funny only because nothing could be further from the truth.

A few days before, our twenty-person crew and five others had assembled at the Duluth National Guard Armory, summoned from various parts of Minnesota, Wisconsin, and Michigan. We were a mix of full-time government foresters (U.S. Forest Service, Minnesota Department of Natural Resources, Bureau of Indian Affairs), and "casuals"—that is, firefighting freelancers. Only a handful of the 120 people present were rookies. Upon our return a few weeks later, the Duluth *News-Tribune* would refer to us as "experienced . . . professional firefighters" in contrast to the tenderfoot hordes recruited through the Job Service and dispatched to the West like so much cannon fodder for Uncle Smokey (much to the horror of veterans, whose crews were taking enough casualties as it was; but such was the mood in the blazing summer of '88.)

At a supply depot established in the Armory, each firefighter was outfitted with gear—everything from earplugs to sleeping bags—then we gathered to fill out the all-important time sheets. As a casual (an "AD-II") in federal parlance), my wage was $7.40 per hour straight time: No hazard pay, no overtime. It's low scale for such demanding duty, but the hours pile up in a hurry. Fifteen members of our crew—Superior-4 (the fourth crew of the season dispatched by Superior National Forest)—were casuals, and I knew we could expect to earn over $2,000 apiece during a standard twenty-one-day tour.

I reminded myself of that as we humped along the steep trails of Shadow Mountain. We were near 9,000 feet, and it was literally breathtaking. As flatlanders we were still acclimating to the thinner atmosphere, made doubly taxing by smoke. The night was fairly clear, but Overhead (the fire management team) seemed ever fond of informing the media that on the smokiest days, when temperature inversions subdue the noontime sun to a pale orange glow, simply breathing is the equivalent of smoking four packs of cigarettes. It's no wonder some fire camps sound like TB wards; it's not unusual to witness coughing jags that drop people to their knees.

Since it was our fourth shift, we were feeling more comfortable, not only with the air supply, but with each other. One of the charms—and challenges—of fire duty is being transported to hazardous locales in the company of strangers. As a veteran, having many friends and acquaintances in the Minnesota wildfire community, I was fortunate to know five other members of the crew when we matriculated at Duluth.

Todd rode with me from home, and we had chattered like high-strung squirrels the entire hundred miles. Though a seasoned Minnesota firefighter, this was his first trip out West, and he was animated by a pulse-quickening blend of joy and anxiety. He was aimed for adventure, high on the prospect of fresh experience, and a little giddy to be leaving his family and taking this blatant risk. I told him what to expect, summarizing the hard-won "fire grunt" wisdom I'd gleaned on other "gigs." The first problem was going to be footgear. His worn, flat-soled work boots had served him well enough in the north woods but would never cut it on a mountain fire. But not to worry; I glibbly assured him the Forest Service supply people would take care of him, and then hoped like hell I was right. Still, it was pure pleasure to play the role of grizzled old vet and take Todd under my wing. He was a freelancer like me. He signed on with the Minnesota DNR during fire seasons, then worked part time at a golf course in the summer, and clerked at an auto parts store in winter. He was twenty-seven, with a wife and kid, and was constantly hunting for a decent full-time job; but, on our early-morning drive to Duluth, we chortled gleefully about the freedom that allowed us to take off like a couple of teenagers, with only a few hours notice, and catch a plane to "the fire of the century." Fire duty is like marriage—you'd better be enthusiastic at the start if you expect to thrive till the end.

The drought had extended our usual spring fire season well into summer, and I had met three others—Tom, Bear, and Lurch—while working fires in central Minnesota in mid-June. Tom was in his early twenties, an ex-marine at war with the world. He was a temporary employee of the Minnesota DNR, working on conservation projects for little better than minimum wage. He was a cynical wisecracker, deeply distrustful of constituted authority, and a self-described "wildass." During our week together in June, I'd learned he was a tenacious, dependable worker but had a weakness for alcohol. When he drank he got mean and had to be watched. Still, I liked Tom. He had a rasping, biting sense of humor that could make fun without offending, and he was often a morale booster. Though sometimes hardbitten, there was no deception in him. He and I had suffered through a particularly cruel day on the stubborn flank of one of the six fires we hit that week. It was ninety-seven degrees and the woods were baked to tinder. Tom and I had emptied about fifteen five-gallon backpack pump cans apiece, fighting flare-ups all day as fire repeatedly rekindled in the dry wind. We were battered—enduring pounding headaches and muscle cramps due to dehydration and exhaustion. One of our crew had collapsed. During a break we had asked each other what we were doing there—seriously, probing for answers. We found a common bond in the simple satisfaction of THE STRUGGLE. We both mentioned money, of course, and Lord knows we wouldn't have been there out of the goodness of our hearts, but I concluded we relished the conflict most. Tom said fire duty sometimes reminded him of the Marine Corps, and he'd hated the service, but conceded that "fire sucks, but it sure beats the hell out of brushing snowmobile trails." I replied that, though it would feel good to be done and head home, it would also be good to be called out again. Tom ran out of cigarettes, and we shared my snuff. "Thank God you've got some left," he said.

Bear was still enigmatic. I'd only seen him a few times during that hot week—never exchanged a word. He was usually driving a J-5 Bombardier, a small-tracked vehicle with a water tank and hose reel. He had a survival knife strapped to his web gear, and I noticed an Army Airborne logo affixed to the sheath. He was built like a fullback, with short blond hair in a military cut, and had a solemn demeanor. He looked like someone to automatically treat politely, and I would discover later that this was wise.

Lurch was as voluble as Bear was taciturn. He was a six-foot-five, 240-pound Finn with a blaze-orange helmet and a personality to match. He was forty-two, a veteran of many fire seasons—in Minnesota and out West—with the stamina of an ox and the mischieviousness of a brat. He seemed to know everyone and, in addition to a penchant for practical jokes, had a gift for scrounging. He could charm and/or bullshit his way into a kitchen or cache that was off limits to everyone else and come away laden with goodies ranging from extra desserts to air mattresses. But the first time I had met him was on an incident he didn't advertise. Our crew had just arrived in central Minnesota, and Lurch was one of the locals, directing us through our first day in unfamiliar territory. He was in charge of his pride and joy, an old two-and-a-half-ton, 6x6 army truck converted into a 1,000-gallon water tender. Lurch had proudly shown us the plywood sidebox he'd recently designed and built for the unit. It was an impressive piece of cabinetry, conveniently arranged for the storage of hose, fittings, and tools—sturdily constructed with tight-fitting doors. Our compliments were genuine. We were using the tender to mop up a peat fire when we were called to a new blaze. Lurch and I jumped into the 6x6, and he blasted off like he was driving a Corvette, not a two-and-a-half-ton military surplus hulk. I had a death-grip on the narrow dash as we careened down dusty backroads toward a burgeoning column of smoke. As we neared a flank of the fire, Lurch veered off the road through a cornfield, slashing for a stand of aspen and pine where the fire was eating through the underbrush. With corn stalks wrapped around the axles, we plunged into the woods, and, almost immediately, there was a horrendous crashing and splintering. In his eagerness, Lurch had shaved it too close between a couple of big poplars, and his new sidebox had been smashed against a trunk and completely destroyed. Hose, nozzles, and handtools were scattered through the woods like discarded toys. I never let him forget it.

So there were some familiar faces in Duluth—Dave was one of them—but I still had to learn the names and abilities of fourteen others. However, bonds fuse rapidly under stress, and Superior-4 had already developed a certain esprit-de-corps. This was due mainly to Tom Schackman, our crew boss. A Forest Service technician with a lot of fire experience, Schackman had our attention and respect from the beginning. Only twenty-seven, and younger than many on the crew, his face had a boyish cast, especially when he laughed. But he also had an air of tempered experience. He was used to command, accustomed to responsibility, and it showed in the way he carried himself. There was no arrogance, but a self-assurance that we would do as he asked. And we did—chiefly because it was clear he knew what he was doing and truly cared about the welfare of his crew instead of the welfare of his ego. There was no guile or manipulation in the man, and soon we were all calling him "Schack." A group of people—no matter how competent—need some focal point in order to form a team, and Schackman filled that role.

As often happens on momentous occasions, our original mission that night on the Hunter was routine. Along with our sister crew Superior-5, we were assigned mop-up along a fairly secure handline. A handline is a narrow trail (anywhere from a few inches to several feet wide, depending on its purpose and location) scratched out of the forest floor with shovels, pulaskis, and specialized rakes known as McLeods. "Building handline" is a fundamental activity of Western fire crews. A standard tactic for controlling a fire is to establish such a line well ahead of or alongside the flames, and then ignite a "burnout," thus creating an effective buffer zone. The aphorism goes: "Make it black and you don't come back."

We had done this the night before in our sector and now had to wipe out any lingering hot spots within fifty feet of the line. It's painstaking, dirty work, and only exciting if you're hit by a falling snag. After a big burn you can hear—and often see—dead trees crashing to the ground for several days. On the previous shift I'd heard three or four an hour, and was reminded by the Safety Officer that being squashed by snags is one of the most popular ways for firefighters to die.

But just as we were deploying along the perimeter, word came down that we were to advance about two miles further east into the mountains and construct a new line. That sounded good, and made up for our disappointment earlier in the evening. We had been scheduled for a shuttle into the fire via helicopter, but it was canceled at the last minute because our crew manifest showed we were too heavy for that particular flight. Nearly half of us weighed over two hundred pounds in full gear. An Alaskan crew, made up mostly of Eskimos—and presumably lighter—had gone in our place, and we were now to march in and link up with them near the head of the fire.

By now it was dark, and we switched on our headlamps, studying each footfall as we scaled a near-vertical slope of loose dirt and rocks. Several times I used my McLeod as a staff or grabbed at the mountainside for a handhold. It's astonishing that more firefighters aren't hurt or killed at night—scrambling over rugged, unfamiliar country, and laboring with sharp tools in the meager light provided by four D-cell batteries and a flashlight bulb. Maybe we automatically take greater care at night, or maybe we're just lucky as hell.

In any case, Overhead got lucky. Our crew noticed two spot fires— blazes started by embers blown out of the main fire—about a half-mile outside the handline. Superior-5 angled off toward one, and Schack led us straight back downslope to the other. It had already consumed a half-acre or so, and fortunately the wind had eased after sunset, or the spot could've made a fast, uphill run and changed the shape of the Hunter Fire considerably. Neither spot had been pinpointed by the air patrols, so we saved somebody's ass—possibly our own.

Starting at the western rim of the spot, a foot or two back from the flames, we dropped into a line-building mode. Those with pulaskis broke ground, slashing at roots and brush. A pulaski is a combination axe and mattock that is the Cuisinart of the fire service. It slices, digs, chops, scrapes, splits, prys, chips, and batters. It can process wood, dirt, or fire. (Legend says the tool was invented by the famed forest ranger E.C. Pulaski, circa 1910, and only Smokey Bear is a more pervasive symbol of wildfire suppression.) Those with shovels scraped and dug, and the three of us with McLeods concentrated toward the rear for the final raking and dragging.

The goal of building line is to expose quickly a band of mineral soil, with each person doing only a small part of the task. A pulaski takes one or two swipes and moves on, making room for the next tool. A synchronized crew is like a mobile factory, or a giant duff-eating worm. In front of us is undisturbed forest floor, in the rear a finished trail. At night it's a bizarre scene: bobbing headlamps and flashing tools punctuate a cloud of dust; there's the ring and thud of steel against earth and stone, highlighted by an occasional curse and the periodic shouts of squad leaders—"Bump up! Bump up!"—to keep tools moving. The tendency is for individuals to do too much in a given spot, trying to build the line themselves. It's difficult, but one must get used to the idea of leaving some work for the neighbor; team-work is critical. The other key is to allow enough room between a person and his buddies so boots or skulls aren't opened with the pulaski. It happens. I recall a fire where a twenty-person crew was reduced to fifteen in the course of four days, and three of the casualties were pulaski gashes. All were self-inflicted, due to the hazards of carrying and swinging edged tools in extremely steep terrain. The crew had been shipped home, since a fifteen-member outfit is generally considered ineffective and awkward in a system designed around units of twenty. Among firefighters' greatest fears is to lose so many colleagues that Overhead sends you home early, significantly reducing your paycheck.

It required twenty minutes to encircle the spot, but there were still some heavy fuels (downed logs, standing trees) burning briskly near the center, so Schack decided to leave Squad One behind to mop-up while the rest of us pushed on to meet the Alaskans. Each crew is organized into three squads, with each squad leader packing a radio. Crews can thus be quickly subdivided into smaller working units with independent communications.

We trudged back to the crest and paused, gazing east. The black horizon of the next ridge was lit by explosions. Trees were bursting into showers of sparks and giant, valley-illuminating columns of flame. They burned furiously for a few minutes, looking like distant oil derricks flaming in the night. Superheated by ground fire, the trees were being consumed in blasts of glory, "torching out" and igniting small chain reactions of crown fire. Fortunately there wasn't enough wind to sustain a full-blown crown—where fire races from treetop to treetop like a twisting orange hurricane. In 1987, at the Silver Fire in southwestern Oregon, I was astounded to see an entire mountain burn up in a few minutes. At the next day's briefing we learned there'd been five-hundred-foot flames ripping upslope at seventy miles per hour; a tough one to outrun.

But we were hiking toward these flames, intending to take them on. Schack reminded us to be aware of safety zones—burned areas or open meadows where we could retreat if the fire turned on us. We each carried a "fire shelter" on our web gear, but such devices were only a last resort. A shelter is basically a heavy-duty aluminum foil pup tent. If a firefighter is about to be overrun by fire, he can rip the shelter out of its case, shake it like a rug to unfold it, and then crawl inside and hold on tight. ("Shake & Bake" as the saying goes.) But a raging fire can generate its own high-velocity winds and snatch a shelter out of a firefighter's grasp. I heard of one who died because he had misplaced his gloves, and his hands got too hot to hold on to the tent. If a person has time, it's also good to clear away as much fuel as possible from the ground beneath. Shelters have saved many lives, but no one's anxious to put them to further proof.

On Shadow Mountain we were approaching the head of an active forest fire, and there are few more dangerous places on earth. Just over a mile beyond the spot fire, the ridgeline dipped down to a fifteen-acre meadow, and there we found the Alaskans, frantically building line at the edge of the trees. The entire opening was bathed in the glow of the fire, as bright as early morning, and headlamps were unnecessary. It was virgin ground, the absolute front. Though there were already over thirty miles of line around the 5,000-acre blaze, this—right now in the meadow—was the seething heart of the Hunter Fire. We had a chance to stop it.

But it was clear we had only minutes. The Hunter was sliding east toward the meadow, part of which was now our safety zone. It was a demonic fire, an incandescent rampart of hell in the midst of the woods. Trees as tall as ten-story buildings were erupting with loud roars, seared into black skeletons almost instantly. The winds were light, so the fire was only creeping, but it extended along a several hundred-yard front, and a gust or an abrupt wind change could thrust fifteen-foot flames into our faces in seconds. Such fickleness is common in the mountains. Schack was clearly nervous, and yelled, "Remember the safety zone!" We were all hopped up on adrenaline and ready to take on the world.

We linked up with the slaving Alaskans and deployed along the perimeter. They were working north, and we took off south, hacking at the ground in a whirl of energized fear. Superior-5 was working toward us from the southwest, and we could dimly hear their shouts and tools. When our crews met, the Hunter would have a new frontline.

Several more trees detonated as we worked, and for a several seconds there was crown fire further back into the burn. It sounded like a jet plane revving for take-off, and it was hard to keep our eyes on our tools. For a moment the entire area was lit as if by noon sunshine, with stark, evil shadows. The temperature was in the low forties, but we were sweating—from fear as well as exertion.

Shortly after our lead elements met Superior-5, Schack's radio crackled, and he received an urgent message. Westby, our Squad One leader reported in from the spot fire that Dave had misstepped and fallen down the mountain. But he was lucky. He'd gone tumbling head over heels for several yards and could easily have broken his neck. As it was, he appeared to have fractured an ankle; he was immobile and in extreme pain.

Dave was one of the five I knew before we staged at Duluth. I'd met him at the Hibbing Air Tanker Base in late June, when we were both on the Minnesota DNR payroll. Dave was a "ramp rat," one of a three-person crew that tended the big water bombers. Their job was to stand by at the airport until an air tanker was needed, then load it as quickly as possible with fire retardant. Things could wax hectic on dry, windy days, when the turn-around time for air tankers can be measured in minutes, but most of the time the Tanker Base was a serene, laid-back haven. We "ground-pounders" accused them of doing little but watching soap operas and tossing horse-shoes. But the day I was dispatched to the Base, Dave was busy. Fire conditions had eased, and the DC-4 was gone. Instead, the tarmac was defiled with a huge mound of wet, dirty fire hose. It was a tangled nightmare— 50,000+ feet of hose in fifty- and one hundred-foot lengths. Our mission was to sort it, test it, wash it, dry it, roll it. We needed the airport runway just for the space to stretch it all out. Dave and the other rats were not happy. Soiling themselves with sooty hose was not an air-operations kind of deal. The only glamourous facet of the task was when joints of hose exploded on the pressure tester, sending nozzles flying off like artillery rounds. I kidded Dave that this job was his penance for viewing too many episodes of "All My Children." We spent seven full days wrestling with that chore, and I learned Dave was a transplant from the West, lured to north-ern Minnesota via marriage. He had taken fire science courses in college and had fought some wildfire in California. His goal was to hire on with a full-time municipal fire department somewhere. We talked about how haz-ardous that occupation was, but on Shadow Mountain Dave now had a de-cent tale to tell about danger.

So we had a firefighter down, and it couldn't have been at a more criti-cal moment. It was a crew boss's bad dream, and for a few moments Schack wavered. Should he go or stay? We had just completed a handline at the head of the Hunter, and there was some doubt we would be able to hold it. But Dave's situation was serious now, and that responsibility finally exerted the greater pull. Schack put Sean Hart, the Squad Two leader in command, and left to take care of his wounded.

Sean took control briskly, stringing us out along the line to beef it up. He had us trench the sections that were sloped, to prevent hot material from rolling out of the burn and crossing the line. Someone yelled "Watch for animals!" It's not unheard of for a burning mouse, squirrel, or marmot to charge out of firey woods and dart across the line. At the Bryant Canyon Fire in 1947, two firefighters burned to death when a flaming rodent scut-tled downslope out of the main blaze and ignited a spot fire below them.

At the moment, however, Sean's concerns were more prosaic. He re-minded us to keep an eye on the unburned forest behind us—it's easy to become focused on the dramatic blaze in front and miss the odd spark or ember that drifts over the line. I didn't envy Sean his position—to be unexpectedly laden with responsibility for a crew in the heat of the fray. Fortunately he was no greenhorn. He was a BIA forester from Ashland, Wisconsin, recently transferred from Colorado, where he had garnered fire experience. I was surprised to learn he was only twenty-eight; I'd pegged him at thirty-five. He had a mature, professional attitude. On a quieter shift, when a firefighter from Superior-5 had shinnied up a snag on a bet to clown around, Sean erupted. While others laughed at the childish antics, Sean boomed, "Hey! Get down, you idiot!" The guy eased to the ground, and we ribbed Sean about being a hardass. But everyone knew it was a stupid stunt, and there's certainly enough opportunity to hurt oneself on the fireground without scaling dead trees for fun. I grinned at him and said, "Now THAT, Sean, was the voice of natural authority. You'll go far." He looked sheepish, but it had been the right thing to do. No matter how much firefighters may put up a macho front or grumble about picky safety officers, most of them (especially the ones who've seen people seriously hurt or killed) instinctively respect leaders who try to get them home in one piece. And in front of the Hunter we needed a professional outlook.

Normally we used our handline as a springboard for a burnout, but there was no time. As we finished the line, the fire was right there—I mean right in our faces. The scariest thing was the huge fir trees just inside the line. All we could do was wait for them to explode.

In a few minutes, three of them blasted into the sky in quick succession, and I was convinced our line was doomed. Imagine a blizzard. Imagine the air filled with tumbling flakes, only the flakes are on fire. A veritable storm of sparks and embers flew high up and across the line. Our two squads and most of Superior-5—about thirty people in all—scattered through the woods like dogs after birds. The brush outside the line was thickly sprinkled with orange specks and curls of smoke, and we scrambled feverishly about on hands and knees, snuffing them in our gloves. It was a desperate game. We flailed at the brush to get at the ground, stumbling from spot to spot as fast as we could, aware that our lives could be at stake.

During the next half-hour the concensus remained "We'll never hold," and I thought about freak winds and fire shelters. Several more dying trees blew clouds of sparks across the line, and we hunted them down with reckless abandon, determined that this would be the final line for the Hunter. The heat was tremendous, but the draft created by the intense fire sucked all the smoke away. We had a clear view of the enemy.

Meanwhile, Schack had reached Squad One, and, taking a page from every Boy Scout manual ever issued, they cut two aspen poles, threaded them through the sleeves of five Forest Service brush jackets, and fabricated a crude litter. It was a long, brutal haul to the nearest point that could be reached by a tracked vehicle, but they managed to lug Dave there without disabling anyone else. It was too dark and smoky to call in a helicopter.

After the trees near our line had been flash-carbonized, the fire settled down to a more even burn, and the storms of embers ceased. The Hunter had shot its wad, and though a good breeze could've changed our lives forever, the calmness held. We let the fire burn itself down to a black no-man's land.

The next day there was some spotting across our line, but the basic front held, and the Hunter Fire was contained at about 5,500 acres. Superior-4, Superior-5, and the Alaskans thus had the rare opportunity to build a line that stopped a major Western fire. Often the fires are so big, the personnel so numerous, that you can only enjoy a small piece of the action.

We passed the rest of the night spread out along a mile of line, scouting for hot spots on the other side. A gibbous moon rose after midnight, stained to crimson by smoke. Trees continued to explode deep within the burn, and it was eerily beautiful to see the dense sky brightened by flashes of fire.

Just before dawn I was alone on a ridge, dog-tired and introspective. I was grateful for the night's triumph and slightly bemused to be on a mountainside in Wyoming, black as a burnt snag and impatient for sunrise. The air was chilly, approaching frost, but I felt warm and potent. I was a well-trained, veteran firefighter. I was proud of that, but I'd never planned it. I reflected on the chance circumstances that led to this moment. It all started on a volleyball court. . . .

The Baptismal Blazes

It was a Sunday afternoon, and I'd been playing volleyball at a community park in Side Lake, Minnesota. Just before 6:00 PM a truck roared up to the court in a cloud of dust, and one of my neighbors yelled out the window: "The DNR's looking for volunteers! They got some heavy fire action."

I'd been a member of our local volunteer fire department for six years, so it was unremarkable to head for an emergency, but I had only meager experience with wildland fire. The DNR pays its seasonal firefighters—called "smokechasers"—but it'd never occured to me to sign on. That day four of us hurried up to Side Lake DNR (Department of Natural Resources) Forestry Station.

We could trace the incident on the wall map. An arsonist was cruising the backroads and lighting the forest on fire, and we listened to the radio spit out fresh reports. Someone in a car or on an ATV was out there "flicking a Bic." From Stingy Lake southwest to Bower Lake, then west to Wolf Lake and over to Day Book—all within a few miles and several minutes. The fires were in young tree plantations choked with tall, dry grass and laced with windrows of seasoned slash; the blazes were fast and hot.

It was the second week in April 1987, and we were in the midst of an early fire season. Below-normal snow accumulations had melted about two weeks ahead of schedule, and a spate of warm, dry weather had cured the woods to tinder. The first fires had been fought in March. It would be another month before grass, brush, and trees "greened up," and there was little or no precipitation in the long-range forecast. Of course some of the DNR smokechasers weren't all that distressed—such conditions meant extra hours and extra pay.

As Bill Schnell, the DNR district forester, monitored the radio and plotted reports on the map, he cocked a rueful eye in our direction and theorized it might be a long night. All his regular crews were deployed, and another fire start would mean a geometric progression of the emergency. It was like listening to the soundtrack of a war movie, or an oldtime radio drama. The static-edged transmissions broadcast an outline of the action and imagination filled in the rest. One engine boss announced that his people were establishing a line a hundred yards in front of a fire, and I could picture them working feverishly in the woods with shovels, McLeods, and a chain saw—pump cans strapped to their backs. At the biggest fire, the one near Wolf Lake, another foreman called anxiously for a bulldozer, and was assured—for the second time—that it was enroute. I envisioned him peering nervously out the window of his pick-up, thumb mashed down on the "transmit" button, sweat beaded on his brow. Another voice announced a legal description to an in-coming helicopter, and I recalled a scene from *Apocalypse Now*. Out there in the brush, flames were surging into the sky, and "armed" men were struggling through the forest. From overhead they would hear the thump-thump-thump of the helicopter approaching for an assault at treetop level with a dangling water bucket. In a moment they'd be blasted with a whipping rotor wash, and a "bomb" of water (about 100 gallons, or 830 pounds) would cascade to the ground and wipe out a regiment of advancing fire.

Bill called out to the scene and informed them he had our volunteer crew ready to go. Did they need reinforcements? Stand by. We waited for a half hour, certain we would be called into action. But the crews had picked up some volunteer labor at the scene, and the helicopter sorties proved effective. By sundown all the fires had been controlled, a couple of the smaller ones extinguished.

We were free to go, but Bill asked who would be available the next day, if needed. I spoke up, and in the morning the phone rang. The Wolf Lake fire required mop-up.

I rode over with Bill, and on the way we checked out one of the other burns. Two game wardens and a fire investigator were already there, combing the area for footprints, tire tracks, or any other telltale evidence. They really wanted to nail somebody for this. As we drove up, they had just determined the fire's point of origin, and the surrounding area would be meticulously examined. In addition to leaving prints, maybe the arsonist had dropped a lighter or a book of matches or something else that could serve as a clue. A conviction was obviously a long shot, but the foresters were taking these plantation fires personally. A lot of time, effort, and dollars had been invested in replanting the cutovers, and it seemed especially dastardly to set seedlings afire, worse than igniting an older stand. Just as people consider it more evil to harm children than adults, the DNR was particularly incensed with the idea of someone consciously targetting young trees. It was a direct attack upon the future. Planting trees is an act of loyalty to posterity, an affirmation of times to come, and a blackened tree plantation is a microcosm of doomsday. You long to punish the destroyer.

When we arrived at Wolf Lake, there was still a lot of smoke. Over sixty acres had burned, but it would have been much worse without the services of the helicopter and the dozer. We could see one spot where the fire had ripped into a thick stand of balsam fir, shooting up through the branches and threatening to "crown out." But a quick storm from the water bucket of the helicopter had knocked down the flames.

Our pick-up, or "engine," was equipped with a two-hundred gallon water tank and hose reel, three five-gallon pump cans, and assorted hand tools. I hefted one of the galvanized pump cans—universally known as "piss cans." They weigh about fifty pounds full, and the cold metal pressing against your back is instantly uncomfortable. Unpadded straps bite into shoulders, and, though there's a baffle in the tank, it still slips and bounces as you move. A half-inch hose is attached to the bottom of the can and feeds a hand-operated slide spray gun, or "trombone." The quality of the stream produced by this unit is probably the source of its nickname. Long ago, some grizzled old smokechaser grabbed one of these new-fangled water cans, gave the gun a few pumps, spat out some snoose, and exclaimed, "Hell, I can piss more than that!" Still it's surprising to rookies how much fire can be snuffed with what is essentially a large, sturdy squirt gun, and when properly applied, five gallons of water can go a long way. And of course the cans get lighter as you use them.

We strode out into black stubble, kicking up gray puffs of ash dust. Bill sadly shook his head at the thousands of incinerated white spruce and black spruce saplings. In most cases only a carbonized stalk remained, with burnt stubs where sleek, green branches had been. Some live trees remained, but they'd been scorched and seared, and many would eventually die. It had been a massacre.

In a stand of mature ash trees we saw a tongue of flame. While Bill pushed on to inspect the perimeter of the burn, I hustled over and found a fallen birch trunk still blazing. The punky heartwood was encased in bark and had smoldered all night until the building heat had mixed with fresh air and ignited. I kicked the old tree apart and doused the flames with a half dozen squirts from the trombone.

I followed Bill out to the north end of the perimeter and found him considering a smoking pile of slash. Before a conifer clearcut is replanted, the logging waste—limbs, culls, brush—is often plowed into huge windrows and piles, providing lanes for seedlings. (It also seems to provide excellent habitat for rabbits and wild raspberries.) One tangled pile of old logs was only twenty feet from the edge of the burn, too close to the dry grass and brush beyond. If the right wind came along and fanned the pile to incandescence, we might have a rejuvenated wildfire on our hands. It made Bill nervous to let it sit there and smolder—like a ticking time bomb—but one heap didn't really justify calling out the bulldozer either, so we went at it by hand.

Mopping up is the grittiest aspect of firefighting. We deal with the stubborn remnants of the blaze—the fugitive, survivalist units of heat that have burrowed into stumps, snags, and hummocks. Ignored, such fire can smolder for days or weeks, especially during a dry season. For instance, a few years later, another smokechaser and I lit off a large pile of slash and wood chips in late March, with twelve inches of snow still on the ground. Over the course of the next month it was rained on several times and even saw another four inches of snow. On April 27 we checked it and found some hot spots. We applied 200 gallons of water and Class A foam, working it vigorously with handtools. On May 10, forty-four days after ignition, it blew out, spreading into the surrounding forest. Fortunately it was a small fire, quickly controlled, but it was a valuable lesson in the tenacity of entrenched fire. We must dig, cut, and chop our way to the deep, lingering heat and painstakingly snuff it.

We were in a low, swampy area, dotted with cold puddles. The fire had roared over them, devouring the covering grass and moss, leaving a dark film on the surface of the water. They looked incongruous now—like tortured, tantalizing oases in the midst of a black desert. But they served us well. As we pried each smoking, half-burned log out of the pile, we'd flop the hottest end into one of the puddles. There the fire finally died—with an angry hiss and a spurt of water vapor. It was a kind of coarse surgery. Layer by layer we peeled away the members of the tangle to get at the source of the heat, the malignant tumor of red coals. Removing a glove, we would gingerly touch the ends of a log, making sure it wasn't hot enough to burn us. We'd pull and heave, lever and roll, and soon our hands were black, our faces smudged, and the area around us strewn with charred logs. It was a steaming battlefield.

After a half hour of sweaty labor, I stuck my hand under a blackened trunk and instantly jerked it back. The cranny was sizzling; I had reached bottom. We yanked a couple more logs away, and a billow of smoke arose as the breeze reached down to embers. I grabbed the pump can, and as Bill rooted and stirred with a stick, I sprayed the rest of my water into that core of heat. It was a satisfying, going-for-the-jugular feeling—the finishing off of a worthy opponent. There were still a few tendrils of smoke when we left, but we had cooled the worst of it and stripped away all significant fuel. The heat would soon dissipate.

We resumed our inspection of the perimeter, and in a few minutes we found another trouble spot. One arm of the fire, a small diversion about ten feet wide and fifty feet long, had somehow burned its way out from the main blaze and snuck under the stump of an uprooted balsam. The area was damp and mossy, and I'm sure that if we had intentionally tried to ignite that spot—if we badly needed a campfire to dry our socks for instance—we would have vainly exhausted a book of matches. It's a backwoods truism that an accidental fire or an arsonist's blaze are at least ten times easier to start than an honest, supper-cooking, hand-warming, Boy Scout campfire. As we struggle to arouse kindling that is only slightly damp, cupping tentative matches and gently blowing on ephemeral sparks, we wonder how in the world the forest could ever burn. But this arm of the fire had worked its way over to the uprooted tree and the deposit of black peat that lay beneath.

Peat is a fossil fuel, a kind of proto-coal that's abundant in Minnesota. It's made up of concentrated, decayed vegetation, and once ignited, a peat bed can burn for weeks or months (in some cases, years). This didn't seem to be a major vein, but we knew it would take some special effort—and more water—to put it out. We trudged back to the truck, where I strapped on a fresh can and Bill grabbed a pulaski.

Most of the smoldering peat was lodged between roots of the fallen tree. Bill hacked away with the pulaski, pulling the mass of fuel completely apart. I hosed down the clumps and granules, and then we dug and probed with our hands until we reached cool material. We sprayed and stirred and poked until the peat on the ground was a muddy slurry with no trace of heat or smoke. I shoved my hand in and groped. It all felt cold, wet, and soothing, so we moved on.

We split up to finish scouting the perimeter, and I angled east, following the firebreak trail created by the bulldozer. The machine had cut a narrow but effective swath through the forest. Several hundred aspen saplings had been torn from the soil and mangled, but fresh earth had been exposed and fire spread checked. Often, the essence of wildfire supression is sacrifice. We concede a certain amount of territory to the flames, depending upon wind, humidity, and fuel, and then dig in and rough out an insurmountable barrier, forfeiting a few trees to save the many. It's a simple strategy, and, providing we have the manpower and the equipment, we can almost always make it work. The idea is to sacrifice as little as possible. It looked like the fire line damage at Wolf Lake had been kept to a minimum; one pass with the dozer had been enough.

As I finished my leg of the circuit I discovered a flaming tree. A thick old ash snag, was burning like a tall torch. The fire had crept into the hollow trunk, simmered all night, and then burst through to fresh air at the top of the tree. It wasn't dangerously near the perimeter, but we'd have to fell it and put it out.

Back at the truck, Bill got on the radio and called to Side Lake headquarters for a chain saw. Speedy would bring one out. While we waited, we sat in the cab and ate lunch. In the space of twenty minutes or so, three drivers passed, slowing down to look over the burn. Bill and I idly speculated that perhaps one of them was the arsonist, returning to the scene of the crime to savor the results of his work. It was possible, though this was a heavily traveled road and a little traffic wasn't unusual. Or maybe, we thought, the perpetrator had been among the volunteers that fought the fire. It's not unheard of for citizens to start fires just so they can help fight them—for the excitement or the pay, or both. In the old days such arson was called "job hunting." A friend once told me of two brothers he knew. As kids, they lived only a half-mile from a DNR forestry station, on the banks of a river. There was a grassy area bounded on one side by the stream and on the other by a highway. It was a relatively safe place to start a fire, and every spring they would light it up, and then run over to the porch of their house. They'd sit on the steps and wait. They knew the forestry chief would respond in a few minutes, and he had to drive right by the house on his way to the fire. Sure enough, as he passed he slowed down and called out the window: "Come on, boys! I need your help." Off they'd run, righteous volunteers battling a fire and earning a bit of pocket money. It evolved into an annual ritual and perennial joke. But at the immolated Wolf Lake spruce plantation it was depressing to be suspicious of every passerby, on a north-woods road where crime and wanton destruction are so alien.

When Speedy arrived, Bill left us to complete the job. We felled the flaming ash tree, and then tore it apart with the pulaskis to ferret out the last vestiges of fire. We made one more pass around the perimeter. The wind had risen as the day progressed, and new hot spots flared to life. I emptied a third piss can, and we did a lot more chopping and digging. By the time we finished, I was exhausted. My boots were black and soggy, my jeans filthy, my hands blistered.

As we hiked out of the burn back to the road, we saw a couple of kill-deers skittering around in the ashes. A variety of plover, common to fields and meadows, adept at feigning injury to lead intruders away from their young, these two appeared to be searching for a place to nest. Perhaps they knew that virile, burgeoning grass would return, that when the rains finally came the ground would fairly burst with fresh green shoots. It wouldn't take long. When killdeer eggs were nestled amid new growth, the mop-up would be truly complete.

But if I thought that cheerful, reassuring scene was the end of my fire season, I was gravely mistaken. I told Bill to keep me in mind if he needed help, but I figured it was only a neighborly gesture—surely the spring rains would come soon.

They didn't. A full month later it still hadn't rained. The brown woods were beyond dry and flammable—they were explosive. Wildfires blazed all over the state, consuming tens of thousands of acres.

One morning in May, we awoke to an acrid, pervasive odor. Outside, a thick haze of smoke blanketed the forest—visibility was cut to a quarter-mile. Alarmed, I phoned the forestry station and learned the smoke was seeping down from Manitoba. A couple of huge conflagrations were out of control—one had burned eighty residences near Lake Winnipeg—and the smoke was detectable hundreds of miles away. It was so bad in our area that the detection planes couldn't fly their scouting missions. That made everyone tense and jumpy. It's hard to spot your own trouble if you're already enveloped by the smoke of someone else's.

The Canadian smoke cleared off next day, but we saw a spate of warm, windy, sunny weather that set people to wagging their heads, clucking their tongues and saying, "If we get a fire on a day like today . . ." There was a pall of inevitability in the air, as thick as the Manitoba smoke. We live in a world of energy; of sparks, heat, flame—both natural and artificial—and the land itself was kindling.

It finally happened on May 12. A thunderstorm passed over, and, though it didn't drop enough rain to rinse the dust off the pine needles, it was seething and kicking with lightning. One of the Side Lake DNR crews was on its way to help out at a fire in another district, when they encountered a small blaze only five miles north of the station. Lightning had struck amidst dry grass in an ash swamp. They piled out of the truck to snuff it and be on their way. It didn't appear to be a serious matter. The fire had obviously been ignited only minutes before, and wasn't too far from the highway.

But the wind was brisk, and the flames rose up and ran. The Side Lakers called for an additional crew. Then one of the smokechasers happened to glance across the highway and saw that another fire had burst into crackling life. Either a spark had jumped the road, or there had been another lightning strike smoldering. In two hot minutes, this new blaze was roaring through thick brush and surging up into a stand of fir. It was less than a quarter-mile away from several acres of seasoned logging slashings that would burn furiously. The foreman on the scene had a two-front fire straight from hell, with nothing but dry fuel between an orange wave of fifteen-foot flames, and the hamlet of Bear River less than two miles north. It had all happened in ten minutes. He radioed for air support and more people.

My phone rang at 5:30 PM. Bill said: "We need help right now. I've got a truck ready to go. Round up someone else if you can."

Sooch's cabin was on the way, so I wheeled into his driveway and vaulted up his back porch. He was just sitting down to dinner.

"You got time for a fire?" I asked.

He grinned and started pulling on his wildfire gear: a yellow, flame-resistant Nomex shirt, heavy boots, a pair of gloves, and his custom-made leather holster that holds a spray can of insect repellent. Sooch hates getting caught out in the sylvan evening air without some high-powered bug dope. He's a firm believer in having the right stuff.

As the screen door banged shut behind us, Sooch called back to his son: "Make sure you keep the sauna hot!" His tone indicated that we would be extremely disappointed if the steam bath wasn't ready for us, the returning (sore, filthy, weary) heroes.

Bill greeted us at the station with, "This is a good one." We jumped into the truck and headed north. We had a pump and hose reel, three piss cans, and hand tools. The radio was buzzing with queries and commands. We heard that a helicopter and an air tanker were on the way, and we could expect at least one bulldozer. The voices of the folks on the ground carried an edge of anxiety.

Sooch took a last drag on a cigarette and flicked the hot butt out the window.

"Oh, great!" I yelled in mock horror. "Here we are on the way to a forest fire, leaving a trail of smoldering butts."

He looked sheepish, but recovered quickly. "Hell," he replied, "We'll just arrive on the scene *ahead* of any fire we start."

We laughed—nervously, and not for long. In a few moments the northern sky was opaque. A monstrous cloud of dense, gray-black smoke rolled over the treetops like a windblown thunderhead come to earth. From a distance it looked like a solid barrier—as if the highway just ended at a dark, ominous wall.

We slowed and eased into the battle zone. There was another DNR engine just ahead. Two men were refilling pump cans. They motioned us forward to where the foreman was dispatching firefighters. We drove on, nervously watching flames on both sides of the highway. On the left the fire was licking at the shoulder, less than fifteen feet away, and it made me think of the twenty or so gallons of gasoline we had in our truck's tank. This was no mop-up operation. We were shock troops, part of the first wave, and we were here to engage the fire at close quarters.

We pulled over next to Bob, the DNR foreman. He was standing in the middle of the highway, a portable radio hot in his hand. He had a good view. At that spot, County 5 runs on a raised roadbed through the swamp. We were about eight feet above the surrounding terrain—a flat expanse of ash, black spruce, and tamarack. To the west was a partially logged area, with stumps and trees right up to the base of the roadway. Between banks of smoke we could see upright trunks flaming like torches in the middle distance. To the east was a wide strip of meadow between the woods and the road. The grass was a couple of feet high and had the dangerous, yellowish-brown complexion of kiln-dried lumber. When that stuff ignited it would rip and race.

Bob was anxiously awaiting his air power, but in the meantime, he directed me and Sooch to grab pump cans and head east. We would attack the flank of the fire and try to slow it before it hit the edge of the meadow.

With the shiny cans on our backs, their hoses curving around from behind to the brass nozzles and plungers with their twin pistol grips (like crude submachine guns), we were reminiscent of Dan Aykroyd (me) and Bill Murray (Sooch) in *Ghostbusters*. As we trudged and tripped along over hummocks of grass, I sang a quickly-fashioned ditty: "When there's big orange flames eatin' up your brush, who ya gonna call? Smokebusters!"

Actually, more like Assbusters. In moments we were sweating and panting, inhaling as much smoke as air. The line of fire was too hot to approach while standing, so we fell into crouches and sprayed at the base of the flames. Sooch tied a kerchief around his nose and mouth. I had rushed off without one.

We worked our way along the line, knocking down the two-foot flames. By the time we emptied our cans we had covered about a hundred feet, leaving a steaming, coal-black perimeter. But there was just too much heat, fuel, and wind. Even before we reached the engine for more water, we could see our line re-igniting and advancing. Piss cans weren't going to cut it.

But a bulldozer had just arrived, and Bob directed Sooch and me and three others to follow behind and hit the hot spots. The dozer slid down the embankment and tore into the woods. The operator held the blade just below ground level, peeling back a strata of vegetation and exposing the wet, black soil beneath. Trees were bashed out of the way, broken or uprooted, and shoved to the side of the line.

We fell in at the rear, like infantry behind armor. The wide steel treads churned up the ground, sloppy mud cascading off the tracks like Mississippi water off a paddlewheel. In several spots there were puddles, ankle deep or better, but the fire would flash right over, consuming the dry fuel above the waterline. We slogged through pungent, slippery mud, the fire to our right. The dozer operator edged close to the flames, conceding as little territory as possible. We strung ourselves out behind, protecting the integrity of the new line. Sparks had ignited spot fires ahead of the main advance, and we knocked down any that were close to the perimeter.

I slipped and fell, and I thought it was mud; but there was a hard, cold surface beneath. I scraped away a film of ooze and saw a sheet of smooth, solid ice. Under the insulating moss the winter cold was still in the ground. It turned out to be a great help—like a stretch of concrete pavement. The dozer operator said later that there was enough ice to support his machine, and he had been careful not to break through the stratum of frost and get bogged down in muskeg.

A small arm of the fire seemed to be moving faster than the main body and was heading directly for a copse of cedars. The cedars were only a few feet inside the perimeter, so I decided to make a stand. I plunged into the brush just ahead of the flames, spraying as I went. The wind was gusty and variable in there, with the fire generating its own air currents. A quick shift pushed out a blast of smoke and hot air that forced me to the ground. For a moment I couldn't breathe, and, as I kept my nozzle pumping out a protective shield of mist, I shoved my face down to mud level to suck air. In a moment I could rise again, the smoke temporarily whipped away. But in less than a minute I had to hit the deck as another searing wave passed over.

For five minutes it was up and down, spray and duck, coughing and spitting, as I briefly stood off an arm of the blaze.

There was a roar overhead. I looked up and saw a twin-engined Cessna dive out of the smoke and bank sharply away to the north. Only a hundred feet up, it was the lead plane for the air tanker. The bomber would be dropping loads of fire retardant just beyond our line. Someone emerged from the smoke behind me and yelled, "We can leave this!"

I retreated to the dozer path and trotted forward to catch up. The fire had burned up to the tracks in a couple of places, but stopped. We had an effective break.

The lead plane screamed by again, directly above. It was canted over on its port wing, even lower than before. I was able to make out a head in the cockpit window before it vanished into a wall of smoke. I heard the deep drone of the heavy bomber coming in behind, but I never did see it.

The dozer trail made a sharp cut to the east, and as I rounded the bend, I caught up with Sooch, Darryl, and Leon. The latter was standing in a crimson puddle, soaked with red fluid from head to toe. For a wild moment I thought it was blood, but then I saw that Sooch and Darryl were laughing as they sprayed Leon's face with their nozzles.

He had taken a direct hit from the air tanker. He had looked up at the plane as it lumbered by, and saw that the bomb bay doors were gaping open. He reacted a second too late, and a massive wave of red fire retardant smashed him to the ground. Mud and pine needles were jammed into his ears and nose, and he never did find his cap.

"I thought the damn thing had only one shot," said Leon. Before he got nailed he had seen it dump a load. In reality, the tanker had dropped its cargo in four stages.

"What's in that stuff?" Sooch asked.

"I don't know," replied Leon, "but it doesn't taste all that great." He was a mess, but at least it'd be tough for his clothes to catch fire. (The fire retardant was a mixture of water, red clay, and fertilizer.)

A few minutes later the dozer completed the encirclement of the fire on the east side of the highway. The slash was coated with retardant, and this section of the blaze was under control.

Just before we cut through a burned-over area on our way back to the road, we heard the helicopter arrive. It landed on the highway to have its Bambi bucket attached, and started making sorties—filling the bucket at a nearby pond.

The dozer crossed the highway to tackle the fire on the west side, and Sooch and I followed. We were soaked and muddy past our knees, our faces smeared with sooty perspiration, our backs cold, damp, and sore from leaky pump cans. We were struggling over rugged, swampy terrain, grunting like chain gang convicts. As he tripped over a fallen limb, Sooch raised his voice in an ironic lament.

"Sure!" he spat. "My old man used to say, 'Go to college! Go to college! Get yourself a *good* job.' Yeah. Now look at me!"

Of course there's nothing keeping a brain surgeon, a district attorney, or an investment banker from hauling a piss can through a northeastern Minnesota ash swamp—it's a free country—but I noticed that none of those people were around. The implication of Sooch's remark was that like other forms of combat, firefighting is reserved for grunts. (A lesson he also learned in Vietnam.) But there was no real bitterness in his voice. If anything, he felt a little sorry for all the white-collar and gold-collar dudes who were not on the DNR's call list. At that moment Sooch wouldn't have wanted to be anywhere else. Me either.

I laughed as I replied, "College? I spent five years in college—and now look at me!"

Yes, it had been a close brush with status and affluence. I had once seriously considered being a scientist. Perhaps there would have been recognition, maybe achievement, probably satisfaction. But I certainly wouldn't have been invited to fight a forest fire. As the helicopter swung by overhead, aiming for the hot vanguard of our common enemy, I felt privileged to be part of the action.

There's a little craziness in the appreciation of discomfort and danger, a bit of macho camaraderie. But in milder form, it's the kind of madness and fellowship that ensures our survival, and serves to make it interesting. We were physically miserable out there on the fireground, but we were having a good time—not giddy, titillating enjoyment—but good in the sense of spending our time well and to the full. We were righteous. There was no ambiguity about the character of our immediate goal. We were doing the right thing at the right time.

About halfway around the western front of the fire, we reached the heart of its advance. There were some big flames charging out of the swamp and into a long windrow of pine slash. The air tanker had hit this area with a load of retardant, coating the surface of most of the available fuel. But the dry pine, saturated with pitch, was fiercely burning, flames shooting up through the coating. The dozer skirted the hottest part of the blaze, grinding back and forth for a few minutes to make a wider fire break before pushing on to complete the perimeter.

Sooch and I lingered, joining four other smokechasers in an assault on this retardant-eating inferno. Despite several wry comments concerning the BTU-output of the government's fire retardant, we momentarily blunted the progress of one section of the fire, then backed off when the helicopter swung in overhead.

The pilot jockeyed his machine into position, bouncing a little in the thermals. We could see his head sticking out the door. This was not a sterile, computer-controlled, laser-guided operation. We were talking seat-of-the-pants, joystick flying—a freelancing joust with fire, earth, and sky.

When he was poised directly over the fire—maybe a hundred feet up—the pilot hit the release. The bucket opened up and collapsed. It looked like a huge orange bladder—the load wasn't merely dropped, it was disgorged. It exited the bucket in a solid column and then splayed out in the wind, hitting the ground in a streaming white cascade. It hammered the flames with a loud *whoosh*, instantly snuffing out 150 square feet of fire, and dampening the area around. Smoke and steam lashed into the air, whirling and hissing in a strobic finale.

The helicopter, a Hughes 500, spun away to dip for another load, and we surged back into the fray, working the edges of the area he'd hit. In less than five minutes the ship was back to douse more of the windrow. After seven or eight runs the worst of the blaze was extinguished, the spreading checked. The official term is "contained." We thought the Hughes should make two or three more passes, but we heard he was low on fuel.

Sooch and I emptied our cans on the remnants of the fire. There didn't seem to be anything left that could easily jump the dozer line, so we headed back to the highway, cutting across the blackened rear echelon of the blaze. Several upright trunks were still flaming—like the candles on Paul Bunyan's birthday cake. These trees would have to be felled. Each gust of wind scattered a flock of sparks from their tops, wafting them off to start new trouble.

We walked past one of the torches—the dead husk of a huge ash—and several seconds later it toppled over just behind us, thundering to the ground with an explosion of sparks and gray dust, a "widow-maker" they call them in the trade. Sooch and I looked at each other and shrugged—another bullet without our names on it.

"Damn!" said Sooch. "We got 'incoming' trees, and they're paying us seven bucks an hour!" But it was only routine bluster; he was in a good mood. Hell, with a first-class wildfire, the DNR could probably charge admission. The smokechaser's rate of $7.33 per hour would do just fine. I sensed that I was working my way into a niche.

And we had a free supper to boot. Back up on the highway, after wading through the cold, therapeutic water of a waist-deep ditch, we discovered a truck had arrived from town with a load of boxed dinners from Kentucky Fried Chicken. We were each handed one and invited to dig into a cooler full of soft drinks.

"How's the grub?" Sooch called out.

A dirty firefighter, clutching a half-eaten dinner roll, gulped and replied, "If you think the weather's been dry, you ought to try one of these biscuits."

But the chicken wasn't bad, and I wolfed it down like a starving dog. Piss can backpacking is hungry work.

Sooch put on a mock scowl. "Did you wash your hands?" he asked.

"Cured by smoke!" I replied, and blessed him with a sooty drumstick.

As we dined by the shoulder of the highway, an old, olive drab bus pulled up. It was filled with uniformed young men. Someone said it was a Federal "Hot Shot" crew, a bunch of firefighters from New Mexico who were up for the northern fire season festivities. They filed out of the bus and were crisply inspected and deployed, moving out like a military unit. Their average age seemed to be about twenty-one. Not surprising. Shuttling around the nation combatting wildfires—for months at a time—is definitely a vocation for young, pliable backs.

It was about two hours since the fire started, and the exciting, "easy" part was over. We had surrounded and blockaded the flames, and now it was time to go in for a messy kill. There were hundreds of hot spots that had to be taken out one by one. The Hot Shots split up and dispatched a squad to either side of the highway, and our crew did the same. At the peak of the blaze, the DNR had about thirty people on the ground, some of them citizen volunteers who were just driving by and had jumped out of their vehicles to lend a hand. But now we were down to a hard core of ten sappers. We waded into the fireground with pump cans, pulaskis, and a chain saw.

The day had been variably cloudy, but at sunset the sky cleared, and a full moon rose to illuminate the havoc. With falling darkness, the tortured landscape was shaded into a bizarre, surrealistic vision. The ground was utterly black, the natural shadow of night deepened by the scar of burning. Flaming snags were silhouetted against the pale luster of moonlit sky, like the ill-omened beacons of some dark, pagan ritual. Forty acres of scorched forest sparkled with pinpoints of orange—scattered embers and tongues of flame feeding on what life and fuel remained.

In the logged area several stumps had been hollowed out by fire and were now glowing from within. At a distance they looked like omni-lucent volcanoes on the surface of some Jovian moon—devilish red mouths gaping in the blackness. Some puddles in the swampy ground were dusky mirrors, dimly reflecting the yellow-orange of nearby flare-ups, transformed into glimmering pools of brimstone. At first fried, the land now baked.

Out on the fireground, we were like shadows ourselves, flitting from flame to flame like great struggling moths. The battle now sounded sharp and wicked—the spitting of sprayed coals, the rasping of blades on trunks and hot bark, the coughing whine of chain saws, the short crack as a tree ripped off its stump.

From up on the highway, looking south, we could see the entire holocaust. It was frightening to consider that the smoldering ashes of this mordant balefire were the offspring of an unpredictable thunderbolt.

While I refilled my pump can for about the tenth time, I heard one of the others say, "If there's such a thing as hell, this is what it looks like." Still, there was a desolate beauty here, a naturally sculpted and fired representation of sublime dementia—a residue of dragons.

We fought until nearly midnight, until the air cooled, the breeze died, and the perimeter was wet and black. We trooped out of the woods like zombies, stumbling, dragging. After six hours of heated, almost constant exertion, even an empty pump can felt dense and leaden.

Of our three engines, two wouldn't start. Since they were parked on the edge of the highway, the emergency flashers had been left on and the batteries were as dead as rocks. With one last surge of energy, three or four of us piled behind each truck and pushed them down the road to turn over the motors. It was an odd scene, like the closing act of an off-beat play. Intricate machines had been the key to stopping this fire quickly. We blessed the fashioned metal prowess of airplanes, helicopters, and bulldozers. There was no doubt that much more would have been lost without air power and diesel power.

But in the end it came down to humans—individual firefighters wiping out the heat, pocket by pocket, ember by ember, spark by spark. The machines didn't endure until the end. The helicopter ran low on fuel and left; the dozer made its pass, then was hauled away before dark. The pickups died sitting. They apparently had less stamina than flesh and blood fueled by fried chicken.

So we pushed them down the highway, resuscitating the pistons with contractions of human muscle. We laughed as we heaved against the tailgates and bumpers, enjoying the irony, enjoying the power we had over machinery.

The trucks started, and we rode south past the burn, deeply satisfied. The fire was beaten and we had earned our ride. Though there was no one along the highway to cheer us, we felt like returning legionnaires—on parade, victorious. Sooch and I figured his sauna was still hot.

The Big One

1.

The phone rang as I slipped into bed. That's when Duty most often calls—after 10:00 PM on a Tuesday night.

"This is Tammy," Duty said. There was a late-hour, caffeine-cheerfulness to her tone. "Uncle Sam *needs* you!" It was a pert, girlish invitation. A summons to arms from a dispatcher named Tammy is the way the real world conducts adventure—no macho Hemingway motifs.

I was surprised. I had signed up for outstate firefighting duty two weeks before, and I had almost forgotten about it. Sketchy news reports indicated that the monster forest fires in California and Oregon were winding down after a three-week rampage that had consumed hundreds of thousands of acres and killed a half-dozen people. Most of the fires started the same day—August 30, 1987—when a dry lightning storm swept over the region igniting hundreds of blazes. (In California alone, 8,860 lightning strikes caused over 1,200 fires in four days.)

Since I hadn't been called to service immediately, I assumed the need for reinforcements had passed—especially for forest firefighters with only modest experience. I was a rookie, with only a dozen northern Minnesota fires under my belt, and none in the mountainous terrain of the far West.

Still, I possessed the primary qualifications: an eagerness to commit for hard service far from home, and a passing score on the "step test." It had confirmed that I was fit enough to be abused out on the fireline. (The government likes to buy fresh. Instead of shipping physical wrecks to hazardous areas, it prefers to send raw material and manufacture its own wrecks on site.)

I had taken the step test at the Department of Natural Resources forestry station in Hibbing. Accompanied by an audio tape with the prescribed metronomic beat, I had stepped onto and off a wooden box for five minutes.

33

The box was eighteen inches high, and the pace was rapid—ninety beats per minute. It was surprisingly strenuous. When the time was up, a forester took my pulse and plugged the number into a table that compared it with my age and weight (thirty-six and 210). It was a quick and crude stress test, and I had heard complaints about its accuracy; but I suppose if a person keels over dead on the box, he or she doesn't have the right stuff. I was sweating and panting a little, but the man said I had passed "with flying colors."

I was supposed to head down to Duluth that minute—to a staging area, an assignment, and a plane, but a timely call from regional headquarters put a hold on the operation. I was sent away with a "thanks, we'll keep in touch." During the drive home, I caught a radio news report of a 10,000-acre fire out of control on Hawaii. "Take me!" I yelled. "Take me!"

But Tammy waited two weeks, and then told me my destination was southwest Oregon. Could I be in Duluth by 7:00 AM next morning? Yes, it was only a hundred-mile drive. Could I promise to serve for thirty days? (As if I would have a choice once I was out there.) Yes, I needed the money. Did I have my own gear? No, just boots. Well, not to worry, Uncle would graciously provide. We would fly from Duluth to Medford, Oregon, then take buses to the Silver Complex, a huge fire in the mountains of the Siskiyou National Forest. Last report: over 45,000 acres.

I hung up and flew into a frenzy of packing. I had had my kit ready to go, but over the course of the past week it had gradually come apart—a shirt here, a pair of socks there, toiletries returned to the bathroom. I had been advised that I should bring plenty of clean underwear and socks. I expected that doing laundry would not always be practical in a fire camp. Warm clothes, particularly longjohns, were also recommended—mountain nights can get nippy, even after a ninety-degree afternoon.

Next morning was clear and frosty. I awoke before dawn, and the sky was thick with stars. The celestial foreground was lit by a pale green curtain of northern lights. They shimmered in a ghost dance against the polar constellations. It was September 23, and my only regret was that I would be leaving northern Minnesota at the peak of its autumn color. By the time I returned, the birches, aspens, and maples would be winter-naked—ready for snow. Everything that was now red, orange, yellow, and fluttering in the breeze, would be down and brown.

The farewell to Pam and autumn added a touch of melancholy to a venturesome morning, but it wasn't nearly so daunting as the roster snafu that confronted me at the Duluth National Guard Armory. Five crews of twenty firefighters each were scheduled to assemble, and rosters had been sent ahead. I checked in and found my name wasn't on any of them. Part of the problem was my "freelance" status. Not being a regular government employee, I wasn't "owned" by anyone. Neither the Forest Service nor the Minnesota DNR had me on the payroll, so my existence was questionable.

(Bureaucratic metaphysics is reduced to a simple question: are you on a list or not?) The clerks on duty wondered why I was there. I mentioned Tammy and emphasized that I had just driven a hundred miles before breakfast. Too bad, but there was no place for me, and I would probably be sent home; nevertheless, stand by. I linked up with a freelancer named Rick who was in a similar fix, and over coffee we commiserated and bitched.

We were saved by Hiawatha-3, a crew from the Hiawatha National Forest in Michigan's Upper Penninsula—known regionally as the "U.P." They arrived in Duluth with only eighteen people, and when Rick and I were offered, they snapped us up. I breathed a great sigh of relief as Larry, their assistant crew boss, wrote down our names, addresses, social security numbers, and next of kin. Once we were on a list, it was *official*—immutably cast. I relished this red-tape affirmation of my being; I belonged to somebody, I was on a payroll.

I hurried to the supply room and checked out my gear: a hard hat, a headlamp with extra batteries, a first-aid kit, web gear (a belt- and shoulder-straps affair that included a small day-pack, and pouches for two water bottles and a fire shelter), goggles, a pair of leather gloves, one package of disposable ear plugs, a sleeping bag, two Nomex shirts (yellow), two pairs of Nomex pants (olive drab), two plastic water bottles, and the fire shelter. Finally, I was issued a large red backpack to carry it all. In a shocking lapse of normal government logic, the latter was called a "red pack."

It was only 10:00 AM and our plane didn't leave until 12:30 PM, so I had plenty of time to get my act together. I transferred my personal items to the red pack, and at the urging of my new comrades I closely inspected my government issue. Sure enough, the headlamp didn't work. I exchanged it for a new one, little realizing how soon I would need it.

I lugged the pack over to the official scale. The allowable weight of a crew (people and gear) is 4,800 pounds, and it's meticulously enforced. If the limit's exceeded, things must be jettisoned. My pack weighed in at thirty-eight pounds, and I didn't see anyone dumping extra socks and underwear, so I guess we all made the cut.

Rick and I were introduced all around, concentrating intently on the eighteen new names and faces. The crew was friendly and in good spirits. They seemed happy to be going out West, and I would learn why as the days passed. We discovered that most of them had been home for only a week. They'd done two weeks of duty in Oregon shortly after the fire started, and were now on their way back. All were veterans, most of them either full-time or part-time Forest Service.

Federal firefighting is a militarized operation, organized under the Incident Command System (ICS). Each crew is divided into three squads—each with a squad leader and a radio. When two or more crews are working together, there's a strike team, and a strike team leader. Strike team leaders and above—that is division supervisors, planners, logistics coordinators, information officers, payroll officers, medical officers, and the exalted Incident Commander (IC)—are referred to as "Overhead." There is a clearly defined chain of command and responsibility, and units from various states and agencies that are familiar with the ICS can simply plug into the system and go to work without a lot of organizational screw-ups and/or turf battles. The system was developed after a large fire in southern California about fifteen years earlier. A number of agencies had been involved, and they couldn't even talk to each other, much less work as a team.

Mike Lanasa, the crew boss of Hiawatha-3 (and a silviculturist in the workaday world), assigned me to his Squad One. Rob Clark, the squad leader, was my own age and had several years with the Forest Service. He had been all over the West on fire duty, and he quizzed me about my experience and abilities. I noticed that he wrote down what I told him. Adding that to the Nomex uniforms, the chain of command, and the obvious prevalence of experience and competence, I was impressed by the fact that this was serious stuff. I was suddenly a part of a professional unit being sent into heavy-duty action—to "The Big One," as I heard someone say. By the time we were bussed to the airport, I was apprehensive. I had volunteered with alacrity, lured by the adventure and the pay, but was I good enough? Did I belong at "The Big One"?

We hiked across the tarmac, packs on our backs, and then passed them into the cargo hold of a United Airlines 727. It was heady stuff. We weren't pampered and coddled like tourists—carefully shielded from noise, dust, and the slightest chance of a minor accident. We were special passengers, allowed the rare dignity of loading our own gear and then walking directly under a wing to the rear ramp and entry. I was delighted. I've always hated those portable corridors that link an airliner with the terminal—antiseptic tunnels joining the gate lounge and the plane lounge, cutting off contact with sun, wind, and rain, as if we're too fragile to survive outside the artificial environment. The devices are safe and thoughtful to the point of decadence. They've always reminded me of the chutes at a stockyard.

Our flight time to Medford was about three hours, and fifteen minutes before we landed we were into the smoke. It was a brownish pall of smog that blanketed thousands of square miles. A Forest Service Overhead man got on the cabin microphone and offered a detailed rundown of the local weather. It boiled down to: hot, dry, and windy, with no relief in sight. The fires were robust and growing.

The small airport at Medford was buzzing. I counted at least five air tankers (old DC-4s and DC-6s) making sorties, with a couple of others on the ground being serviced. Their huge bellies were stained red with fire retardant.

While we lolled on the grass, waiting for the busses that would carry us into the mountains, I learned about the favorite pastime of firefighters—speculation. Would we go directly onto a night shift when we arrived at the fire camp? Would we be "spiked out," that is sent into the wilderness and supplied by air for days at a time? Would we be assigned to mop-up? To initial attack? To a hot line? Everyone had a theory and reasons to believe it. Being a rookie, I had no basis for a strong opinion, but an "assault" into the wilderness sounded good for starters.

I also learned that like Napoleon, the Forest Service believes strongly that personnel march on their stomachs. We had been fed a hot breakfast at the Duluth armory, and then handed a sack lunch as we walked to the plane. United Airlines had provided another meal en route, and when our busses finally arrived at the airport, our first stop was a restaurant in downtown Medford. A sign at the door read: OUR SPECIALTIES: BANQUETS, SENIOR CITIZENS, GOVERNMENT CONTRACT FEEDING. We duly filed in to be systematically fueled (buffet style)—to be fattened up for what I hoped wouldn't be slaughter.

Near sundown our five school busses headed west in a convoy. We were told it would be a three-hour ride. The smoke-shrouded sun faded from dim orange to dusky purple, and we slowly gained elevation. Farmland gave way to wooded hills, and a double-lane highway to a narrow, winding, gravel road. After an hour, we encountered a stenciled sign forbidding passage to the general public, and we drove into the heart of the Siskiyou.

Soon we were climbing past mountainsides of smoldering stumps and snags, and the forest was blackened as far up as we could see. After dark, the night was sprinkled with sparks and hot spots, and as we neared camp we were treated to a distant overview of an entire mountainside on fire. Across a deep ravine we could see trees bursting into flame with great showers of sparks and twisting columns of illuminated smoke. Turbulent orange balls rolled from the core of the fire and unfurled into long sheets of flame, roaring upslope in unstoppable blazing waves. Neighboring peaks were dimly lit by the fire, and, against the background of stars, it was a spectacular show. The "oohs" and "aahs" from the veterans on the bus indicated that this was above-average action. I pondered the fact that this conflagration was only a few miles from our camp.

Agness, Oregon, is at the confluence of the Rogue and Illinois rivers, about fifteen miles from the Pacific as the raven soars. It's not really a town—more of an outpost. There's a restaurant/resort/store, a Forest Service ranger station, and a couple of homesteads. The fire camp was set up on sloping fields that straddled a narrow county highway—just paved within the last few years by the look of it. The only flat ground was reserved for helicopters, and the chief complaint at Agness was the irritation of trying to sleep comfortably on a hillside.

It was late when we arrived, and they didn't send us out on a night shift. We were told to pick a place in the field and bed down. By the bouncing light of headlamps, we hiked across the meadow to an unoccupied spot. On the way, one of our people bent over and shined his light into the grass.

"What is it?" someone asked.

"Scorpion."

"Oh."

There were over a dozen crew-sized "tents" scattered over several acres. They were makeshift affairs fabricated out of plastic sheeting and two-by-fours. Rather than risk stumbling into an occupied one, we chose to lay out our bedrolls on bare, unadorned sod. We had been issued foam backpackers' pads in Medford. We placed our red packs at our feet to minimize the nocturnal, downslope creep, and once I got used to the noise of a couple of generators that served the camp, my first night in the Siskiyou was peaceful. Scorpions or not.

✳ ✳ ✳

2.

Next morning the sky was low and gray, obscuring the surrounding mountaintops. Oh, great, I thought, it'll probably start raining, and they'll ship us home. I already displayed symptoms of the traditional firefighter's ambivalence: you want to conquer the fire, but you also lust for the action and the money. The attitude was summed up by a wry little motto I heard the first day: "We came to save Oregon, but we'll settle for a check." Because it was so huge and dangerous, this Silver fire was ideal. Everyone had room to exercise their professional best—work like pack animals—and there'd still be plenty of fire to go around.

Breakfast was served by a mobile catering outfit that often worked on movie sets. It was decent grub, and there was tons of it. Afterwards, we gathered around Mike for a briefing. He told us that the Silver Complex now encompassed just over 50,000 acres. There were forty-nine crews from fifteen states, and a total of 130 personnel. We had ten helicopters, ten water tenders (or tanker trucks), nineteen fire engines, and two bulldozers. In spite of that impressive order of battle, we weren't here to extinguish the fire. Our goal was to hold the line, to contain the blaze until the drought ended. Only heavy rain or deep snow was going to kill the fire completely, and given the long-range weather forecasts, it would probably be the latter.

We were assigned to the night shift, on a section of fireline known as Division "D." There were political strings attached to our mission. Not far beyond the current line was an eight-million-dollar-timber sale of prime Douglas fir. The credibility, and perhaps the careers, of the local Forest Service Overhead depended on saving that sale.

It was a sensitive area. Earth First!, the militant environmental group, had "spiked" trees in the neighborhood, and the loggers were incensed. A tree is "spiked" by driving several long nails into the trunk at sawing level. Hitting a nail with a chain saw is a quick way to ruin a day, perhaps a life. The theory is that if several trees are randomly spiked in a given stand, anyone but a lunatic would think twice before logging them off. As usual, the Forest Service was caught somewhere in between the "eco-guerillas" and the loggers. Officially, the Feds were trying to strike a balance between conservation and production. To Earth First!, the Forest Service is part of the exploitative establishment, the government arm of the logging industry. To the loggers, the Forest Service is the overbearing, mismanaged, regulatory agency cramping their style and cutting into profits. (Among loggers, the generic label for a Forest Service employee is "piss-fur Willy." To rangers, a logger is "pine-shit Johnny." And so it goes.)

"We may be guarding that area tonight," Mike said, referring to the prime fir.

"From who?" one of our sawyers asked. Ironic laughter. These people were used to being in the middle. Some folks in Oregon didn't even want them fighting this fire, but more about that later.

Mike spread out a map. It was a recent infrared aerial survey of the Silver Complex. About ten miles south of our assigned area was the heart of the Kalmiopsis Wilderness. The head of the fire was moving in that direction, and the hope was that it would stop at the Illinois River. The terrain was too rugged and remote for effective counter measures, so Overhead was relying on that natural barrier. They expected the river to be a stopper, but if it wasn't. . . .

Mike said we would board the buses at 5:00 PM, so we had the rest of the day to set up our own little camp. We migrated uphill, and found a flat spot in a grove of madrone and mountain holly overshadowed by scattered Douglas firs. We scrounged some rope, plastic sheeting, and two-by-fours, and constructed a crude shelter. Since rain wasn't likely, our main goal was to provide shade during the day, when we would be sleeping.

Our site was bordered by a swath of dense blackberry bramble, and there were still some berries amid the thorns. We discovered a huge pile of fresh bear scat, sloppy and laced with berry seeds, only a few feet from our shelter. It seemed likely we would have visitors. The major concern of the veterans though, was some nearby poison oak. It's often the bane of firefighters in the West. The two chief campsite protocols were: don't get the poison oak oil in your sleeping bag (by wearing contaminated clothing to bed), and check your boots for scorpions in the morning.

Bobby Caldwell, one of my associates on Squad One, found a large jawbone amidst the bramble—probably from an elk—and he hung it by the door of our shelter to ward off "evil spirits," like poison oak . . . and rainfall.

A few of us preferred to be out under the sky (and away from any snorers or screamers), so we worked at setting up some "nests" back in the brush. I had just established a comfy, level spot where I would have some shade, when Mike returned from another briefing to announce that we were going to be "spiked out," that is transferred to a smaller, rougher camp up near the fireline. The word was that we would be up there for three days, and naturally we had to take everything with us. Our newly-constructed shelter would go to some other crew. There was a little grumbling, but it was good-natured. That's one of the attractions of fire crew work—never being sure from day to day (and sometimes from hour to hour) where we will be or what we will be doing. On the fireline, life is in a continual state of flux. At any moment we could have been ordered to the LZ for instance, and whisked away in helicopters—a sort of Federalized rapture.

We boarded buses in the late afternoon, and they carried us higher. The road was a maze of hairpin turns and switchbacks. It was skimpy, with nothing between us and steep, thousand-foot banks but the skill of the driver and the integrity of the tie rods. Fortunately the roads were controlled—only official Forest Service vehicles were allowed. It was a scenic jaunt, with high-country vistas backlit by the setting sun. But the air was permeated with smoke, and there was an undercurrent of tension beneath the usual banter.

By the time we arrived at the end of the road—literally—it was dusk, and darkening quickly. We were at Drop Point (DP)-13, one of the many access points to the fireline. In the valley below, and up the far side toward the next peak, we could see tall flames. The sky was suffused with a red-orange glow. Some of it was the residue of sundown, but most of it was the sinister effulgence of the wildfire.

There were four crews gathered at the southwest terminus of a long, high ridge called Sugarloaf Mountain. The Division Supervisor beckoned us into a large huddle and gave us our instructions for the night. There was a handline, that is a trail cut with chain saws and scraped down to mineral soil with shovels and pulaskis, which ran the length of Sugarloaf. Most of it was just below the crest on the side of the mountain away from the fire. It was about fifteen feet wide, and we were to patrol it and hold it, making sure the line wasn't breached by sparks or embers. We were to snuff out any hot spots that remained, up to a hundred feet inside the burn. There was a tool cache at DP-13, and the "order of the shift" was to be fifty percent—half of each squad would carry shovels, half pulaskis.

When I first heard the term "pulaski," I thought it might be associated with Casimir Pulaski, the Polish cavalry officer who fought and died for the patriot cause during the American Revolution. Properly balanced, the pulaski might have made an effective, though unromantic, cavalry weapon. But it's been a firefighting implement from the start, and seemed the tool of preference in our squad. Being a rookie, I got a shovel.

The crews formed up and moved out in single file. In the lead was a crew from Colorado who called themselves "The Yellow-jackets." Behind them was Superior-18, from the Superior National Forest in northeastern Minnesota (with some members from the U.P.) They had flown out with us. We were third, followed by Minnesota-4, a crew of Minnesota DNR employees who had also been on our plane.

It was fully dark, and we all switched on our headlamps. The lights ahead bobbed and darted, then winked out of sight as the crews eased into the forest. We were reminded to stay ten feet apart, and to carry our tools on the downhill side.

The trail was precipitous and abrupt, a treacherous cross-contour route that aimed straight for the top of the ridge. In the glare of headlamps, the rugged terrain was either fully lit or utterly black. Sharp edges of rock jutted out of deep shadow, and massive roots reached in out of the night. It was like a black and white moonscape—a narrow tunnel of starkness bordered by the abyss.

We were forced to concentrate on that trail, to focus on each footfall. It was beyond "watch your step," it was *plan* your step, especially in the spots where the ascent was nearly vertical, and the climbing was just that—a groping for handholds and the meticulous placing of toes and heels. At a couple of steep walls I felt stirrings of adrenaline. My body was on full alert as I clung to bare purchases of stone and sensed an airy chasm just a few inches to the left.

It would have been a hazardous hike in daylight—a welter and rummage of loose rock and tangled roots. At night it was an abstract sculpture, a rebus of a track where obstacles loomed suddenly out of darkness. It was crazy. Eighty people, burdened with web gear, packs, and tools, were ascending a mountain trail which none of them had seen before. Would there be casualties? It was clearly dangerous. Did the division super or the strike team leaders expect an accident? I did. But the veterans seemed relaxed enough—at least so far as I could tell in the surreal light of the headlamps.

Each crew was assigned a sector on the line, and after about twenty minutes of walking, we were more or less in position. Accompanied by the crackling of radios and occasional shouts, we fine-tuned the operation, "bumping up" or "bumping down" the line as we subdivided into squads, then into pairs.

Our squad took a short break just below the crest, and everyone switched off his lamp. It was breezy, and swaths of clouds and smoke edged raggedly across the sky, intermittently exposing patches of stars. We were facing the Big Dipper. Behind us, to the southeast, an orange glow silhouetted the ridgeline, as if we were poised at the rim of a seething caldera. The actual flames were a few hundred feet below, and everything in between was burned. We were fairly secure—at least for the moment.

Each team of two ended up responsible for about a hundred feet of line, and in a few minutes we all moved off into the burn to search for hot spots. Just over the crest we ran into a landscape of charred manzanita. It was a tenacious brushfield, a veritable maze of black, twisted limbs. The twigs and leaves had been incinerated, but all the larger branches—chest-high and tined with burned stubs—remained. They were like earth-tentacles, tortured claws that stabbed, scraped, and clung. "Black barbed wire" I heard

Steve, our Squad Two Leader, call it. It grew out of loose and tricky talus. Stumbling and cursing, we fought our way into the midst of the tangle.

The hot spot hunting procedure was simple. We turned off our lamps and looked around. Live embers sparkled like beacons in the burned, double-black night. I was teamed with a Forest Service vet named Al Andrews, and we found a half dozen hot spots in the first hour. Some were little more than single sparks, and we simply snuffed them in our gloves, or buried them with a single scoop of the shovel. But there were some larger patches of smoldering duff, their intensity and potential for fresh fire maintained by a heart sink of blackened rock beneath. The night wind could fan the duff into flame, whipping sparks across the line into tinder-dry fuels.

Al's preferred method for handling these spots was to grub a line around them with his pulaski, and stir up the embers to release the worst of the heat. Then I could use the shovel to mix it up with mineral soil. It's one of the many techniques that come under the category "dry-mopping"—that is extinguishing fire without water. In the mountains, water is often at a premium, and with enough trained people firefighters can handle a lot of fire by hand.

It was quite a contrast to some of the fires I had fought back in Minnesota. Take a peat fire—what's burning is the actual ground beneath your boots. The flames burrow down and form cavities, sometimes several feet deep. The only effective weapon is water—in mega-doses. I recall one small peat fire that was scattered over no more than three or four acres, and we pumped 10,000 gallons an hour for two days to kill it. On Sugarloaf we had only cold steel.

Our squad spent about two hours extinguishing all the hot spots we could find in our sector. Then, well inside the burn, we used a fusee to kindle a small campfire. (A fusee looks just like a highway flare and is used to ignite backfires and burnouts. We had all been issued a couple back at DP-13). Our elevation was 4,800 feet, and the night was cold. We stoked our fire with pre-burned manzanita, and then hunkered down to warm our hands and eat our lunches. Later, Rob set up a watch schedule, and, each half-hour, two of us would patrol our line for fifteen to twenty minutes.

Al and I took the first shift, walking slowly, and pausing every few paces to switch off our headlamps and scour the darkness—especially on the green side of the line. We examined not only the ground, but the treetops as well. Al pointed out that a blazing, windblown spark could easily land in high branches and kindle a fire.

The evening breeze had planed out to stillness, and the forest was quiet. It was a good time to talk, to stay alert with words. For me it was a familiar time, those graveyard hours after midnight. I had survived ten years of shift work, and I knew the seduction of circadian rhythms, the powerful narcotic of drowsiness and the tricks of passing time. Stewart Brand once said that everyone ought to "do time." He knew of three ways:

in prison, in the military, or in a job you hated. I had done my time, slogging through a decade of swing shifts in a job that was sometimes hazardous, always dirty, and often excruciatingly boring.

Al and I spoke softly, telling stories. We liked each other. First impressions had been mutually positive, and we had slipped into comfortable roles. Al was four years older, had nine years with the Forest Service, and was an experienced firefighter; he was my elder, a mentor for the younger greenhorn, and he had tacitly volunteered to tutor me in the craft of battling wildfire. He was also a Vietnam combat veteran, a machine-gunner with the 101st Airborne. He relished the fireline.

"I was in Vietnam for a year," he said, "and this [firefighting] is basically infantry work. I love it!"

It was more than the inherent danger and the occasional excitement. Al revealed that there had been a healing experience as well. He had been embittered by Vietnam, made cynical not only by the verities of a brutal war, but by the neglect and resentment he had perceived back home. The war was a lost cause—if not on the battlefield, then at least in the minds of his countrymen. To many people he was tainted; he wasn't an elite, wounded and decorated American soldier but a bloodstained mercenary of the discredited Establishment. He was viewed not as a warrior but as a killer. Battle-tested veterans always feel a certain ambivalence toward civilians. The British soldier-poet Wilfred Owen, killed in World War I, summed it up best. Addressing the folks back home about the men in the trenches, he wrote: "Weep, you may weep, for you may touch them not." A returning soldier expects honor; he feels deserving of respect. There may not be a full-blown, ticker-tape parade, but there should be an obvious deference, an overt expression of gratitude. A disability payment from the Veterans Administration is not enough.

Al felt cheated and abused—taken advantage of and then disowned. He didn't whine about it, but the feelings were there. Then, on a previous firefighting job in Oregon, his crew had been bussed through a small town that sported handmade signs on lawns and in windows: "Thank you, firefighters," and "Good job, fire crews!"

"For the first time ever," Al told me, "my government service was appreciated." Fireline duty was suddenly more than a personal adventure and some extra money; it was a crusade.

Back at the campfire, the stories were about campaigns past, or "old flames" as someone quipped. Collectively, members of our squad had fought fires in Oregon, Idaho, California, Nevada, and the Carolinas, as well as in Michigan, Wisconsin, and Minnesota. This Sugarloaf Mountain gig was a slow start, but there was hope that the Silver fire would produce a fresh batch of lore—both drama and slapstick.

Al told of a time on some other Western fire when his squad was sitting on a fireline, exhausted. From their resting place they could see a sign nailed to a tree on the green side. It was low, and partially obscured by brush, and nobody could read it. If someone had stood up and taken three steps, they could have seen it clearly, but no one stirred.

"Wonder what that sign says?" his partner mused, but everyone was too tired to expend the effort.

Finally they got the order to light some fusees and start a burnout. They rose to go to work, and since they were up, his partner ambled over to the sign and bent low to read it, flaming fusee in hand. The brush at the base of the tree ignited, and in a moment they had a blaze on the green side that scared the hell out of everyone. Al didn't remember what was on the sign.

"It was probably Smokey Bear and 'Only you can prevent forest fires,'" said Al.

The hours before dawn were long and cold, and the last stars rose over an eerie atmospheric inversion. A mass of cooler air had flattened out the columns of hot gas from the valley, "capping" it like a close-fitting lid. The dense smoke dispersed in a vast, even sheet, engulfing all but the highest neighboring peaks. It was as if we were on the shore of an ocean, the mountaintops reduced to mere islands poking above the surface of a gray-white sea. But it was weird ocean—lit from below by flames, its depths suffused with a devilish glow. It was something out of a fantasy epic, perhaps a valley in Mordor, before the evil walls of Barad-dur.

Just before sunrise, as early-morning breezes tore at the inversion-sea and peeled off great tidal waves of smoke, we re-formed into crews and hiked down Sugarloaf. Back at DP-13 we returned our tools to the cache. Later in the day they would be trucked back to camp and sharpened— shovel blades as well as pulaskis.

Each crew climbed into the back of an Oregon National Guard five-ton truck—those six-by-six monsters with the canvas tops. Our driver looked young, perhaps eighteen, twenty at the most, and that seemed to make a couple of the veterans nervous. It was a downhill run all the way back to the spike camp, and everyone had heard the stories about trucks and buses careening off the mountain trails and tumbling for a quarter of a mile over rocks. Out on the fireline we could be active, have input into the nature of our fate. In the back of a truck we were helpless cargo, and there wasn't much faith put in brake shoes or teenagers.

Sure enough, we were less than a mile down the road when the truck began to accelerate. Out the back flap we could see the shadowy trunks of the firs whipping past. Or so it appeared.

"We're going pretty fast," said Steve. His voice was solemn, just a tad edgy. There was a profound silence, a quick darting and meeting of eyes. I learned later that Steve had been in a near-accident in such a truck a couple of fires before. Everyone knew that, and deferred to his tension. And, as I had noted from news reports, most of the half-dozen Western fire deaths so far had involved motor vehicles. It seemed that traveling to and from a DP was more hazardous than being on the line.

All we could do was hang on and sweat, but when we finally pulled into camp one of the veterans took the driver aside for a few polite, but forceful words. We weren't interested in exploring the operational limits of the Army's five-ton trucks; slow and easy was the ticket, especially downhill.

✳ ✳ ✳

3.

During the night our red packs had been shipped up from Agness to the spike camp, a small mountain meadow called Burnt Ridge. It certainly wasn't wilderness. There was a catering truck with a generator and hot breakfast, but compared to Agness it was definitely low-rent. And a better place to live. It was quieter, and we were closer to the action.

After eating, we collected our gear and found a relatively level spot in a grove of mature Douglas fir. It was amply shaded, with a ridge between us and the local helispot, and was far enough away from the generator to be tranquil. I flopped my pack and sleeping bag on the ground and slept until 3:30 PM.

I awoke to a new world. Burnt Ridge was being reinforced, refined, expanded, and as a camp, generally degraded. Our intimate, unpretentious spike camp was growing like a tumor. While we slept a veritable convoy had arrived. The food operation had tripled in size, and there were now showers (a semi-trailer with its own generator and water supply, plus a tent-annex), a finance tent (for timekeepers, accountants), a medical tent, mounds of tools and supplies, and a lot more people.

At our pre-shift briefing, Mike told us that this was our new base—that stuff about being up here for only three days was history. As far as he knew (and no one ever seemed to know anything for certain beyond the span of a shift) we would be on night duty indefinitely—nocturnal creatures.

By 6:00 PM we were back at DP-13, feeling like we had just left. A thirteen-hour shift can really munch up a day—or more accurately, a twenty-four-hour period. "Day" has little meaning to those prowling the woods all night and sleeping in the sunshine.

Our assignment was precisely the same as the night before. Our squad found *one* hot spot—a single spark, really—early in the shift, and that was it. We spent the rest of the night patrolling and sharing coffee and stories around a campfire. We were next to Superior-18 again, and on our patrols Al and I stopped at one of their campfires, on the boundary between their sector and ours. It was the highest point of Sugarloaf, on bare rock and exposed to the wind—the coldest place on the mountain. The two firefighters stationed there were both named John, and to keep them straight we dubbed them John-1 and John-2. Because it was so windy they had kindled a small fire and ringed it with rocks. John-2 was usually lying down, wrapped around the rocks and trying to stay warm between patrols. We invited them to stop in at our squad's fire (a blazing inferno that was completely sheltered and well within the burn), and John-1 followed immediately.

We fell into a vigorous joke exchange with the rest of the squad, and John-1 provided us with a catch phrase that would endure for the rest of the campaign. He would start to tell a joke and then get lost in the extraneous minutae. He'd say: "There was this guy named Bill . . . maybe it was Ed . . . but [pause] it doesn't *really* matter." The narrative would progress for a moment, until he got to another variable: "He had this red Corvette . . . or a GTO; well, maybe it was a Jaguar. But [pause] it doesn't *really* matter." By the time he limped through a joke in maddening fits and starts, the punchline was irrelevant. But we now had our fatalistic, debate-ending aphorism. Any conundrum could be resolved, any troubling question answered, any doubt assuaged, any philosophy summarized. With the proper inflection, and a well-timed, utterly resigned shrug, you might end an incisive critique of the situation at hand by intoning: "But [pause] it doesn't *really* matter."

At around 3:00 AM we noticed a few flakes of snow, but by morning the sky was clear, and nobody at lower elevations believed us. Claims of precipitation were being taken with a grain of salt in the Pacific Northwest. It had been so dry for so long that weather reports were items of gossip—sources of ugly rumor. Humidity readings (usually very low) were savored as if they were the latest tidbits from a sleazy tabloid.

Metropolitan Burnt Ridge now had an Agness-like din about it, so most of the crew took to sleeping with the aid of government-issue foam earplugs. They were okay if they didn't give you a headache, but as Al said, "it didn't *really* matter."

We awoke to more changes. A layer of hay had been spread out over the "business district." Its purpose was environmental—a buffer between the humans and the dirt, mainly to protect the dirt. The Forest Service was a lot fussier than I expected about easing our impact on the land. The hay was a cushion for heavy foot traffic, and every day it was hosed down to prevent an inconvenient backfire from being ignited by an errant cigarette butt or some such, and embarrassing (or frying) us all. The straw blessed the camp with a carnival-like aspect, except for those unfortunates who were allergic to it. No one needed any further irritation of the nasal passages.

Another addition was an official bulletin board. There I learned that in the twenty-seven days since the Silver fire had begun, there had been eighty-four casulaties: "thirty-four reportable injuries, and fifty occupational illnesses." The latter included carbon monoxide poisoning, heat exhaustion, and simple viral infections. The fire camps were like giant petri dishes, or grade-school locker rooms—great places to raise and propagate viruses. Virtually everyone in camp was coughing, choking, and spitting. It was dubbed "the Rogue River hack" and was the common cold (or walking pneumonia) encouraged by hefty concentrations of smoke, dust, and the odor of your socks.

It was considered declassé, and a general pain in the ass, to shower every day. The rule of thumb was that "real firefighters" only showered on the third day. (It was appropriate timing for an event that resembled resurrection.) It was alleged by one of the oldtimers that enough dirt on the skin mixed with natural body oils, will make you waterproof. Perhaps, but that wasn't one of our problems. What would have been handy was a way to make ourselves fireproof.

The Forest Service had tackled that problem and had come up with a gadget called a "fire shelter." We all carried one on our web gear and weren't allowed on the fireline without it. Rick and I had never practiced with a shelter, so after dinner we had one of the veterans give us a lesson.

As mentioned, the fire shelter is basically a reflective foil pup tent, folded into a tight rectangular wad and stuffed into a carrying pouch. When secured on your belt or webbing, it's little bigger than a quart canteen. If about to be overrun by flames, we are supposed to jettison everything but the shelter. If we happen to be carrying a gallon of saw gas, that's especially important. Rip the fire shelter out of the pouch and unfold it by means of vigorous shaking—like snapping the dirt out of a rug. Since the flames may be screaming uphill at seventy miles per hour, haste is of the essence. The material is fairly stiff, allowing one to stand the tent on one end and step into it. Then, with feet planted on that end, a firefighter firmly grasps the other and drops forward onto the ground. It's critical to have a firm grasp on the shelter. High winds and fire-generated air currents can combine to whip up one-hundred miles per hour blasts that would rip the shelter away. "If possible," says the instruction sheet, "you should also clear the ground of leaves, twigs, and other combustibles, and any obstructions that might prevent a semi-tight seal between the fire shelter and the earth." And of course, if pigs had wings they could fly. The terrain we had been in to date was so rough and tangled that it would take the Corps of Engineers to fashion a textbook fire shelter site.

Still, it's better than nothing. I later saw a Forest Service training video where a volunteer had crawled into a shelter that was tightly ringed with piles of dry brush. With charged hoses standing by, the piles were ignited. In a few moments the shelter was in the midst of an inferno, but the volunteer remained unhurt, though uncomfortable, and increasingly nervous by the sound of his voice on the radio.

It can reach over 200 degrees inside the shelter, and a firefighter might have to dig a hole for his or her face, but it seemed like a real option—if one could get into it fast enough. I did it in less than a minute in practice, but I wasn't beset by the terror and confusion of reality. In any case, it was comforting to have one hanging on my belt.

The training had been timed well. That night our squad was exposed to imminent danger for the first time. We were sent on a smoke hunt into a potentially explosive draw far from the fireline. We were on Fishhook Peak, a 5,000-foot summit just across a burning valley from Sugarloaf. A scout on the peak saw an intermittent, phantom-like flash of fire about halfway down the mountain—just below a wide tract of unburned brush and trees. It was difficult to pinpoint exactly, but it was clear that if the hot spot blew up, a large section of Division "D" line would be jeopardized.

Mike posted Kevin as a lookout, and he was to watch intently for the on-again, off-again flame. He would serve as our radio guide and warn us if it looked like the fire was going to take off. With Rob in the lead, our squad started down a trail that led into a draw, or chimney. It was above the hot spot, and, in effect, we were descending into a furnace flue. If the breeze freshened and/or made a sudden shift in direction, the fire we were after could blast up the mountainside, confined and intensified by the natural forge-like draw. There'd be no way we'd outrun it.

Each step was an advance into peril; Rob and Al repeatedly emphasized the seriousness of our position. We were relying entirely on Kevin and a sometimes fragile radio link to keep us out of trouble. By the time we sensed danger ourselves, it might be too late. Soon we were in an area that was green on both sides of the trail. We were surrounded by fuel. We paused, using our headlamps to signal Kevin, trying to mark our position. He was supposed to talk us into the vicinity of the hot spot, but though we were less than a half-mile away, he said he couldn't see our lights. We backtracked until he could, and he gave us fresh instructions. We descended again, angling down the mountainside for a quarter-mile, but saw only blackness. The trail seemed to be veering away from where Kevin said the fire was. Having us out of sight made him nervous, and he called us back to the top.

Rob and Al dropped their packs and went scouting along the crest of a ridge that sloped off the summit of Fishhook in the direction of the phantom flame. In a few minutes they had it scoped out. The trail did turn away from the hot spot, because the stump or snag or whatever was smoldering, was sitting near the bottom of a long, near-vertical drop. In order to reach it we would have to traverse an acutely steep talus slope for a quarter-mile, or climb down a literal cliff for several dozen yards. The fire couldn't safely be reached and engaged on foot, at least not at night. Rob reported such to Mike, and he passed it on to Overhead. We withdrew. (A few days later the spot did indeed blow up. From Sugarloaf we saw a stand of fir burst into a fireball. Two helicopters, including a twin-rotored Vertol with a 1,000-gallon bucket, knocked it down, and there was no breach of the line.)

We rejoined the crew, patrolling a handline just below Fishhook. We found one hot spot that was only a few feet from the line—an interesting little smoke that encompassed a nest of yellowjackets. It was another cold night, but the rocks below the smoldering duff were still warm, keeping the yellowjackets active and angry. We would have gladly left them alone, but the line was just too near, and the embers had to be extinguished. It was a two-man job. While I sprayed the nest with water from a bladder bag, Bobby stirred up the duff with a pulaski, releasing heat and raging insects. There was no way to knock them all down with the spray, so after about a minute of furious activity we had to retreat. We waited a half-hour for the yellowjackets to settle, then returned for another minute of action. After four or five quick sorties, the spot was finally cold and the yellowjackets subdued. We didn't get stung.

In addition to a patrol sector, our squad was also assigned lookout duty on Fishhook Peak. Relieving Kevin, we took twenty-minute turns up there with a radio, ready to warn the rest of the line about any dangerous changes in fire behavior. We could see most of Division "D."

The wind had picked up, a sharp northwesterly blow that was pushing thirty-five-degree air. It was bitterly cold atop the peak, but the panorama was stupendous. The smoke was being driven away to the southeast, and the fire was in full view directly below. There were actually dozens of separate fires—intense, blazing pockets in the midst of blackness. I was reminded of World War II aerial photos of fire-bombed cities at night. Occasionally one of the pockets exploded. A gust of wind would push a simmering ground fire up into dry treetops, and the fire would "torch out." There would be a whooshing blast followed by an eruption of sparks, and then the tree was a giant flare—a brief, but brilliant mini-sun that lit up its section of the valley. When one tree went up, another would often immediately follow, and another, and so on, in a violent pyrotechnic chain reaction.

But the fire, as grimly fascinating as it was, paled in comparison to the sky. As it had been for weeks, the sky was cloudless. From our pinnacle at 5,000 feet, a significant portion of the earth's dense atmosphere was below us, and in terms of the wavelengths of visible light, we were much closer to the stars than we were back in Minnesota and Michigan. Despite the turbulence of the wind, there was a breathtaking clarity to the air. The constellations were crowded with stars, and the Milky Way was a luminous white band. If we had had a pair of binoculars, we could have resolved the celestial haze into tens of thousands of distant suns, the swarming core of our galaxy.

Fishhook Peak is a high point in the region, and we enjoyed an unobstructed 360-degree horizon. This imbued the sky with an especially dome-like character. I had a vivid sense of being at the focus of vast hemisphere, at the center of our world—raised above the land and fully exposed to the well-traveled light of the heavens. It was a place of power, where everything could be seen, a place that usually belonged to eagles and wind.

Far off, in the translucent haze of the eastern horizon, we could see the faint glow of Grants Pass, and a little to the south, Medford. These traces of civilization emphasized our grand isolation. The rest of the horizon was dark, a testimony to the surrounding wilderness. Rising up over the dim lights of Medford was the gleaming expanse of the coming winter constellations—from the sparkling star-patch of the Pleiades, down through orange-eyed Taurus, into the brilliant asterism of Orion with his spangled belt and blue and red beacons. And just above the rim of the planet was firey Sirius, the brightest of stars, glittering like a diamond turned in the light. All night we took our turns at the vigil, a rotating watch that carried us to dawn as if gliding on the axis of the earth. It passed too quickly.

✳ ✳ ✳

4.

The following afternoon, just as we were preparing to go on duty, we were pulled off the night shift. We had been switched to days at the last minute, and we would start the next morning. In essence, we had a little time off—though nobody wanted it—and I took the opportunity to wash some socks and underwear. There were some tubs and washboards set up near the showers, and for the first time in my life I saw how the world was before Maytag. Pretty grim. But it beat wearing crusty socks and mutating briefs. I still had extras, but I wanted to stay ahead of the game if I could. (Our Nomex shirts and pants could simply be exchanged for fresh units at the supply area.)

That evening we heard the big news: the fire had jumped the Illinois River. In a day's time it had consumed over 2,000 acres in the Kalmiopsis Wilderness. The concensus was that there was no stopping the blaze until it burned itself out of the wild country. The Kalmiopsis was just too rugged and remote. Once over the Illinois, the fire was guaranteed to consume at least another 20,000 to 30,000 acres. It must have been a helpless, anguished feeling for the Forest Service Overhead Team to concede that much territory—hoping for heavy rain but seeing absolutely nothing in the forecast. In a local press report the Incident Commander was quoted as saying that the only moisture he had seen for weeks was "my own tears when the fire jumped the Illinois."

But, as was mentioned in more than one story in the *Mail Tribune* out of Medford, the fires were not unmitigated disasters. Wildfires, it was pointed out, are often natural processes. They are nature's way of clearing dead undergrowth and stifling brush, and preparing the forest for new life. It was argued in one editorial that the Forest Service itself was responsible for the severity of the present blazes, because the forests had been overprotected. Since the Service had begun fire detection and suppression efforts in the early 1900s, large quantities of fuel had been allowed to collect on the forest floor. Previously, there'd been *more* wildfires (just about every time there was a dry lightning storm), but they'd been far less intense. There simply wasn't as much accumulated fuel. It takes a big fire to hurt the mature pines and firs. Their thick bark can protect them from a small fire that doesn't crown out in the upper stories of limbs and needles.

Back in Minnesota, there had been widespread support for a new Superior National Forest policy of allowing most natural fires in the Boundary Waters Canoe Area Wilderness to take their course. A fully protected wilderness area is not really wild. Besides, an over-mature forest can be a breeding ground for devastating pests and disease and is not as rich and diverse a habitat for wildlife as younger, more vigorous woods.

In Oregon, some people wanted the Forest Service to leave the fires alone. It was contended that fire control efforts sometimes did worse damage than the fires themselves. Heavy use of bulldozers for the construction of firelines had left significant scars in the past. However, changes were being made. A spokesman for an environmental group in Grants Pass said that in battling the Silver complex, the Forest Service was "sensitive to protecting wilderness values." Indeed. In one of the wilder areas of the Siskiyou, firefighters were forbidden to cut down smoldering snags because Overhead didn't want to leave behind any *stumps*—obvious man-made objects. (Some on our crew thought that was going too far.)

Next morning we were up at 5:00 AM, ate breakfast, and were on the trucks by 6:00 AM. From DP-13 we hiked back up along the spine of Sugarloaf. Four crews were strung out along the crest, "lizarding out." (We are said to "lizard out" when we hunker down on hot rocks in full sunlight.) Our job was to watch. Sugarloaf was basically cold, but the Forest Service wasn't taking any chances. Fire was still burning in the valley below, and though the odds were against a "slop-over"—a breach of the line—there was that eight million dollar timber sale to think about. Besides, for the moment there were too many crews on hand. Overhead didn't want us lounging around camp, so they sent us out on the line to sit. It was a temporary hiatus, and they didn't dare send anyone home. When the fire finally came roaring out of the Kalmiopsis, they were going to need as many people as they could get. And there already had been some embarrassment. Hiawatha-1 (the previous manifestation of our crew) and several other eastern crews had been sent home, only to be called back out the next week—at great expense. It was much cheaper to "store" us out on the line than to pay our airfare prematurely. Everyone was sure there was going to be a lot more action, and soon. Facing south, we could see the awesome, sky-engulfing columns of smoke rising out of the Kalmiopsis.

There were two helicopters making sorties all day, and watching them helped the twelve-hour shift to pass. One was a twin-rotored Vertol, a downsized version of a Chinook (or "shit hook" as it's more popularly known), and I'd never seen one in action before. It and a much smaller Bell 204 were dumping buckets of water on the slopes directly below us, and we had a unique perspective—looking *down* on the helicopters, as if we were airborne ourselves.

Occasionally I would walk over to Al's post, and we would talk military history—one of his passions. We ranged from Pickett's charge at Gettysburg to the Tet offensive, and Al slipped into the realm of his personal experience.

During our first night shift he had suffered a severe headache, and now he told me why. One day in Vietnam, his machine-gun squad had been involved in a vicious firefight. "There were 1,500 people at forty-acre hill, trying to kill each other," he said. In the midst of the fury, a bullet hit Al in the face. He saw it. The slug ricocheted off a log, and the action snapped into slow-motion. He actually watched the projectile dart in toward his eyes. It seemed to take a ridiculously long time to travel a few feet, but he couldn't move. It struck him just above the nose and knocked him down.

His initial reaction was rage. He jumped to his feet, pissed-off, and suddenly disgusted with the whole scene. Strangely, there was no pain, but he was bleeding profusely. "Fuck this shit!" he yelled, and dropped his web gear. He had had enough. He walked toward the rear. All day men had crouched and crawled in that area—one of his ammo-bearers had been shot dead only minutes before—but Al was beyond caring. He simply strode to the rear in full view of the world. (He shook his head at the memory of it.)

He didn't like the way the medic looked at him, and he figured he was going to die. But while he was lying there waiting for a medevac, his mind did another flip-flop, and he tried to get up and return to his unit. The medic wouldn't let him. At the hospital the surgeons cut the bullet out of his head, and much to his surprise, he didn't die. He was left with impaired vision (correctable with glasses), and with unpredictable, recurring headaches that were sometimes incapacitating. He complained bitterly of his treatment at the Veterans Administration hospital, and how he felt his condition had been taken lightly by the doctors. Apparently he was just supposed to feel grateful he was alive, and not bother people with the life-altering nature of his wounds. (He also had had a leg shot up, and it hobbled him occasionally.)

At the end of a fervent diatribe against the system, he suddenly grew embarrassed. He abruptly stopped talking, looked at me and shrugged. "But," he said, with a twisted grin, "it doesn't *really* matter."

"Bullshit," I replied. "You've been telling me it matters for the past half-hour."

"Hell, man, I've just been telling stories." And we dropped it.

The next day we finally got to a hot line. As the sun was easing up over a ghostly inversion, we marched down a dead-end road directly below Sugarloaf. We were down where we had seen the helicopters making bucket drops the day before. A handline extended off the end of the road, heading for the remote bottom of the valley. For the first time, we were close to open flames. Numerous spot fires were burning in deadfalls and stumps, occasionally spreading into the lower branches of young firs and incinerating them in quick, firey blasts.

A Washington State crew hiked down the line first. Their assignment was to push on to the end and construct more line, extending our front all the way to the creek at the base of Sugarloaf. We teamed up with Minnesota-4, and both crews were split into squads. Some did mop-up on the hot spots at the high end of the line, while others assembled a long hose lay down the side of the mountain. Our goals were clearly outlined: 1) we would extinguish all the fire we could find, 2) we would ignite a burnout in the remaining greenery on the uphill side of the line, and 3) we would hold the line with nozzles and hand tools. The overall purpose was to create a buffer zone to save a large tree plantation that abutted the line. Our water supply was two portable 1,000-gallon tanks back up at DP-13. Known as "bird baths," they were supplied by tank trucks, which shuttled water from a creek several road-miles away. People did their best, but we had to be aware that our water supply was subject to unpredictable interruptions.

I was teamed up with Rob, and we started in on the spot fires. We had an inch-and-a-half hose, and we took turns—one guy on the nozzle while the other hacked away with a pulaski, exposing embers and digging around stumps. The morning sun was already hot, and we were working in the midst of scorched forest, treading on heated rock. It was a double oven— fried from above, baked from below. In moments we were drenched with sweat and black with soot. We took periodic breaks to run hose water over each other's head and neck. But it was satisfying, hands-on labor. We were killing a lot of fire in a hurry.

And we were also TV stars. Early on, we were still working close to the road at the head of the line and easily accessible to the media. Within minutes we were interviewed by two news teams from competing Portland stations. They were both trolling for drama and controversy, baiting us with questions like: "Are you concerned about your safety out here?" (Intent: "Tell us a harrowing but short and video-friendly story about how six of your buddies were gruesomely killed, how emotionally distraught you are from the terrible experience, and how the Forest Service might have prevented the tragedy.")

But the telecasters were disappointed. Though they dutifully recorded our names, I had the feeling they wouldn't be using the tape. Rob and I were two simple grunts-in-our-glory, happy to be living and fighting in the mountains, enjoying the camaraderie and making good money. What petty complaints we had weren't worth mentioning, and we didn't. The TV boys wanted images of battle-weary, slightly dispirited troops thrown into the

breach against their will and were now exhausted and terminally homesick.
It's too bad they didn't run into our Squad Three. One of their guys had his
professional motto printed on the back of his helmet: "Think OT!" (as in
OVERTIME).

While we were being interviewed, a Forest Service information officer
hovered nervously in the background, no doubt wondering what kind of in-
anities we were spouting into the microphones. He seemed relieved when it
was over, and Rob and I grinned at each other as we resumed our work.

Barely an hour after they went in, the Washington crew was ordered
out. They came trudging back up the mountain—drenched, winded, and
ruefully grinning (or cursing, depending upon individual temperament). A
spot fire had crept into some fresh fuel and blown up, torching out in some
bigger trees. We had heard the roar—like the ignition of a distant jet engine. The crew was forced to retreat, and the Vertol and a 204 were called
in.

We paused to gawk as the Vertol howled directly overhead at treetop
level, then dropped out of sight into the valley. We could not see flames, but
we saw the payload of water cascade through a wall of shimmering heat
waves rising out of the forest. The fire was very hot, and there was little
smoke.

We did not find out till later that the water was being dumped on the
rest of our squad. Al, Bobby, Dave, and Larry, the assistant crew boss, had
been dispatched as a saw team to clear snags from the line, and they had
been surprised by the sudden flare-up. Someone above had screamed, "Get
the hell out!" and they had scrambled back up the handline. In places the
slope was about seventy percent—veritable cliffs—with loose rock and exposed networks of roots. The going was mean, and they were about to jettison all their gear when the helicopters began to drop water practically on
top of them. They ran/stumbled/climbed at full bore for only about a hundred yards, but the line of retreat was nearly straight up, and Larry said
later that they had been prepared to use their fire shelters; though he ad-
mitted it would have been a real trick to find a spot level enough to deploy
one. Fortunately, three or four loads from the helicopters eliminated the
immediate danger, and the other squads began advancing hose lines to
knock out the rest. The Washington crew humped back down to the end of
the line and resumed cutting and digging.

Rob and I finished mopping up our assigned sector, and I was sent
down to help haul and lay hose. We were running an inch-and-a-half feeder
line, installing a gated wye every one-hundred feet, so that one-inch attack
lines could be connected wherever needed. We wanted a lot of nozzles ready
when we touched off the burnout.

The job was almost done when we heard another blow-up down ahead
of us. Radios squawked all along the line, and in a moment we were madly
uncoupling the hose we had just laid and dragging it back uphill. The heli-

copters descended, circling in like raptors and hammered the new flare-up. But it was far upslope, halfway to the top of Sugarloaf. We lugged our hose back into position, laughing a little in the midst of our game of musical couplings.

By noon, everyone was low on drinking water. Most people were packing four canteens plus a couple of cans of Gatorade, but the temperature was near ninety, and we had been working for six straight hours. Supplies had been sucked up. The strike team leader called for extra water, and two plastic cubees were delivered to the end of the road. Mike asked for a volunteer to run one of them down to the Washington crew and some of the people strung out along the way, and I elected to make the trip.

The cubee held five gallons and weighed just over forty pounds. A handgrip was molded into the top, but it would have been awkward, and, therefore, dangerous, to carry it a mile down the mountainside like a piece of unwieldy luggage. There was a broken pulaski handle lying near the tool cache, so I slid the end of it through the handgrip, and then slung it over my shoulder. I looked like the traditional hobo, his bundle of possessions tied to a stick. The cubee rested comfortably—in a manner of speaking—balanced at the middle of my back, and I still had one free hand.

About a quarter-mile down the trail, I started dispensing water. People from our crew and Minnesota-4 were scattered along the hose lay, holding back a fresh surge of flames. At one spot the blaze was only a few yards from the line, with flames ten and twenty feet high devouring a stand of small firs. A grand old snag had also caught fire, and it was obviously being undermined. It was partially hollow, and we could see the flames shooting up inside, eating away what remained of the trunk. It was leaning slightly in toward the burn, but it had the potential to topple perilously close to the line.

One of our crewmen was manning a nozzle, tracking it back and forth like a machine gun, from one end of the fire to the other. At the moment it was a stalemate. A professional sawyer stood by, waiting for things to cool off. He needed to drop that snag. In the meantime they were both crouched in the shelter of a huge fir which shielded them from the intense heat, and served as some protection if the snag should topple of its own accord. I filled one canteen per man, and then hurried on, feeling the radiation of the fire on my back. I hoped that, when I returned, the line would still be intact. It seemed to me there was reason for doubt.

The trail turned into a goat path. It was so steep that at times I was in danger of falling forward and careening straight down. I hugged the ground, feeling for handholds and cautiously selecting each step. The trail was mostly loose rock, and there were people somewhere below. If I dislodged a large stone there was no telling how far it would tumble. It amazed me to realize that crews had *worked* on this winding, treacherous line—with chain saws and pulaskis—cutting away trees and the worst of the brush.

As I descended, the rocks turned wet and slick. The line was following the bed of an intermittent stream, and rivulets of cold water seeped out of the mountain. Scattered patches of moss thrived on damp stone, and they were like banana peels thrown on a sidewalk. I scraped at the moss with a boot before placing full weight on a given rock. It would be simple to fracture an ankle, or worse, and getting out of that hole would be hell—by whatever means. A helicopter wouldn't be able to help.

Soon, all sound of the fire above had faded away. There were little pools in the creek bed, and the fir had given way to dense, jungle-like stands of myrtlewood and maple. I kept an eye out for snakes.

I entered a stretch of fresh cuttings, and could hear the roar of chain saws and the ring of pulaskis ahead. These people were working hard. They grinned when they saw me. "Gunga Din!" someone yelled, and, with a chorus of genuine gratitude in my ears, I filled canteens and water bottles until the cubee was dry. It was pleasant duty.

Far above, the line held, and, by the time I struggled back to the end of the hose lay, the sawyer had felled the hollow snag and was working on others. The spot fires were out, the initial mop-up was complete, and we were ready to make some fire of our own.

We spread out along the line, and a half-dozen people stuck fusees onto the ends of sticks, lit them, and then walked slowly through the brush, scattering fire. There was a gentle breeze to our rear, and the fire rose up instantly, leaping out of crackling pockets to form walls of flame that rushed away uphill. We spent the next several minutes tempering the fire. We wanted it to burn as freely as possible, but if an area got dangerously hot, it was lightly doused to keep it under control. It was a highly subjective judgement, based on the gut feeling of whoever was on the nozzles. The rule of thumb: if it got scary, hit it.

As soon as the edge of the handline was burned, it was hosed down thoroughly. The fir plantation, choked with dry grass, was just across the line, and a single stray ember could nullify our efforts. It would be an extremely hazardous place to be if the fire jumped the trail. It's a matter of record that most forest fire facilities involve the sudden ignition of "light fuels," like grass or brush, that burn hot and very swiftly. A wind shift is a common culprit, and, in the mountains, the wind can do freaky things.

Near our squad's sector, the fire crept inside a live Douglas fir. There was a cleft in the trunk extending from the ground up about twenty feet, and the flames found it convivial. The huge, mature tree was less than twenty yards from the line, and leaning toward it. We moved in with a hose to extinguish the fire around the base, then called for a sawyer. We thought he would drop it, but instead he just cut around the lower part of the cleft, "surgically" removing the worst part of the burn. He had us hose down the rest, explaining that one Doug fir like that was worth thousands of dollars, and it was now Forest Service policy to save as many individual mature trees as possible without endangering human life.

By the end of the day, our burnout was just about complete. A few hot spots remained, but the night shift could handle them. As we collected our tools and donned our packs, the Washington crew trudged up out of the hole, filthy and exhausted. But no one on any of our three crews had been hurt—not so much as a twisted ankle—and, given the assignment, it was surprising. However, as we waited for the trucks, we learned that other strike teams hadn't been so fortunate. One of the Superior crews working up on Fishhook had suffered two casualties—a broken arm and a collapsed lung—caused, we were told, by being struck with falling rock. And on the other side of the fir plantation, a sawyer had his shoulder broken by a widow-maker—a falling tree limb. It had been a rough day in Division "D."

✳ ✳ ✳

5.

Next morning we hit it again. Along with Minnesota-4, we were sent back to the plantation. The night shift had mopped up our burnout, so we were dispatched to the end of the handline where the Washington crew had been cutting. Our mission was to extend the line "all the way to the bottom," that is, to the banks of Indigo Creek. We didn't know exactly how far that was, but the strike team leader believed we could do it in one day. We had two saws per crew, so we broke up into four groups, each taking a fifty-yard chunk of territory. As each swath was cleared, groups would leapfrog ahead to start on another segment.

But that plan was engendered by morning optimism. The trees and brush formed a thick, almost impenetrable tangle. Our initial cutting was like burrowing into a green wall. We were following the deep gully formed by an intermittent creek, and it was a wicked jumble of boulders and criss-crossed deadfalls. The sides of the gully were steep and loose. In our sector we found a four-foot vertical drop concealed by brush, and we had to scout cautiously the way ahead to avoid similar mantraps. And it was hot. The forecasters had promised another ninety-degree day, and we were methodically felling our own shade trees.

It was simple, savage work. A sawyer and a swamper (an assistant to watch for hazards, pull branches out of the way, push on trees) would take the point, felling trees either downslope or dropping them onto the green side if possible. (We *never* toss fresh fuel onto the burned side—no matter how cold it looks.) They would limb them and saw the trunks into manageable pieces. The rest of the crew followed behind, stacking the remains on the green side and hacking at the smaller brush with pulaskis. Normally, we would also scrape the ground down to mineral soil, but the creek bed was all rock and gravel—and wet besides.

It was sad duty. We were slashing our way through a beautiful stand of myrtle and maple, killing young trees and casting them aside in ugly heaps. If not for the fire, no one would have disturbed this remote creek bed for years, perhaps decades. Without our crude trail, it wouldn't even be accessible. I reminded myself that our goal was the protection of the forest as a whole. At least we weren't in there with heavy equipment.

We shared the slaughter, taking turns with the chain saw and slaving away in merciless sun. The strike team leader had made arrangements for extra water to be brought down, but it never arrived. We conserved what we had and talked about temporarily damming one of the rivulets and taking a chance with the native product. The main concern was contamination with giardia, a common waterborne intestinal parasite, and we discussed it long enough to talk ourselves out of it. Among all those Forest Service employees we sported too much biological expertise to allow ourselves the bliss of ignorance.

Mike told us to take our lunch break in shifts, so the saws would never stop running. With only four sawyers it was hard to keep everyone working steadily, and Mike wished to put out a maximum effort. He wanted our crew to be noticed by Overhead, to develop a reputation as "a good crew," and, therefore, land more active assignments. Or so he hoped. Since this was a Western fire, there was a bias in favor of Western crews, and Mike felt we would have to labor hard to overcome it.

We tried, but our sedulous advance was cut short by the clock. Usually the day shift ran until 6:00 PM, but this was our sixth shift, and on the Silver Complex that meant we were due for a day of R & R. We had to be back at the DP (drop point) by 4:00 PM to catch our ride into town. From where we were, it would take at least forty minutes of hard hiking/climbing to get out, so we donned our packs at around 3:00 PM and headed up. Each saw team had finished its first swath, but no more. We had advanced the line about 600 feet.

We were met at the top by some Overhead dude who asked how far we had "progressed." From his manner we could tell that it was a formality—that he didn't consider our day's efforts to be of critical importance. Our commanders were erring on the side of caution, and I was suddenly glad we hadn't "built" more line than we had. It was my impression that, though our new handline could be strategically justified, under normal circumstances there wouldn't have been enough manpower available for the job, and the IC's plans would've survived without it. But he had the people, and he needed to keep them, at least for a while.

My buddies told me it was also unusual to have R & R after only six shifts. It was more common to labor for two weeks before a big break, and they had been on fires where they never did go on leave. We all could've handled a few more shifts without a day off, but we didn't complain.

They bussed us into the Pacific Coast town of Gold Beach, a small port at the mouth of the Rogue River. We hauled our red packs into a motel—an incongruous setting for a camp—and tried to transform ourselves from fire grunts into civilians. A long shower and a clean pair of blue jeans was the first step. (It was considered boorish to wear Nomex in town, clean or not, and only nerds blatantly advertised the fact that they were firefighters.) The second step was to add alcohol.

The United States Government paid for our meals in town—up to a point. We were allowed five dollars for breakfast, five dollars for lunch, and thirteen dollars for dinner, but Uncle Sam wouldn't allow one penny for booze. It's a priorities problem when you think about it. They call it R & R—rest and recreation—right? Well, what one thing would assure us more R & R than any other? Right. But this nation is still wrestling with its puritanical roots, and the Forest Service wouldn't buy us a drink. Even the bible notes that ". . . wine maketh glad the heart of man . . ." (Psalms 104:15), and the apostle Paul advised Timothy to "Drink no longer water, but use a little wine for thy stomach's sake . . ." (I Timothy 5:23). Now there was a man who understood R & R. I suggest that the Forest Service hire an Official U.S. Taxpayer to monitor each big incident. An honest, upstanding citizen could be picked at random from the files of the IRS and be paid AD-II wages to make judgement calls on government expenditures. In the grey areas, or in matters of controversy, he or she could be brought in and asked: "Hey, should we spend your tax money on this?" They might quail at some of the helicopter operations (the biggest ships cost the Feds fifty dollars per *minute,* or $3,000 per hour), but would they neglect to buy us grunts a few beers? Not if they were a true patriot. In any case, we weren't depending on Uncle Sam to get us drunk—we had our own pocket money for that.

In a way, we had more responsibility in town than we had out on the line. We had to balance having a good time—that is, vigorously celebrating survival and camaraderie—with displaying good manners. It had been made clear to us by Overhead that any crew causing the least bit of trouble in town would be shipped home—immediately. And they had activated that time-honored automatic enforcement mechanism: even if only one member of an outfit screwed up, the whole crew would be penalized. I was assured by the veterans that the Forest Service meant business. They were chronically involved in controversy, and good PR is apparently high on the priority list. A drunken brawl in a local tavern is not an efficient way to court the goodwill of a community.

About half of Hiawatha #3 ended up in a semi-ritzy bar across the road from the motel. It wasn't the homiest joint in the world, but they had tap beer at a reasonable price, and we didn't need much more than that. A good jukebox, maybe, and theirs was acceptable.

We pounded down the beer, clinking toasts to somebody's birthday and to the economic opportunity offered by a major forest fire. We were loud but non-violent, about as innocent and clean-cut as possible without being so-ber. But I could see that Mike was holding back, still on the job. A good crew boss never rests. He was casting an occasional, nervous glance at Bobby, who was steering at full throttle for the painless land of "Ten-Beer Obliv-ion."

I was holding back too—not out of a sense of duty but because more than four or five beers steers me to a toilet. I decided I should be Bobby's chaperone, a self-designated drunk-roper. Around midnight I saw him tense up. He had been galvanized by some sudden inspiration. No telling what—maybe he was just going to pass out. He rose, mumbled something about dancing, and started stumbling between the barstools and tables. I jumped up and grabbed his arm, deflecting him toward the door. He tried to dance, but I was a lousy partner. Instead, joined by Al, we sang our way across the parking lot ("Do wah ditty, ditty dum ditty doo!"), across the road, and to the door of Bobby and Al's room. A security guard told us to shut-up, and we did. I apologized to the man, and Al dragged Bobby to safety.

Mike and the rest had followed us out, and Mike slapped my back and said, "Good man." At that moment I felt I was really a part of Hiawatha-3. Guiding Bobby to his room had been a small task—he might even have made it on his own (though I doubt it), and Mike hadn't made a big deal of it. But the message was clear: crew members looked out for the crew. I was now a full member.

The next day we did a little shopping—mostly for some cheap paper-backs—though I also searched for a new pair of boots. Mine had seen a lot of rugged mileage before this gig, and the Siskiyou fire lines were finishing them off. I was certain they wouldn't last another week—the soles were just about to start flapping. And without decent boots I could be confined to camp, helping the caterers do dishes or some other equally depressing task.

But Gold Beach was a footwear wasteland. It boiled down to two choices: a pair of logger's high-topped, spiked boots, which I didn't need and couldn't afford, or, at the same shop that sold used books, a pair of "re-conditioned Malaysian army boots." I asked Al what "re-conditioned" meant, and falling back on his military experience he instantly replied: "Fumigated and polished." I could afford those, but I didn't think they'd last a single shift in the mountains. I'd have to order boots through the commissary back up at Burnt Ridge.

Late in the afternoon I wandered down to the Pacific, touching it for the first time. The beach was wide, and surprisingly clean. I spent a couple of restful hours watching seals cavort in the surf, and pelicans and cormo-rants skim the whitecaps.

The haze-filtered sun laid a dull sheen on the waves, and for a few moments I had a strange conviction of déjà vú. Briefly, the scene was utterly familiar, and I decided the perception was "historical" in nature. As a young boy I had been fascinated by the tales of World War II in the Pacific theater.

In those years, just before heavy United States involvement in Vietnam, the Christmas catalogs were full of war toys, and my friends and I were weaned on submachine guns from Mattel. One year I received a Landmark Book entitled *From Pearl Harbor to Okinawa*. It was a history of the Pacific war, and I read it five or six times. I *studied* the photographs and maps. I fantasized about being a Marine Corps gunnery sergeant, or a Naval fighter pilot. I grieved for having been born too late. In my mind I could *smell* the Pacific Ocean. It was "the smell of victory!" One of my most vivid childhood dreams involved traveling from California in a submarine—heading for Japan. Pacific waves rolled over the bow, sparkling in the sunlight.

A few years later my generation had its chance—we had our own Pacific war. One of my high school teachers had fought against the Japanese on Saipan, and, one day in class, circa 1967, he briefly reminisced about his wartime experiences. He closed by saying, "It looks like you boys are going to take your turn." Some did. But, by the time I graduated in 1969, my head had been turned by a religious cult that forbade military service. It's another story—a long one. Suffice it to say that I've never crossed the Pacific. But there in Gold Beach I finally smelled it, temporarily wistful about a naive little boy exhorted to dreams of glory. In the end, however, it was the seals and pelicans that impressed me most. A twinge of regret at having missed "my turn," was quickly tempered by the realization that if I had crossed the Pacific in 1969, I might very well be long dead.

Just before we left town, Jim and Randy, both EMTs, performed a valuable PR service for Hiawatha-3. At dinner time in a local restaurant, Jim rushed to the aid of an old man who had recently suffered a stroke. The guy was suddenly unsteady, and appeared to be in trouble. While waiting for an ambulance, Jim and Randy monitored his vital signs and comforted the man's wife. It turned out to be nothing serious, but the incident made the local paper when the restaurant management sent a grateful letter to the editor. And it ultimately helped more than Hiawatha-3. Back at Agness, we discovered that further R & R in town had been canceled. One crew had two of its members engage in a downtown knife fight, and another firefighter had tried to forcibly enter the wrong motel room. He was deadass drunk, and honestly mistaken, but the solitary woman inside was not amused. All three ended up in jail.

From now on, said Overhead, R & R would have to be taken in camp. But Mike made sure that the IC heard about our EMTs and the appreciative response, and we hoped it might sway his judgement, eventually. We were all disappointed, but Jim was particularly chagrined. The restaurant manager had given him a handwritten chit—the next time Jim was in town, the drinks would be on the house. We kidded him about his lost beer—especially on the searing afternoons to follow.

Throughout the next week we were shuttled around like tourists, becoming intimate with every inch of fireline in Div. "D."

✳ ✳ ✳

6.
OCTOBER 2:
A Forest Service Overhead man got us up at 4:30 AM. He sounded like he relished the onerous chore—his voice teetered on the edge of glee. Everyone instantly hated his guts, but it was still pitch dark, and we couldn't see his face. (The next morning they sent a woman. She was a lot gentler, but just as effective. You know: "If you want someone's attention, whisper.")

After a groggy breakfast, we were bussed back up to Burnt Ridge—or rather, directly past it to DP-2. We spent the day hunting for smokes (and finding a few) on a largely cold mountainside just below Fishhook Peak. It was a long, tedious day, but at least we wouldn't have to go back there. Just before quitting time, we got the order to break down several hundred feet of hose line, pack it back up the mountain, and out to the DP. It was messy, cross-contour, cross-country work, but we were glad for the heavy activity after patrolling for the most of the shift.

The strike team leader said there were several hundred more feet of hose at the very base of Fishhook—maybe 2,000 feet below, and a half-dozen miles by trail—and he needed a crew to hike in, collect it, and arrange to have it lifted out via helicopter. Mike volunteered us with alacrity. It would be good, shift-eating duty—far better than searching for small hot spots that may or may not exist. Okay, said the strike team leader, that would be our assignment for the next day.

Back at Burnt Ridge, I ordered a new pair of boots from the commissary—a $100 pair of Red Wings with eight-inch tops and Vibram lug soles. The favorite boot of the firefighting fraternity is the legendary White, a boot that apparently never gets discarded, but rather sent back to the factory for "re-building" when needed. I met a career Forest Service man from Alaska who had been wearing the same pair of Whites for seventeen years (rebuilt once), and he thought they were the greatest thing since the pulaski. But he did mention that the secret to leather boot longevity is the use of a boot dryer, a device designed to dry boots from the inside out, and so prevent cracks in the leather.

I lusted after a pair of Whites, but they cost $220, and I was already intimidated by the cost of the Red Wings. The woman at the commissary said they would arrive in two or three days. I hoped so; my soles were shipping dirt. I had glued them in Gold Beach, using a hoity-toity, super-something cement, but they hadn't lasted one shift.

The IC was in camp that evening, and I listened to his briefing. He said the Sugarloaf timber sale was still number one priority, and that's why so many of us were working out on cold firelines. Overhead was simply not going to take a chance on pulling out too soon. Some Hot Shot crews—the storm troopers of the fire service—had been airlifted into the Kalmiopsis to construct some initial lines, but they were almost certainly going to be overrun, and the lines would be abandoned the next day. A five-man helitak crew in California had been trapped in a flare-up generated by a freak wind, and four had made it into their fire shelters. The other was dead.

OCTOBER 3:

Back to the familiar environs of DP-13 and Sugarloaf Mountain. At the last minute, we were aced out of our potentially interesting hose-retrieval mission by a Western crew. Mike was disgusted. We had worked diligently at every task we had been given, volunteered for everything in sight, and among our veterans we had as much, if not more, mountain fire experience than many of the younger Western crews. Nevertheless, we were still treated as second class. Western people were calling the shots, and they looked out for their own.

The aerial infrared survey from the night before had registered two hot spots near the old slopover on Sugarloaf, so we were dispatched up there to hunt for them. Mike gave us a pep talk, and we spent a long, hot day crisscrossing old, cold, ground. We found nothing.

Late in the day, we heard a helicopter descend deep into the valley below Fishhook, and then watched it rise out of the forest with a great spaghetti-like tangle of hose dangling at the end of a longline (cable sling). That Western crew obviously wouldn't make it out of there until well after dark; they were going to rack up a lot of valuable hours. Hiawatha-3 was not happy. The highlights of our day had been 1) birdwatching at lunchtime (Kevin was well-versed in things avian, and we identified a couple of varieties of nuthatch and enjoyed the antics of a brilliant blue Stellar's jay), 2) we found a section of a week-old newspaper lost by another crew, and the crossword puzzle was intact.

OCTOBER 4:

We were sent marching far down a line below the tree plantation—across the valley from where we had been cutting new line a few days before. We broke up into squads, and then into two-man patrols, hunting for isolated smokes. Our squad decided to keep score, but each "kill" had to be confirmed. A smoke didn't count unless it was seen by at least one other person.

Dreamer and I teamed up, and began slowly scouting our territory. We had about fifty yards of line, and we were supposed to check as far back as 300 feet into the burn. Early in the morning I smelled smoke near an old deadfall, but I couldn't find the source. I passed the same spot twice, and caught the faintest whiff. I searched the immediate area in depth—feeling inside snags and stirring up suspicious piles of ash. Nothing. We were definitely into detail work, but we had all day, and as the ground and air were warmed by the sun, the invisible hot spot might flare up. Such was our manpower density, that each firefighter had about one acre of ground to cover. We had the time to examine literally every square foot, and that's what we were supposed to do.

Just before noon, I happened to glance in the right direction, and saw a curl of smoke. There was the spot I'd smelled. Deep in the bole of a burned out snag was a major heat sink. The core of duff was too hot to touch. Bobby confirmed my "kill," and I tried to dry-mop it—scraping out the smoldering wood with my pulaski. But there was too much material and no safe place to put it. The snag was within a few feet of a pocket of unburned brush, and it would be a catastrophe—and highly embarrassing—to ignite a reburn this late in the game. Especially if it was started by an Eastern crew.

There was a charged inch-and-a-half hose deployed along the handline, so Bobby and I hooked up a one-inch hose and nozzle to the nearest wye, and dragged it up to the snag. We filled the bole and stirred, generating a cloud of steam. We worked the water in until everything we could feel was cold, and I was happy. We'd had some serious heat there, and honest-to-god embers were becoming pretty rare in Division "D." Undetected, that snag would have smoldered for days.

That was the apex of the shift. However, our squad tracked down a total of six hot spots, and, between patrols, we stalked a covey of blue grouse, played several hands of Bullshit Poker (a game of lying, bluffing, and deceit well suited to the personality of our squad), and laughed uproariously at the strike team leader. It seems someone tampered with his backpack while it sat unattended on the line. When he climbed, huffing and sweating, back up to the DP—a steep and torturous ascent—and reached into his pack for a canteen, he broke into a fluent stream of profanity. "I thought that damn pack was too heavy!" he cried. And in front of two crews he pulled three rocks from the depths of his kit. The man was a good sport, but no one confessed.

That afternoon Mike had gone on a scouting mission. He found the source of some substantial smoke that we had seen from the DP, and scoped out a route that a crew might follow to reach it. Its source was a dangerous pocket of fire that could easily mushroom into a major blow-up with the right wind. He reported it to the division supervisor, and said he'd be happy to take Hiawatha-3 in there with chain saws and bladder bags to mop it up—or to direct an aerial assault, or whatever. Again he was promised the job. Reaching and eliminating that isolated fire would be our assignment for the next day. Our spirits rose.

That evening Kevin and I walked to the rim of Burnt Ridge to watch another sunset. A combination of smoke, elevation, and low coastal clouds had produced several spectacular light shows, and usually a dozen people gathered at that spot after supper. Other than a third-day shower, it was the best entertainment at Burnt Ridge.

The sun disappeared into a streaked yellow haze fringed with bluish-purple, and we lingered to watch the first stars wink on. We were looking up at the Big Dipper when someone yelled "Look at that!" The man was pointing toward the southwest horizon.

"Wow!" was the only appropriate response. A mountain had just exploded. A distant peak—perhaps ten miles away—was engulfed in monstrous flames. Even as we watched, the fire devoured the mountain. We could see the flames ripping upward until they reached the summit and licked at the stars. From far away the orange tongues were feathery and undulating—like solar flares at the rim of an eclipsed sun. Was anyone on that mountain? Was there a handline at the top? It was a horrifying thought. We were witnessing a hellish, unstoppable fire, a raging storm of heat so intense that trees as tall as skyscrapers were bursting into instant, all-consuming destruction. It was a terrible kind of beauty. We heard the next day that there had been 500-foot flames traveling upslope at sixty to seventy miles per hour. Fortunately nobody was in the way.

OCTOBER 5:

Several news items caught our attention. A thirty-eight-year-old firefighter died on the line in California—heart attack. A firefighter on another division of the Silver Complex suffered eye injuries when the alkaline batteries of his buddy's headlamp exploded in his face. A new fire had been ignited several miles north of us, started by a deer hunter. It was already up to 600 acres, and the Oregon DNR had mounted the initial attack. And, closer to home, the Burnt Ridge fire camp was going to close; we would be transferred back to Agness the next day.

Once again we teamed up with Minnesota-4 at DP-13. Once again—at the last minute—we lost a plum assignment to a Western crew. Only that morning, Mike learned that the fire he had scouted the day before was going to be handled by someone else. Instead, our Eastern strike team was dispatched to a mop-up job at a backburn that had already been mopped, and was nearly cold. Mike and our strike team leader (a Minnesotan), were bitter.

We hiked for about a mile and a half along a narrow handline that ran along the eastern flank of Sugarloaf, about a thousand feet below the crest. I walked up front with Mike and the strike team leader, and they monitored the progress of the usurping Western crew on their radios—sarcastically commenting on the lack of initial progress, and severely criticizing the crew boss involved. Mike, usually calm, mild-mannered, and willing to roll with the bureaucratic punches, was tired of being pushed around from one relatively dead arena to the next. I was surprised to hear the vehemence in his voice. It reinforced my impression of the firefighters' attitude: though paid the same no matter what we did, most of us lusted for action—wanted to be where we could have maximum effect. We wanted to be busy. Part of it, of course, was the fact that the more we had to do, the faster a shift passed, but we also had a sincere desire to make our mark on that fire, to be able to exercise the full range of our skills.

Even so, the hike out to the backburn was particularly charming. We were hugging a contour line on a precipitous slope, winding around the mountainside through a labyrinth of roots and rocks. The path was loose gravel—caving for long stretches, and each footfall was critical. In a half-dozen places it was a matter of carefully coordinating handholds and foot-holds, chests pressed against bare rock. In a couple of spots we slid our tools ahead and used both hands for scaling. It wasn't a sheer drop to the bottom, but steep enough to make the angle academic. Not OSHA-approved activity. Once again I was surprised that forty people with packs and tools could rapidly negotiate such a wicked trail without incident. I had to keep remind-ing myself that this wasn't an average sample of the general public.

Clearly the native residents weren't expecting us. We flushed a mule deer at close range, and found bear tracks so fresh that I expected to en-counter the beast around the next bend. The animals presented a special hazard. Since there was so much slope above us, we were fully exposed to a great many potential falling-rock projectiles. The startled deer bounded upslope and triggered a small avalanche of gravel. There were several shouts of "Rock!" as the entire team froze to watch for stone missiles. Even a frightened squirrel dislodged a few small rocks. But smaller rocks hit big-ger rocks and so on, and a deer or a bear, or even a marmot, could easily start a dangerous chain reaction that might knock loose a mankiller.

Once we reached the backburn, we broke up into squads and spread out to look for smokes. We found a few minor ones and snuffed them, but spent most of the day on longsuffering patrol. Al taught me the smoke-hunter's trick of looking for small clouds of bugs. Insects often gather over a warmer area, allowing us to locate a hot spot even when it isn't smoking. I actually found one like that and was very pleased. That's the kind of pro-fessional arcana that separates the veterans from the greenhorns.

Over Rob's radio, we heard the Western crew check in with Overhead when they finally reached Mike's pocket of fire. They ordered a helicopter to make several bucket drops and then waded in with handtools to finish it off. A couple of hours later, we heard them congratulated by the division su-pervisor for eliminating a dangerous threat to Division "D." We sourly bitched about how it should have been us.

Late in the shift, our squad took turns climbing to the lookout post we had established on the northern shoulder of Sugarloaf. From there we could see how the hot winds were stoking the great conflagration down in the Kalmiopsis. Towering mushroom clouds of smoke filled the southern sky— "money bubbles" they're called in the trade—ensuring more paychecks for somebody. It was all the more spectacular because the flames themselves weren't visible and hence left to the imagination. The distant skyline buzzed with air tankers and helicopters, and we certainly felt like a rear-echelon unit.

OCTOBER 6:

At dawn we were trucked out of Burnt Ridge for the last time. Our redpacks were sent down to Agness, and we were shipped to DP-5 over in neighboring Division "C," on the opposite side of Fishhook Peak. But our driver got lost, and we spent two hours bouncing around on hard wooden benches in the back of a five-ton truck, eating dust and nurturing hemorrhoids.

When we finally pulled into DP-5—the only crew there—we were greeted by the Division Supervisor herself. Some of the crew expressed surprise to see a woman in command of a division. It was apparently unusual, but I expect they'll be seeing a lot more of that in coming years. I estimated that about ten percent of the firefighters were female. We had only one woman on our crew, and that appeared to be an exception. Of the several dozen crews I observed, only one other had a single woman. All the rest had two or more, and one of the Washington crews had six, or about thirty percent. They could obviously do the work, and I suspected they were an effective civilizing influence as well. I think the operation would have been a lot cruder—physically, temperamentally, aesthetically—if all we had had out there in the bush were a bunch of macho dudes, bachelor pigs, and hypermale adolescents in their early twenties. Because of the female presence, I'm convinced that most males displayed a better part of themselves, and the Silver Complex was, therefore, more orderly, more efficient. There was also something to look at besides finely formed Douglas fir—for both sexes.

As far as I could tell, there were few, if any, overt sexual problems. As one veteran of many fires and fire camps told me: "I've never even heard of anyone 'getting any' at a fire." Basically, there would be little opportunity for either time or circumstance (or energy), and it would be an unprofessional thing to do—especially for a woman. They had to prove themselves—individually, and as a gender. But there are always exceptions, and in a couple of years I would witness a bizarre case of sexual "scandal." More later.

The division supervisor assigned us to patrol and mop up on another cold line (where we found zero smokes), but she did provide us with one diversion. She gave us a meteorological kit, and every half-hour we took turns at taking relative humidity measurements, and recording them for the edification of Overhead. We discovered that, in three hours, the air temperature rose from sixty-eight to eighty-four degrees, and humidity dropped from fifty-one percent to twenty-four percent. It was easy to see why forest fires turn aggressive during the afternoon.

The fireline paralleled a bouldery creek bed, and I patrolled it for a while, jumping from rock to rock in the middle of the stream. It had shrunk to a mere trickle joining deep, limpid pools, and I searched for trout while keeping an eye out for snakes. It was a cool, moist, soothing place to be, but I learned later that my personal sojourn there had been rather mundane. Dreamer walked the stream toward the end of the shift, and he was momentarily overcome by a sense of deep-time déjà vú. For a little while the place was haunted, and he could see the ghosts in his mind—the Coos and Tillamook hunters, the prospectors and fortune hunters, the pioneer timber cruisers—all the people who had passed that way before, using the creek bed as a passage into the heart of the mountains. "I could feel it," said Dreamer. Over evening coffee, he described a gut-level sense of "oldness" in himself as he walked up that remote pathway in the wilderness. People nodded as they listened. Most of us felt privileged to be poking around in the nooks and crannies of the Siskiyou.

At the end of the shift, we were trucked back to Agness, and we took up residence at our original campsite. I found the flat spot next to the mountain holly tree that I had claimed twelve days before but never had had the chance to use. I settled into my sleeping bag under the warm light of a high, deep orange moon—screened by smoke to the rich color of fire. I drifted off quickly.

OCTOBER 7:

Next morning it was back to Division "D" and the familiar firelines below Sugarloaf. We assembled at DP-13, and Mike felt compelled to openly acknowledge our rearguard status.

"We came out here," he said, "for three reasons. One: to fight fire. Two: make some money. Three: to see some country. Well, two out of three ain't bad." He smiled. "Besides [pause] it doesn't *really* matter."

There had been some bitching about the lack of action, and Mike urged us to cultivate a psychological mode of "hunkering down"—a mental toughness to overcome the monotony of patrol. Constant vigilence, he reminded us, was a lot tougher and more demanding than constant action. He said we were doing the hardest work around. I believed it.

But Squad One, at least, got some action that day. There were two huge fir stumps still smoldering on a mountainside below DP-13, and while the rest of the crew marched off toward Fishhook for more patrolling, we laid siege to the stumps.

As is a lot of Western forest fire work, extinguishing the fire was an excavation project. The fugitive heat had burrowed into deep cover, slowly gnawing at roots. The fire had been alive for several days, planted like a time bomb. With pulaskis and shovels we started down, vigorously pressing the attack. It felt good to be putting our blades and edges to use.

The strike team leader had dispatched an engine to be at our disposal; a one-and-one-half ton truck with 300 hundred gallons of precious water, a pump and hose reel, and two "engine slugs," that is, crewmen. The driver was from Seattle and had been on fire duty for five weeks. He had just about had his fill, but he managed to laugh at us—humping like earnest maniacs, working as if the integrity of the entire Silver Complex depended on exposing and snuffing those two stumps.

"You guys been bored lately?" he asked.

Well, I guess so, because laboriously moving over two cubic yards of rock and gravel—some of it piping hot—seemed like big entertainment. For the first time, I actually had the opportunity to wear the fine pair of goggles I had been issued in Duluth. When cold water hits hot gravel, bits of debris blast off like shrapnel, and it's not unheard of for stressed rocks to explode in your face. Eye protection was mandatory, but a side benefit of the operation was the dense clouds of steam being generated. We inhaled the moist vapors with genuine relish. The hot, dry weather, coupled with heavy doses of smoke, had rendered our nasal passages raw and bleeding. Being temporarily engulfed by steam was pure heaven. It was like the soothing mists of a sauna, and for the first time in two weeks I felt as if I was drawing a full breath.

We worked continuously for half the morning, and I figured it took twelve to fourteen man-hours to dig out and extinguish the stumps. The fire was at the bottom of the roots, hot and stubborn. They had to be completely uncovered and then soaked. The smoldering wood was actually charcoal, crusty and pitch black. The roots would have probably cooked for several more days, eventually breaking out into open flame. But we nailed them; it was a fine morning.

At the end of the shift, as we waited for the Army trucks at the DP, we heard of a new strategy for Division "D." A Forest Service fire behavior technician had spent the day hiking the firelines and talking with the folks most familiar with "D"—like us; nobody knew the Sugarloaf-Fishhook area better than we. He came away convinced that "D" was a ticking bomb. With the right wind, the remaining pockets of fire deep down in the valley would explode. "The fire," he said, "is going to come out of (Division "D"), and when it does you better be the hell out of the way!" In the meantime, he added, there was no reason to have several crews patrolling cold lines—they were simply in harm's way for no good reason. He told us he was going to propose to Overhead that all crews be pulled out of "D," with only a few scouts left behind to monitor the situation. That sounded good to us—as long as we weren't the ones left behind. We were itching to move south, down where the big fire was scorching the Kalmiopsis Wilderness.

7.
OCTOBER 8:

We didn't need it, but another day of R & R was on our schedule, so we were duly shipped to Gold Beach. The ban on crews in town had been lifted, and Jim got to collect his free beers after all. It was crazy for the townspeople to keep us out of their motels, bars, and restaurants for too long, and the Forest Service had made its disciplinary point.

For me, the highlight was watching the Minnesota Twins beat Detroit in the second game of the American League playoffs. As fans will recall, they eventually knocked off Detroit en route to a stunning upset victory in the World Series. I wisely chose to watch the game with a bunch from Minnesota-4 in *their* motel room rather than with my Michigan crewmates. If I had a gambler's soul (or more confidence in the Twins) I could've made some big money. The Detroit supporters on Hiawatha-3 were so confident of a Tigers' triumph that Dreamer offered me a $100 wager, double or nothing, and almost everyone was willing to go at it for five or ten bucks. I might've ended up with a fat bankroll—or a pulaski in the back. As it was, Dreamer agreed to root for the Twins in the Series, and I admitted I was surprised by the outcome of the pennant race.

OCTOBER 9:

The jovial woman at the shoestore/bookshop had admonished us, "You be sure and get a good night's rest, now!" I guess most of us did. But, truth to tell, I was sleeping just fine on the ground under the stars and wasn't reluctant to leave Gold Beach and head back up into the mountains.

We returned to Agness around noon, and speculation ran high. We heard that most of the crews had been pulled out of Division "D," and hopes rose that we would be transferred south to the firelines on the rim of the Kalmiopsis or maybe dispatched to northern California where a fire had now claimed over 200,000 acres.

But it was considered a bad omen when we were unassigned that day, allowed to lay around camp, enduring what was essentially another day off. We passed a hot afternoon reading, napping, or plugged into radios (or trying all three at once). We feared the worst. The word was that a few crews would remain wedded to Division "D," and who knew that terrain better than Hiawatha-3?

There was a crew boss briefing early in the evening, and Mike returned with the official bad news: back to Division "D." There was an outburst of moans and curses, but little did we imagine what challenge awaited.

OCTOBER 10:

We returned to DP-13 at daybreak. In contrast to the hectic mornings of two weeks before, there was only one other crew, a contingent of Eskimos from the Alaskan tundra. They were quiet but bemused, as if sharing some secret or an inside joke. We would see more of them later.

As the Alaskans marched off down the line, Mike called out for me and Kevin. We walked over to where he, the Strike Team Leader, and the Division Supervisor were bent over a map laid out on the hood of a pick-up.

"We need a couple of scouts," Mike said. I was flattered, but it wasn't for our eagle eyes, map skills, or knowledge of woodcraft and navigation that we were chosen. Mike said he just knew that Kevin and I "liked to walk," and this assignment would require a cougar's share of covering ground—cross-country, cross-contour.

The Division Super wanted us to do a "burn intensity survey"—that's ranger-talk for "what's burned and what ain't." We were to follow two miles of fireline below Sugarloaf, stopping every 150 feet to penetrate the black for 500 to 1000 feet. We would record our impressions on a map—in detail— and then report to Overhead that evening so they could transfer our data to a master map of the Silver Complex. Apparently they couldn't map accurately enough from the air.

We were given maps of Division "D," and Kevin took a radio. I borrowed a compass and pencil from Rick, and we set off ahead of the crew, orienting ourselves with the topo (topographical) maps and planning a strategy. Essentially, we were cartographers, filling in maps and documenting the changes the fire had created in this portion of the Siskiyou Range. It was a formidable task, so we split up. While I made a foray into the burn, Kevin paced off 150 feet and dropped a piece of orange engineer's tape to mark the spot where he entered the forest. When I completed my survey and emerged, I followed the trail until I saw his ribbon, then paced off another 150 feet. I left my own marker, and re-entered the burn. When Kevin returned to the trail he did the same, and thus we leapfrogged down the line. Periodically we paused to compare notes and record each other's observations.

I could see why Overhead wanted the area mapped. There was wide variation in the extent of the fire damage and potential for reburn. A few swaths were totally consumed, but most of the forest had only its ground cover or its understory burned, with plenty of available fuel higher up. Some acreage was untouched, but lying above partially blackened draws that could possibly re-ignite and spread upward to endanger the handline.

We gradually worked our way downward, heading for the nadir of the valley and Indigo Creek, about 3,000 feet below. As usual, the trail was treacherous—steep, crumbly, and studded with freshly-cut staubs, and each trip into the burn was a struggle. We were either traversing the slope, fighting through brush while treading on edgy, ankle-busting, boot-munching igneous rock, or we were sliding straight down the mountain, grabbing for handholds, then shortly turning around to scrabble back up. We were covering some of the meanest miles around, but it wasn't unpleasant work. Mike had chosen his scouts well. Kevin and I truly enjoyed our in-depth examination of the mountain and the forest.

The quiet and solitude allowed me to focus on individual trees. Since my logging days in Oregon fourteen years before, I had forgotten how stunning and humbling the mature firs could be. I leaned against one of the gargantuan trunks, my chest pressed against the bark, my head as far back as it would go, until my hard hat fell off. Staring upward that way was dizzying. It was a squirrel's-eye-view of infinity. The fir was a living ziggurat that reached for clouds and wind. It was older than the United States, and its top, invisible from the ground, defined the border of the sky. I hugged the fir and my long arms subtended only a modest arc along its circumference. If I could only climb as well as an ant! I laid an ear against the bark. Nothing. That's always a marvel to me. Here was this giant living thing, a thick pillar of organic substance with a million miles of capillaries—a green creature that sucked tons of water out of the soil and pumped it up to the clouds—and there was no heartbeat. Why doesn't such a massive plant—the great whale of the mountains—throb and hum with the energy of life? If it were such I suppose the woodlands would roar like stadium crowds or rumble like rolling thunder, and the deer would be deaf. Instead, the great trees creep up on the centuries, ripening through silent generations until they span a forest empire. They need the wind to speak, and fire to be reborn.

While we were on one of our forays into the burn, the rest of the crew passed by, bound for a smoke-hunting mission near Indigo Creek. We didn't expect to see any of them until the end of the day, but about halfway along our designated route we ran into Randy and Dreamer, headed back toward DP-13. Dreamer was limping, using a shovel as a crutch; his right ankle was wrapped. He had stumbled and sprained it, badly enough to justify evacuation, but not badly enough to justify a helicopter. Randy was along as escort and aid. We clucked our sympathy and moved on. It was the crew's first "reportable injury," and, considering the work and the terrain, that was amazing. Dreamer could just as easily have broken his neck.

Kevin and I figured we had walked over ten miles—mostly off the trail—by the time we reached the Alaskan crew, just a few hundred yards above Indigo Creek. They had found a standing, flaming snag only 300 feet from the line, and were waiting for the Hiawatha-3 saw team to join them. Our crew was apparently off inside the burn, strung out in a skirmish line searching for smokes. Most of the Eskimos were taking a break, gathered in the middle of a small clearing that encompassed the line. We walked through their midst, nodding. They were quiet people—not unfriendly, but reticent. Their demeanor compelled me to remain silent myself, only gesturing as we passed. The Strike Team Leader told us later that the Alaskans had been astonished and a little intimidated by the towering Douglas fir and ponderosa pine. Many of them were away from home for the first time, and they had never seen a tree larger than a tundra spruce. They always took their breaks in as open a spot as they could find.

In less than an hour, Kevin and I were at the creek, our survey complete. The trail had guided us to another world. We had left the coniferous, boreal forest far above, and were now in a lush defile of madrone, myrtle, and maple. Indigo was a narrow stream, twisting between huge boulders, and shrunken by the drought, but it still supported a jungle-like tangle of vegetation that clung to sharp, rocky banks and hung out over the creek bed. There was no trace of the fire. The water was crystal clear and icy cold, and we even spotted a small trout in one of the pools. It was a quintessential mountain stream.

We had been told that once we reached the Indigo, we were to follow the handline until it crossed over, and then climb up the other side of the valley to DP-3 and a forest road. A bus would meet us there. A wide, unmistakable fireline had led to the creek, but then it trailed meekly off upstream, a mere path. It was faint, and in some places traversed bare ledge rock. If not for pink ribbons tied to limbs and bushes, the trail would have been all but undetectable after the first several yards.

The ribbons stuck out like headlamps at night, but we began to doubt their worth. The trail quit the bank and the pink markers led directly upstream, from boulder to boulder. The creek now cut through a canyon, and there were no banks to follow. Some of the rocks were as big as small houses—mossy, damp, slick—and we clung to them like spiders, or scaled steep faces on all fours. In one spot we had to hug a rock wall and edge around a corner, our feet gingerly probing for half-submerged stepping stones. Every move had to be considered. It was a grueling course, and in many places the only way to advance without swimming or wading in the rushing current, was via a dangerous leap from rock to rock. For 200 yards we were like rats in a maze, scrambling over and around the boulders and numerous fallen snags scattered among the rocks at awkward angles. Surely Overhead didn't expect crews to come this way. It was one thing for Kevin and me, happy hikers unencumbered with tools, to scamper freely along; but it would be quite another for entire crews to be jumping around like goats while clutching shovels, pulaskis, and chain saws.

Finally we encountered a sheer rock wall. The creek itself was in a rapids mode, and the ribbons had shunted us over to the left "bank." There was a cleft in the eight-foot wall, and a river-beaten log, about six inches in diameter, was jammed into it at a sixty-degree angle. Its limbs had been ripped down to wicked little stubs, and we could see scuff marks on the trunk. Someone had used this ridiculous, half-rotten stick as a "ramp" to scale the rock wall. The pink ribbons at the top clearly indicated we should do the same.

Kevin and I looked at each other and shook our heads. It was a challenging hike, and we appreciated a little adventure as much as the next fire grunt, but this certainly couldn't be the way we were supposed to go. We decided it must be a scout trail—an initial route into the fire that had since been abandoned. Not long after entering the creek bed we had noted another trail that led directly up from the stream on the other side. We hadn't seen a ribbon, but now it seemed logical that that was the intended route to DP-3.

We backtracked until we found it, and crossed the stream on a dry gravel bar. The trail rose directly up the mountainside. Kevin went first, kicking footholds into the dirt, and grasping bushes as handholds. Enough loose gravel and dirt cascaded down to form a talus pile at the base of the slope, and Kevin struggled every inch of the way for the first hundred feet. When he finally reached some easier ground and quit dislodging rocks, I started up behind. His passage had destroyed many of the tenuous purchases, and I had to creep up, burrowing into the soil with fingertips and boot lugs.

I was about twenty feet up and seriously doubting I could get much higher, when I heard voices across the creek. I slid back to the bottom on my heels and butt. Just emerging from the woods onto the trail of ribbons was the Strike Team Leader, the rest of our crew, and the Alaskans. It was quitting time and they were heading for DP-3—and they weren't going our way.

The Strike Team Leader pointed upstream. "We follow the ribbons," he said.

"You're kidding," I replied.

He laughed. "You've been up there, eh? Well, I *have* seen better trails."

I yelled for Kevin, and in a few moments we all watched as a small avalanche of dirt, rock, and small bushes roared down the mountain. Kevin was close behind, barely in control as he skidded down to the creek. He smiled crookedly and brushed the dust off his pants. He was glad, he said, that we didn't have to go that way, but he and I were still skeptical about the ribbons.

We fell in behind the Strike Team Leader, and all thirty-eight of us steered up the middle of Indigo Creek. I figured it would be a minor miracle if no one got hurt, and it was a good thing Randy and Dreamer had gone out the other way. Indeed, how *would* we get a casualty out? The valley bottom was basically a chasm, and it would be impossible for a helicopter to get in there. It was a sobering thought, and I took extra care with my footing.

I was near the head of the column, and I could glance back downstream and see most of the others. It was a weird scene—like a line of yellow ants twisting over and around a jumble of pebbles. I saw one of our people jump from a rock, hit the wet portion of the next boulder and slide. She plunged into the river waist-deep, partially wedged between the rocks. A squadmate quickly offered a hand, and Barb emerged unhurt, but she could just as easily have broken an ankle. I hoped that Dreamer's injury wouldn't initiate a trend.

We reached the sheer wall with the log "ramp," and one by one we safely scaled it. I thought that would be the worst of it. Once we reached the trail up the mountainside, I supposed we would just have a long, if steep, hike. There was no valid reason for this assumption. I had been looking at the map all day, and I had seen how the trail up to DP-3 cut straight across the contour lines for a good 2,000 feet. This data didn't register until we slipped and hopped across Indigo one last time and stood at the base of the trail. Al and I chuckled. It was dry, mirthless laughter—the kind of noise made by a suffering patient when the surgeon cracks a joke.

The trail aimed—as the Strike Team Leader quipped—"due upward." Actually, it was a seventy to seventy-five degree slope, but for crews with packs, tools, and no rope (and why not? that was a good question), it was virtually a cliff.

The Alaskans went first. They seemed as agile as cats, climbing with a sureness and energy that belied their tundra background. They were enjoying it, but watching them climb gave us additional perspective. They seemed to be scaling a perpendicular rampart, disappearing into a vertical tunnel of vegetation about 100 feet up. We saw hands and feet slip several times, and it was scary. We waited until the last one was out of sight, and the dirt and pebbles had quit falling; Squad One went first.

Pulaski in hand, Al started up. I jumped in behind, and then came Bobby—lugging a big McCullough chain saw with a twenty-four-inch bar. It was madness. The first thirty feet were just easy enough to lure one to the point of no return. I grasped at semi-exposed roots, frantically digging with my fingertips—trying to expose a handhold before my toehold gave way. Twice my foot slipped out of the loose dirt "steps," and I held on with a thumb and forefinger, my other hand ripping away at the hillside for a grip of anything. Once I just burrowed a quick hole, stuffed my fist inside, and hung precariously onto the soil itself. And this with two free hands. What about Bobby?

I glanced back. Our eyes met, and we concluded a silent agreement. Slowly, carefully, Bobby passed up the chain saw. I braced myself and then grabbed it by the bar. Bobby climbed up beside me. I handed the saw back, and then struggled a few more feet upward and dug in. Bobby pushed the saw up the slope and I grabbed it again. He climbed up past me to where he could secure himself, and I passed the saw up.

And so it went. We ascended in a grim relay, yard by yard, risking life and limb for a stinking government chain saw. Even as we climbed, the absurdity of it hit me, and I seriously considered letting the saw drop to the bottom—the hell with it! But it was too late. The rest of the crew was strung out on the mountainside below, and there was a good chance the damn saw would nail somebody.

By the time we were a hundred feet up, my head was buzzing and my chest throbbed with adrenaline. How had the Alaskans scampered up this face so quickly? I was impressed. Even after the path finally "leveled" to the point where we could walk/climb in a more or less upright position, each step was painful. But then, I reminded myself, Kevin and I had already hiked over eleven miles since morning.

Once we got off all fours, Bobby and I took turns carrying the saw—about 100 yards at a crack. The trail was rocky now but still loose. Each footfall was critical. It would be easy to knock a rock free and send it careening downward—a deadly projectile for those below. It was terrifying how a stone could build up momentum, ricocheting as it tumbled from free fall to ragged bouncing, and always picking up velocity. A fist-sized rock could kill a person outright—even before it knocked him back down the mountain, bowling over others on the way. I morbidly speculated about the possibility of a single rock wiping out an entire crew. It kept my feet in line. I did stumble and kick a rock free, but I flopped onto it before it could get away, and jammed it securely into a crevice.

About halfway up to DP-3—which increasingly took on the aspect of an unreachable nirvana—the Alaskans were bunched together, taking a break. It was their turn to be impressed. Bobby had the McCullough slung over his shoulder, and two of the Eskimos pointed at him and hooted. Their crew boss shook his head.

"How in the hell did you guys get that chain saw up the cliff?"

I pointed at my right ear and made a circular motion. To complete the explanation I snorted and uttered a weary "shit!"

They all laughed.

I was near exhaustion and knew I would have to play some mind games to get to the top with any kind of dignity. The trail ahead was a daunting, ski-jump of a slope, angling out of sight toward the clouds. Each step was going to hurt—my legs, my lungs, my head. I decided to race. My goal—the means to keep the pain and weariness at bay—would be to beat all the Alaskans to the summit. I firmly resolved that the lead elements of Hiawatha-3 would be the first to the top.

I rested until the Alaskans showed signs of moving on, then I rose to my feet, took the chain saw from Bobby, and resumed the climb. I pretended that this was an Olympic event, that there was a gold medal (and a cold beer) awaiting the winner at DP-3. The Alaskans, of course, didn't know they were in a race, but soon they were on my tail, only fifteen yards behind. Were they gaining? I opted for a simple strategy. Since no one had enough energy left to continuously climb, I would wait until I saw them pause. That was my chance to rest. But I never let them resume the climb before I did. Through eyes stinging with sweat, I studied the three closest Alaskans. When it looked like they were about to decide to make a move, I set off, gaining a half-step each time. I imagined them vying with each other for the silver and the bronze. It was almost fun, and it got me through a thick haze of misery. My clothes were soaked with sweat—it actually dripped off my cuffs. I felt as if I were suffocating through my skin, as if my shirt weighed twenty pounds. My leg muscles were like twisted steel bands, and I knew they were near spasm. The saw was a ton of iron biting into my shoulder, and my chest heaved at every breath.

Phil, our Squad Three leader, overtook me on one of my short breaks, and offered to take a turn with the saw. I surrendered it without argument, and thus lightened, I made a final "dash" for the top. I could feel a heavenly breeze dropping from the open roadway above, and as I finally clambered up the last ten feet of trail, I prepared to let out a whoop of triumph. And then I saw Kevin. He was already there, stripped of his pack and grinning. Somewhere along the way he had passed us all, and was the first to reach the Promised Land. I laughed at myself and the little psychological game that had guided me to the end. "All right, Kevin!" I yelled. At least I had "beaten" the Alaskans.

A bus was waiting for us, and Randy had hitched a ride. Before he had escorted Dreamer back to camp, he had had a taste of what we were in for, so he had seen to it that the bus was equipped with two cases of ice-cold soft drinks. Now there was an example of a heads-up fireground tactic. Since we had expected to endure the hour-long ride back to Agness sucking on hot canteens, we blessed him profusely.

Within ten minutes, most of us were shivering. Our body heat was being wicked away by our sopping clothes, and the late afternoon air on the mountain was cooling quickly. By the time everyone reached the summit (spent, but all in one piece) and we were ready to leave, the bus driver had to turn on the heater.

That evening Kevin and I accompanied Mike to the daily Overhead briefing to pass along our dearly gained cartographic data. To our chagrin (but not surprise), our ten hours of sweat and meticulous observation were reduced to one minute of discussion, and a dozen pencil strokes on the master map. We had to laugh.

Toward the end of the meeting someone asked the IC for his opinion about how long there would be crews committed to the Silver Complex.

"Well," he replied, "let's put it this way: I booked Bob Hope for the Christmas show."

My new boots had still not arrived at the commissary, and it was the opinion of the clerk that they weren't coming at all. There had obviously been some snafu, and she could trace no record of my order. A fresh order might take at least a week, but I had no choice. She said she'd put a rush on it.

I walked over to the supply area and asked for some heavy-duty strapping tape. But it was a tight operation. In order to get anything, you had to either trade (ie., an old, worn pair of gloves would get you a new pair), or you had to be some kind of Overhead. The supply officer on duty was reluctant to give some tape to a mere grunt. I showed him my sorry boots and related my tale of woe, trying to make my voice simultaneously say "pretty please," and "give it to me or I'll rip your throat out and steal it." He finally offered me half a roll, though it was probably out of pity rather than fear.

Before I turned in, I wound several wraps of tape around the instep of each boot, hoping they'd hold for at least a few more days.

* * *

8.

OCTOBER 11:

Dawn. We were back at DP-13 (where else?) with an Alaskan crew. This one was Tongass-4, a regular Forest Service outfit that had arrived at the Silver Complex only four days before. But they were already veterans of the Indigo Creek/DP-3 scenic walk.

On their second day out, they had been treated to the toughest Division "D" had to offer, and when the Strike Team Leader announced that we would all be hiking to DP-3 again, some on our crew were startled to hear a few of the Tongass people exclaiming "All right!" and "Good!" It seemed they had a competition going. They were *timing* people as they raced up the mountainside to DP-3. It was my little mental first-aid fantasy of yesterday turned into living nightmare. What I only dared to suggest to myself, these folks had made into an actual diversion for the entire crew. I had guessed that it had taken me about forty minutes to make that climb, but we overheard the Alaskans saying that their champion had done it in twenty-nine minutes. One of their toughest goats was named Heather, a petite young firefighter who wore her Whites with authority.

With a few exceptions—notably Squad One—Hiawatha-3 was *not* enthusiastic about another extended patrol down to Indigo Creek. It was our seventeenth day on the line, and, while morale was not a problem, it was certainly not as high as it had been the first day. Another difference between our crew and the Tongass people was that our average age was in the low thirties. Their average age appeared to be in the high twenties. "Glory" was near the top of their priority list, while the chief concern of Hiawatha-3 had shifted toward timekeeping, payroll, and weather reports from the U.P.

We were just a mile down the trail when the tape on my boots wore through and separated. My soles flapped like coin snatchers on clown shoes. I paused to re-tape, and one of the Alaskans said he had some "serious glue" back in camp that might get my boots through a few more shifts. I resolved to look him up that night, assuming my footgear didn't disintegrate completely on the arduous trek ahead.

About halfway down to Indigo, we huddled with the Strike Team Leader and received our assignments. Each crew would deploy into a long skirmish line and mount an extensive cross-country smoke hunt all the way down to the creek. The aerial infrared survey had revealed at least three small hot spots within a thousand feet of the line. In addition, there was still that flaming snag from the day before, and the plan was to snuff it with an air attack. The Strike Team Leader needed a couple of grunts to help him with that, and since Kevin and I had put on so much mileage the day before, we were chosen to help him with the air show. Overhead had treated our hard-earned map data lightly, but the effort was appreciated by our peers, and the "helitak" duty was our reward.

While the two crews split up and disappeared into the charred forest, Kevin and I and the Strike Team Leader hiked down the trail to within a quarter-mile of Indigo. A ribbon on the fireline indicated the location of the snag, and we found it as advertised—less than two chains (one chain equals sixty-six feet) off the line.

It was the shattered remnant of a huge Douglas fir, about twenty feet high and nearly five feet in diameter at the base. It was hollow, and smoke poured out the top like steam from a volcano. It was a dangerous situation. The right wind could stir up the fire in the bole, wafting a shower of sparks off across the line and into fresh fuel. Al, Rob, and Bobby had been there the day before, and had contemplated felling the snag with the twenty-four-inch McCullough I nearly threw off the mountainside, but they had decided the saw was too small to handle the job. Instead, they had secured the area, clearing away potential fuels, and digging a "cup trench" on the downhill side of the snag. If it should tumble over, it would roll into the trench and harmlessly burn instead of careening downhill into unburnt territory. Or such was the hope.

The Strike Team Leader was a genial Forest Service career man named Otis. He was originally from Wisconsin but was presently working at a national forest in Arizona. He was beginning to take this snag personally. He had been with our boys the day before, and it'd really bugged him to be forced to leave it smoldering overnight. He was determined to nail it. He established radio contact with the local air force, and while waiting for a helicopter to be dispatched, we tried to knock down the upper portion of the snag. It looked thin and shaky, and if we could tear it down we might be able to reach inside the bole of the tree with handtools. We found a small log to use as a battering ram, and grunting and shoving, we pounded on the snag until it was clear that it was sturdier than it looked.

In a few minutes we could hear a helicopter approaching, and while Otis talked them down to our position, Kevin and I lit a couple of fusees to serve as beacons. We had already strung out several feet of fluorescent pink ribbon in a little corral around the snag, trying to give the pilot every advantage. Pinpointing a spot fire on a wooded mountainside—much less hitting it with water—is no mean feat. The ship had to swing down into the narrow valley, fighting updrafts and essentially hugging the steep rampart of the mountain. Even at treetop level, he would still be over a hundred feet off the ground, and the small plume of smoke would be all but invisible.

The pilot started from downslope and cautiously drifted upward. It was like a storm rising out of the depths. The engine noise swelled to an intimidating roar, then we felt the gust of rotor wash as the helicopter finally steered into view. The ship filled the constricted patch of sky we could see from the forest floor, its running lights blinking like baleful eyes. I was reminded of the dramatic scene in *Close Encounters of the Third Kind,* when the alien spacecraft slowly rose from behind Devil's Tower. We all waved our arms.

A crewman in a white flight helmet and orange jumpsuit hung out the door. He gave us a "thumbs-up," then dropped a roll of toilet paper. It unfurled in the breeze, snaking down like a party streamer. It draped over the forest canopy almost directly above. That would be the marker for the bombing run. Another wave, and the helicopter disappeared, screaming away over the mountain. We were now an official target—ground zero for a bucket drop.

When we heard the next helicopter approaching, we lit two more fusees, laid them on the ground, and took cover. A hundred gallons of water weighs over 800 pounds, and we never knew what else might fall. If a bucket was filled in a lake or river, we might have anything from rocks and sticks to live turtles falling out of the sky. We moved off and huddled behind the fortress trunks of live firs, helmets on and tools secured.

We heard the "whoosh" as the bucket opened, and then the musical sound of a sudden rainstorm in the upper boughs. In a moment I was soaked. A deflected shower burst through the branches above and cascaded onto my head. The pilot was about forty feet too far to the east. Still, for the first run it wasn't bad, and Otis called in the correction. At least the area around the snag would be damp for a while.

The pilot made four more sorties and scored two partial hits before he was dispatched elsewhere. Though it was wet all around, the snag was still smoldering. It wasn't a wasted effort, but not total victory either. Otis was frustrated. The snag would have to come down. He radioed the Division Super and requested a saw team. Through a small opening cut out of the forest a little further up the mountain, the sawyers could rappel down from a hovering helicopter and hike to the snag.

It sounded like an interesting operation, but the Super said it was too late in the day for that kind of air show, and since the snag and its environs were wet, we could leave it for another day. Otis swore. He vowed that he would pack a big saw down there himself if necessary. After clearing away more brush and debris to make a wider circle of safety around the snag, we regretfully hoisted our packs and headed down to Indigo Creek.

Hiawatha and Tongass were waiting. They had snuffed three smokes between them, and, except for our stubborn snag, that section of the line was now secure. After a short break, we fell into single file and headed up the obstacle course toward the trail to DP-3. There were more close calls on slick rock, and then another torturous climb up the mountain. Without the chain saw, it wasn't quite as hazardous. Instead, I was packing a pulaski, and in a few spots I used it like an ice axe on a glacier, hacking into the mountainside for footholds. It wasn't an approved Forest Service safety technique, but it beat digging in with fingernails and prayer.

The Alaskans conducted their race, and we heard that Heather made it to the top in twenty-seven minutes—a new personal record. No one from Hiawatha did it faster than about thirty-five, but a portion of the Tongass crew lagged behind Kevin and me and a few others—it was some small comfort. When I reached the summit, though, I found a half-dozen Alaskans vigorously kicking around a Hackeysack—as if the whole thing was a school picnic. As I said, they were young. Still, there was exhilaration in it, even for us "oldtimers," and most of us weren't too wasted to sing on the bus all the way back to Agness. The lyrics—and it didn't matter what they were—knit us together like a jovial congregation of brethren.

After supper I strolled over to the Tongass camp and fetched the "serious glue." It was a pungent concoction dubbed "Shoe Goo," and I hoped it was more "serious" than its name implied. Mike was debating whether or not he would leave me in camp the next day. My sorry-ass boots didn't belong on the line, he said, and he was right. But I practically fell to my knees and begged not to be left behind to wash dishes or sling hash. I sang the praises of Shoe Goo (though I hadn't tried it yet) and absolutely promised him the boots would hold for one more day. I was pathetic, and he relented. But at the briefing that evening Mike publically complained about my trouble with the commissary, and no less than the IC himself said he would personally drive me into town (Brookings, Oregon) the next morning to get a new pair. Boots were solemn business.

But it would not be necessary, for we also learned that the next shift would be our last. Hiawatha-3 would be "de-mobed" (that is, demobilized) and sent home. We had been out for three weeks, and that was now the limit.

OCTOBER 12:

Most of us weren't ready to go home. We had psyched ourselves up for at least a month-long tour of duty, and, aside from Dreamer's puffed ankle, we were still physically intact. Our big hope was that we would be shipped to the hot lines around the Kalmiopsis. We wanted more action—more money.

Just after breakfast, about half our crew gathered around one of the portable orchard heaters. There were three of these weird fuel-oil units, and they had become *the* place to hang out for a quick cup of morning (and evening) coffee. Word had spread around Agness that this was our last shift, and, as the Tongass people trooped by on their way to a bus, one of them called out, "Ready to go home?" He intended it as a jocular, rhetorical question. He expected a chorus of "Yo!" or "Right on!" or "Yippee!" He was taken aback when eight or nine of us yelled in unison: "Hell no!" But gung ho or not, Overhead had spoken. My boots only had to last for twelve more hours. The Goo looked good.

We were bussed up to DP-13, a spot now utterly familiar. This was our natural habitat. I tried to conjure up how I had felt on that first night shift, surrounded by people I had known for just over twenty-four hours, the sky lit by flames, and not knowing what the hell to expect. It was as if I had suddenly been plopped into someone else's dream; I was an alien. That seemed like a year ago. I was now surrounded by friends, and DP-13 was a congenial and well-worn background. For the first time, we were the only crew there.

Our assignment required that we split into three groups. Mike needed one "rehab" team. These people—the bulk of the crew—would "de-construct" a section of handline, build some water bars (anti-erosion ditches), and sow grass seed. A second group of three would snuff a known hot spot just down the line from the DP, and then patrol the length of Sug-arloaf. The third group would make yet another run all the way down to Indigo, and then climb that terribly righteous path up to DP-3. There were groans from some of the crew, but Squad One wanted that mission. It was mostly a matter of machismo, but we knew that it was also a way to pass an interesting and speedy, though rugged shift. It sounded far superior to pre-paring rocky ground for grass seed.

Since we were the only squad that displayed any interest in another long, hot march, Mike awarded us the job. But he wanted only four people to go. That meant one of us would have to volunteer for the rehab detail. Silence.

"Okay," said Rob, "we'll flip for it." As squad leader he was already in, so the coin toss was between me, Al, Bobby, and Dave. We each dug out a coin and stood in a tight circle. "Heads are winners," said Rob. We all flipped. Four tails! We flipped again. Bobby and I came up heads, and I breathed a sigh of relief—I wanted to march. It was now between Dave and Al, and I was amused to see that the normally unflappable combat vet was actually nervous. Al truly desired to hike to DP-3 again, half-gimpy leg and all; he wanted nothing to do with grass seed. They flipped. Dave, tails; Al, heads. He whooped for joy. "Hey!" he chortled, "that's the first time I've won anything in my life!" We all burst into laughter. There was no trace of irony in his voice. He was as happy as a kid with a sack of candy.

"Won!" hooted Steve. "Won? Are you kidding?"

Indeed. Al had just won the "opportunity" to slog and slip back down to what had become known as *the hole,* and then struggle and scrape 2,000 feet straight up the other side. There would be sweat, pain, and a fair chance of injury. Al grinned.

We set off with a spring in our step, a happy little band of brothers. Al dug into his seemingly bottomless reservoir of movie trivia and dredged up an appropriate cinematic metaphor. "We are," he said with a sanctimonious flourish, "on a mission from God." Yo! The Blues Brothers.

Actually, we were on a mission from the Division Super. We were to patrol the line of course, but our main function was to check out that smoldering snag. No saw team would be dispatched that day either, and Overhead was hoping the damn thing would just burn out and disappear. I didn't know where Otis was, but I figured he was cussing about it.

It was a gorgeous autumn day—sunny and smoke-free, but not too hot. Though arduous, this was largely a joy-hike. We had been hardened by three weeks of work in the mountains, and could kick back and enjoy the majesty of the Siskiyou. We had pulaskis, but they were snugly sheathed.

The snag was still burning, and the surrounding area was again desert-dry, as if the bucket drops had never been. The top looked even more eaten away and precarious, so we hoisted the battering ram and pounded away again. This time we knocked some chunks free, and they fell into the cup trench. We chopped them up and buried them. That was better, but the snag was still a threat, and Rob would report it as such.

We hit Indigo Creek around noon, and stopped for lunch. Without the clutter and hubbub of two full crews, we could appreciate the quiet enchantment of this remote valley. Not many humans had ever been this far back into the forest, and we found some sun-dappled boulders on which to lounge and savor this privileged ambience.

The maples were golden, a rich understory of color beneath the dense canopy of primeval fir so far above. The pools were coated with fallen leaves, slowly floating downstream—the departing fleet of summer past. The fire hadn't touched this spot, and the thick green moss on the boulders was moist and alive. There was humidity—honest-to-God moisture—a luxuriant balm for seared nostrils. The creek was liquid emerald, here and there pierced by a shaft of sunlight. We saw silvery trout swimming in a deep pool. A tiny waterfall churned part of the pool into a storm of clean white bubbles. Here was a patch of Eden, or a hideaway for unicorns.

After lunch, Al and Bobby stripped the webbing from their hardhats and used the shells to pan for gold. These streams that feed into the Rogue River conceal more than trout. The town of Gold Beach wasn't christened that because of the character of the evening light. We had packed in one shovel, and Rob and I took turns using that as a pan, sifting through the coarse sand along the bank. There were several glitters in each scoop, but it was only quartz or reflections off wet pebbles. Nevertheless, it was fun to play prospector out there in the wilderness, and I found that it wasn't easy to stop. Each false gleam led me on to another shovelful. Maybe we could turn up a nugget. I could see how people got hooked. It was like the compulsive dropping of nickels into a slot machine. But alas, we would have to rely on Uncle Sam's payroll for our riches.

Before we began our final DP-3 anabasis, I inspected my boots. To my surprise the glue was holding. The soles and uppers were still tightly bound, and I was ready to do a commercial for Shoe Goo: "Listen, citizens, if good old Goo will do for a fire grunt's kickers, just think how it'll spruce up your Guccis!"

In some ways that third ascent was the worst. There was no other crew to "race," and I focused on the pain. Halfway up I couldn't recall just why we had all been so eager to win the coin toss. Only after I felt the sweet breezes at the summit did I fully recollect the pleasure of such torture. We had wanted this assignment because most others didn't. We were the only firefighters in Division "D" to walk into *the Hole* for three shifts in a row. It was a small enough triumph, I suppose, and it didn't make an iota of difference in the overall scheme of the Silver Complex, but it's usually the little challenges and victories that get one through life. "Nothing in life," wrote Winston Churchill, "is so exhilarating as to be shot at without result." As long as I live I shall never forget Bobby and me battling up the mountain with that damn chain saw, and how we amazed the Alaskans, and how we went back there two more times.

My right boot had come apart again, finally beaten. But then I hadn't allowed the Shoe Goo its mandate of a full twenty-four hour drying period. I wasn't complaining—it'd been enough, and the left boot was still okay. It was a fine afternoon.

That night there was a black bear in camp. It was a huge bear, and, given the odor of the catering trucks (and the garbage bin), I was surprised we hadn't entertained one every night. It was nosing around our sleeping area as we prepared to turn in, and some guys who had been sleeping out under the stars retreated into tents. The bear was last seen only thirty feet or so from where Phil and I had our bedrolls on open ground, but I was too tired to move. I shoved my pack up into a tree and called it good. (It reeked of sandwiches and fresh fruit.) Besides, the only "safety" in the tent was the spurious "safety of numbers," and too many folks had stashed candy bars in there. Phil and I stayed put and loudly razzed those who retreated. I had slept in the neighborhood of black bears several times in my life, and none had crawled in with me yet. There were rustlings in the nearby brush, but I fell asleep shortly. Any bear with half a brain (and half a nose) was going to head for those caterers.

OCTOBER 13:

Nobody got sentimental about leaving Agness. Burnt Ridge had been our real home, and it had already been "rehabbed" and returned to the forest. There was a hint of swagger though, as we trooped through the camp toward the bus, our gear slung over our shoulders. People watched. They waved and wished us well. We were obviously a veteran crew, and I walked as a seasoned fire grunt—even with a boot sole flapping.

The bus took us back to Medford via U.S. Highway 101 along the coast. The scenery was spectacular, and we stopped to eat our bag lunches and watch Pacific combers break against craggy rock towers. The Oregon coast is like a long castle wall, shattered by the millenial siege of the ocean. We cut back into the forest just east of Crescent City, California, and drove through groves of monstrous redwoods. We paused at a wide spot in the road, and all gathered in front of a massive trunk for a crew photo. A fire crew from Virginia was there doing the same, and we exchanged cameras, performing the photographic honors for each other. The woods and roads of the Northwest were thick with fire crews.

Unlike our first visit, the sky at Medford was clear. The apocalyptic shroud of smoke was gone, and the sun was hot and unfiltered. We had heard news reports that the U.P. and northern Minnesota had already seen snowfall, and we realized that this southern Oregon afternoon would be our last taste of summer-like temperatures for several months.

The four other crews with whom we'd flown out were also at the airport, and, after weighing our gear, we boarded the jet together—up the rear ramp like the aerial insiders we were. The plane lifted off an hour before sunset, flying east into the creeping dusk. The Cascades quickly dwindled behind us, with Mount Shasta's sunlit pinnacle among the last to disappear. Somewhere over snow-sprinkled Idaho mountains we eased into blue-black darkness.

Two hours later, above western Minnesota, the pilot banked the plane over on its port wing and told us to look north. The cabin lights were shut off and out the portholes we could see a shimmering, greenish-white curtain of northern lights. It was a full circle then—from aurora to aurora—the lights had blessed me coming and going.

A local TV crew was waiting for us at the terminal in Duluth, and, when they approached us, Randy dodged the lights by pointing at me and telling them I was the "crew spokesman." I snickered at his joke, but what the hell. As had the Oregon media, the local TV people seemed to be fishing for some comment about how we had suffered terribly out there in the Western fire wars. There had been a moderate amount of physical discomfort, of course (though reporters seem incapable of using the word "firefighter" without the adjective "exhausted"), and certainly a significant exposure to hazard—in the end, ten firefighters were killed at various locales. But when asked if I would be willing to go back, I instantly replied with a tactful form of "damn right!" What else? How many other people get paid for travel, adventure, and camaraderie? Hard work? Certainly. Dangerous? Absolutely. Worth doing? Most of the time.

Walker Percy wrote: "Why is a man apt to feel bad in a good environment, say suburban Short Hills, New Jersey, on an ordinary Wednesday afternoon? Why is the same man apt to feel good in a very bad environment, say an old hotel on Key Largo during a hurricane?" Yes, why *do* we often relish hardship, danger, and conflict? Because, at least for a little while, we can be outside ourselves. Under pressure, our consciousness expands. The common expression is that you *rise* to a challenge. Paradoxically, when hemmed in by struggle, pain, and disaster, we often feel lighter, freer, and more potent than ever. And if these sensations can be shared with others who are "in the same boat" (battered by waves and perhaps listing), they are intensified. It's why the Forest Service will never lack for firefighters, nor the military for soldiers—at least when there's actually a war to be fought. The simple fact was that saying good-bye to Hiawatha-3 was going to be far more difficult than anything we did out on the fireline.

We spent the night in the Duluth armory, sacked out on Army cots that weren't half as good as a foam pad on bare ground. *No* bed is better than half a bed, and that goes for civilization in general, but I was glad for a one-night reprieve on the farewells.

The next morning it had to be faced. One by one I sought out the crew members to shake hands, to trade our names one more time. Each grasp was warm and tight. After three intimate weeks, it seemed I had known some of them for years. Their faces were imprinted in my brain, and there'll be no difficulty in recognizing them several years hence.

I saved Al for last, and we embraced. To make it okay, he let out a loud wail of mock despair. We shook hands and laughed.

"I'll see you at the Big One," he said.

I resolved that if there was any way I could swing it, I'd be there. With new boots.

"Fire is a prodigal; its furnaces abound in jewels which they scatter to the winds; and it is to some purpose that charcoal is identical with diamond." — Victor Hugo

Hellroaring

1.

Those twenty-one days at the Silver Complex served as introduction to Western fire and mountainous terrain tactics, and ten months later on Shadow Mountain, I was grateful for the experience.

Five days after our harrowing night at the head of the Hunter Fire, Superior-4 was assigned to a bus and dispatched north to Yellowstone National Park itself. The big time.

We were shocked to discover that this bus was not of the school variety, but rather a luxurious motor coach, normally a charter, and we didn't have to share it with anyone. After several days of jostling shoulder-to-shoulder and butt-to-butt in Army trucks and school buses, the coach seemed as spacious as a 747, and we stretched out on two seats apiece (with headrests), happily crowing over our good fortune.

"I don't *believe* this!"

"Gotta be a screw-up. Gotta be."

"Quick!" someone yelled to the driver. "Lock the door, and let's get the hell out of here before Overhead changes its mind."

But no one came to ruin the party, and, to our delight, the driver, a rotund and jovial fellow who was tickled at having a fire crew aboard ("a nice change from yuppie skiers"), switched on the coach's superb stereo system, and we cruised out of Hunter camp accompanied by Johnny Horton crooning "Commanche," "North to Alaska," "Whispering Pines," and other appropriate tunes.

I marveled at the contrast between our brutal baptism on the Hunter Fire, and this almost whimsical departure. Our plane from Duluth had landed at the Jackson Hole Airport in late afternoon, and we had lugged our gear across the tarmac and boarded an old school bus that made a brief stop at the camp so we could drop off our red packs and fill our canteens, then delivered us directly to a drop point. We were issued handtools and fusees, and by dusk were marching down a fresh bulldozer line towards a free-burning flank of the fire. We fell in with two other crews and struck off the dozer trail up a ridge, constructing a three-foot wide handline. The wind was down, and we worked close to low flames, digging and scraping a buffer at the edge of the black.

We kept at it for seven hours, slaving in the dust, smoke, and heat by the glare of headlamps. I mused that a mere twenty-four hours before I had been rolling out of my bed in Minnesota, and was now in another time zone, somewhere in the Teton National Forest sharing the hazards of a hot, nighttime fireline with people I had known for less than a day. As weariness increased, so did a sense of not-unpleasant wierdness—an impression of transcending self and experiencing this intense slice of life from a distance. In front of this semi-stranger was dense, midnight-black forest; behind were dozens of pockets of bright flame silhouetting the stark skeletons of burned snags. To either side were sweating, grunting firefighters, grimly hacking at the ground. Earlier there had been banter and occasional laughter, now was mostly silent determination to manage the pain and endure the shift.

By 3:00 AM our crews were spent, and we huddled around some hot spots near the line, groggy and half-dozing for about an hour. A hard frost had descended, and our feverish sweat turned cold. Abused muscles and joints tightened up, and, when the Strike Team Leader roused us to head back down the line, there was a chorus of groaning and cursing as we all eased up into stiffness.

We improved the line here and there as we hiked to the drop point, loosening up and getting warm again—briefly. Just before dawn, we gathered at the base of the slope to wait for Army trucks. It was twenty degrees, and none of us were dressed for it. The start of our shift had been high summer—we had baked in the bus from Jackson Hole—and as often happens in the mountains, we had cycled around to a late autumn ambience over the course of the night. We awkwardly hopped around in our fatigue, trying to keep toes from going numb. There was wood nearby, but the Strike Team Leader didn't dare let us kindle a bonfire. "Our transport will be here shortly," he said. But it wasn't.

A half-hour later a couple of us heard a strange clicking noise. My first thought was a woodpecker, but then we realized it was Fass. His teeth were chattering so violently that we could hear them from thirty feet away. He was stalking back and forth and swinging his arms. "Th-th-this is n-n-nuts!" he spat.

"Keep movin', man," someone said, "you're freezing."

"N-n-no shit!"

Then Tom pointed and hooted. "Fass! Look at your canteen!"

One of the water bottles on his web belt had apparently sprung a leak, and there was now a two-inch icicle hanging from the pouch. Fass looked down and moaned. We shook our heads in amazement and kept stamping our feet. The trucks were an hour late.

We hit the chow line in a stupor, but noticed that the scrambled eggs were green, not tinged with chartreuse, but truly, unmistakably *green*. Caterers, harried and under pressure, can be forgiven the occasional culinary faux pas, but the green eggs proved to be symbolic of the general quality of the grub, and, by next day, a new food outfit was in camp. One thing the Forest Service bureaucracy fully appreciates is the necessity of well-fed firefighters.

That afternoon, as we prepared to board a bus for a return to the drop point, there was general laughter when Fass appeared in our midst. He looked like the Michelin Tire man, plump and bulging. Beneath his brush coat he was wearing every shirt and sweater he'd packed. "Go ahead, laugh," he said, "but my teeth won't chatter tonight."

"Yeah, but can you bend over?"

Fass didn't care. He vowed never to be underdressed again.

A few days later I had my own problem with clothes. Before we were sent north to Yellowstone, we had been given a day of R & R in Jackson. It was clear that laundry was a universal priority, but over 100 firefighters were going to be in town sharing the same notion, and everyone was dreading the prospect of a hot, crowded, over-taxed laundromat—especially when saloons, restaurants, and gift shops beckoned. I saw an opportunity to make a little extra money. I offered to do anyone's laundry at three dollars a head, and Tom, Sean, Todd, and Westby (our Squad #1 leader) took me up on it. I collected the cash and dirty clothes, figuring to clear five or six bucks and get my own wash done free.

The bus paused at the laundromat and I stumbled off, burdened with two sacks of pungent underwear and socks. Sean and my other clients congratulated themselves on a wise decision—the laundromat was a hellhole. The way depressed patrons were crammed in there, was like they were dropping coins into slot machines rather than washers. The front door was propped open for heat and steam to escape, and there were even laundry bags stacked out on the sidewalk.

The bus pulled away, heading downtown to the taverns and tourist traps, and I girded myself for an ordeal that promised to be uglier than expected. But as I reached the fetid doorway I was approached by an Oriental man who identified himself as the owner. He explained that due to the booming business he was instituting a new policy for firefighters. All I had to do was label my sacks, pay a set fee in advance, and he and his associates would do the laundry. I could simply pick it up before we were bussed back to camp that evening.

"You, sir," I said, beaming, "have made my day." I peeled off a few bills and ambled away feeling like a Wall Street bond dealer who's just made a killing in a bear market. Several minutes later—a double-scoop ice cream cone clutched in my fist—I ran into Westby and Sean. They gave me a quizzical look, wondering at first, I'm sure, if I had simply deposited their duds in the nearest dumpster. They hadn't expected to see me for two or three hours.

I couldn't resist a smug, shit-eating grin as I detailed the recent operational change at the laundromat.

"You son-of-a-bitch," said Westby, but he was laughing. "Well, that's the American way; you took the risk, you reap the profit."

But it turned out not quite that elegantly. Several hours (and a few beers) later, I picked up the laundry and climbed aboard the bus. Back in camp my clients gathered round as I dumped the wash onto a clean tarp and people pawed through the pile to find their stuff. (It was a self-service business.) When the sorting was done, it was revealed that Westby and Sean were missing significant portions of their wardrobe. Accusing stares. My modest venture had gone sour. Being short on socks and underwear is no trivial matter on the fireground. A refund would be meaningless.

"I'll track this stuff down," I promised. Right. It was 11:00 PM, and it was a "closed camp." Even if I had means of transportation, I couldn't just waltz out of there. Schackman suggested I consult our Liason Officer. After several inquiries, I learned he was camping with a Chippewa National Forest crew. He was also sound asleep. I eased into the tent and paused over his sleeping bag. It was now 11:30. How was he going to react to lost underwear? A cardinal rule of fire camp is that you don't deny people their sleep. Still, dealing with such pesty problems as mine was supposed to be one of his duties. I gritted my teeth and gently shook his shoulder. "Yes?" His instant alertness surprised me—as if rude awakenings were routine—and I stammered a little as I explained my crisis. He didn't even sigh. "Let's go to town," he said, and unzipped the bag.

He drove me the twelve miles to the laundromat, making cheerful small talk. Here, I thought, is a guy with a professional attitude. I would have accepted surliness, or a reprimand, but he was only interested in handling the task at hand, awarding priority to the socks and underwear of fire grunts over his own sleep. Such seemingly small sacrifices—easily avoided or brushed off—are what cements the system. Any system.

It was past midnight when we got to Jackson, but the laundromat was still open, and I found the rest of the laundry. A triumph. The Liason Officer and I were both relieved—not to mention Sean and Westby. My profit margin appeared miniscule by then, and I resolved to stay out of the laundry business.

Our motor coach ride was a trek that many people commonly travel thousands of miles to take. We cruised up the Snake River valley on U.S. 89, gawking again at the always improbable pinnacles of the Grand Tetons. They're the kind of exaggerated peaks appearing only on the covers of paperbacks about mountain men or wizards. I first saw the Tetons from

30,000 feet, on our flight back from the Siskiyou the previous autumn. With snow sparkling in westering sunlight, they were the brilliant jewels of the Rockies, and I vowed to take a closer look someday. That day had arrived sooner than anticipated.

We skirted the shore of Jackson Lake and the vast expanse of open water was startling in this Western setting. For the past week, water had been a rare and precious commodity. Up on the line we had carefully nursed five-gallon bladder bags, milking every drop as we mopped up hot spots. To spray water was a luxury; the bulk of our extinguishing was painstakingly achieved with dirt.

We crossed into Yellowstone at the South Entrance and quickly realized how privileged we were. Most tourists had been evacuated from the park, so we viewed its splendor from an empty road, unimpeded by traffic. It had probably been a long time since anyone passed as pleasant an August 31 in Yellowstone as we did. Initially there was the staccato clicking of shutters and excited shouts as we spotted wildlife: moose, elk, antelope, mule deer, a black bear. But soon it was routine—astonishingly so—and Sean mentioned that he had always considered Yellowstone National Park as a huge, outdoor, drive-through zoo for the urban masses. And so it seemed. In an hour the sight of magnificent elk was utterly unremarkable. I could see value in that. Like it or not, we are a fully mechanized society, and if casual tourists (that is, the majority) are able to view such abundant wildlife with relative convenience, perhaps it aids the cause of conservation. It's easier to doubt the worth of something never seen, and the more people who experience the life and grandeur of Yellowstone, the better chance it and other preserves have of continued protection from those who would develop and/or exploit wilderness. Or so one hopes.

We reached Old Faithful around lunch time, and everyone piled out of the bus for a toilet stop. We couldn't linger long, but we did see the geyser spout. Massive smoke columns in the distance reminded us we weren't tourists, but for a while it was hard to tell. Folks were running out of Kodak.

In early afternoon, having traversed the length of the park, we pulled into a campground at the north end, about four miles south of the Montana border. With four other crews, we spread out amidst the developed campsites, taking special note of the heavy-duty steel food boxes designed to foil the grizzlies that occasionally turn up in search of goodies.

But our more immediate irritation was the Park Service ranger with a Smith & Wesson .357 on his hip. He clearly regarded us as riffraff, a necessary evil. Throughout the Yellowstone fire operations, there'd been tension between some of the Park Service people and elements of the Forest Service and state fire teams. The Park Service resisted the use of bulldozers and other heavy equipment within the boundaries of Yellowstone, maintaining that such machines could do more damage than fire. The Forest Service people felt they were being compelled to battle the fires with one arm tied behind their backs, and, as the blazes grew and costs escalated, there was protest and conflict. Both sides had a point, of course, and it boiled down to how much time, energy, and money should be expended on fires that many claimed were doing more good than harm. The wild card in the deck, however, was that blazes originating in the park could spread to lands outside—both public and private—so supression strategy was an ongoing debate. More on that later.

We were barely off the coach (a vehicle we would sorely miss) when this ranger read us the riot act, obviously working under the assumption that we were vandals, litter bugs, and outlaws. It's possible he had had a bad experience with some other fire folks—Lord knows there was a sprinkling of malcontents and idiots in the wildfire ranks—but it's more likely he simply confused the shiny .357 with his brain (or his penis), and indulged in a garden-variety power trip. A big pistol can do that. We listened and chafed but held our tongues.

✳ ✳ ✳

2.

First thing we did was build a bridge over Slough Creek, a pristine trout stream flowing through the campground. I felt strange—digging and hammering in a wilderness area, spanning water that had been protected since 1872.

But fighting wildfire is a military operation, and armies boldly advance where others dare not tread. At Slough Creek we faced a fire named "Hellroaring," after a stream in the Absaroka Beartooth Wilderness of southern Montana, where the "man-caused" blaze had started two weeks before. It was now over 30,000 acres and eating into Yellowstone from the north. As we nailed the decking of our crude bridge, we could see dark mushroom clouds of smoke billowing over a ridgeline a couple of miles away. It was windy, and the fire was making a "run," gobbling up forest at the rate of ten chains per hour on a one-mile front.

Just before sunset it rained—not water, but thousands of black pine needles. They settled over camp like an evil harbinger of apocalypse. Massive convection currents were surging out of Hellroaring, sucking charred debris into the sky and scattering it for miles. By dark we had to shake out our sleeping bags. The northern horizon was suffused with a deep red glow. Now and again the color intensified, and we could hear the roar of our enemy. I was happy to have the creek between us and the fire, but that night I had a bizarre dream about being overrun by a herd of flaming bison.

Soon after dawn our five crews tramped across the bridge toward the fire. Beyond Slough we hiked uphill for a mile and a half, following a pack trail. At one point I was startled to see a huge buffalo staring at us from a scant twenty yards away. I was gratified to note he wasn't on fire. Near the crest of a wooded ridge, with a meadow at our backs, we started building handline. We were in grass at first, and the going was easy. The crew bosses kept us well choreographed, and our line of one hundred or so firefighters resembled a fast and sinuous Rototiller.

Since we had about three miles of line to build, the Strike Team Leader requested that we "keep humping." As usual the trick was to work like a fiend but pace ourselves. We were facing a thirteen- to fourteen-hour shift, and it would be wise to have a reserve of energy in case we had to mount a hasty, prolonged retreat.

For nine hours we slashed through the wilderness, the rumble of Hellroaring growing ominously louder as we advanced. It was bull work, a muscle-wearing, mind-taxing endurance run. It helped to slip into an altered state, a locale in the brain where the mechanical labor can be shunted into auto, and conscious thoughts slip off to more congenial territory—like how to spend the fat federal paycheck. Fat by grunt standards, that is.

As was common at Yellowstone, we were supplied via pack train, and around noon a rider with a three-mile string brought us extra cubees of drinking water. It was a convivial way to be served, and it always lifted my spirits to see these sturdy, attractive animals and note that we were co-workers. (And speculate who was treated better.) I was amazed at their footwork. A few days later I would witness a thirteen-mule string pass a stretch of fireline that was so crisscrossed with hose that it resembled a spider web, and yet not one of the fifty-two hooves so much as brushed the lay. (I had just tripped over it twice.)

By early afternoon we had run into a vein of duff. It's not unusual for the litter of needles, cones, leaves, and humus on the forest floor to be four to six inches thick. This cushion of biomass is an excellent medium for supporting smoldering fire that might endure for several days or longer. To construct an effective line the duff must be cleared away to expose mineral soil and is not a huge problem. However, that day we found ourselves literally trenching through a strata of duff that was nearly four feet deep. The entire strike team effort bogged down as it mutated from fireline "scratching" to a mining operation. A few inches beneath the surface the duff turned tight and spongy, and pulaskis bounced back in our faces. We didn't dig so much as rip, rake, and chop. It was slow and nasty and seemed futile. How could such a line be a fire-stopper? But still we grubbed on—bitching—and I've never seen a fire crew that looked more like a chain gang as we ditched our way through the trees.

Fortunately we had line scouts out ahead and lookouts posted at critical points, and late in the day they all agreed our work was indeed useless. We had one and one-half miles of line in, but the Strike Team Leader decided we would be overrun before we could finish. The fire was moving too fast, and another blaze, the Storm Creek Fire, off to the east, was expected to close in. Aside from being a rigorous workout, the day's mission was for nought. Most of us laughed—a tad bitterly to be sure—for such is the nature of combat. The proposed line had been a gamble, an aggressive attempt to save more forest. But the fire—now less than a mile away and a steady roar in our ears—had outmanuevered us. Instead of a fireline, Yellowstone had another hiking trail. We backfilled our duff trench, then straightened aching backs and withdrew to Slough Creek.

For some reason not clear to me, the Strike Team Leader decided that rather than follow our line/trail back to camp, we should take a cross-country "short cut." I considered it significant that one of the first curiosities we encountered as we angled into the woods was a picturesque, but slightly unnerving bear skeleton. A few chains further on we passed an elk skeleton. Bones in the forest are a poignant keepsake of Mother Nature, a remindful souvenir of death, and it was compelling to view these two collections as a bad omen. The terrain cooperated with this pessimism, and we were soon descending a steep defile peppered with loose rock, made trickier by our weariness. A member of another crew took a wicked tumble and twisted his back. (The next day he was shipped out.)

We stumbled down to Slough Creek, some distance upstream of our bridge, and the Strike Team Leader led us across, hopping from rock to rock. Easy for him—he had no tool and wasn't fatigued after several hours of line digging. Our crew was outraged, and there was open, loud dissension.

"What's this bullshit!"

The Strike Team Leader must have heard but gave no indication. He was fully aware that his "short cut" was a fiasco.

It seemed unwise to go rock-hopping over wet stone while grasping a pulaski, so several of us simply waded—knee-deep (ah, yes, soaking wet boots—shit!)—through rushing, icy water. Hazard and suffering are part of the job, but there's a difference between necessary danger and pain, and needless, avoidable travail. We had had a *trail* that led to a bridge, and we didn't take it! A firefighter had been forced out of the game, and we were merely lucky there hadn't been more. For a while I *hated* that Strike Team Leader.

Morning brought a fresh strategy. The creek would be our line, and we would backburn from there. While the other four crews were trucked out to improve a line a few miles to the west, our crew crossed the stream to clear out "ladder fuels." These are any combustibles—brush, lower limbs, saplings—that will allow ground fire to climb into trees and "torch out," perhaps initiating a crown fire and broadcasting sparks and embers for long distances.

For half a day we used pulaskis and a chain saw to clean up a zone forty feet back from the creek, transforming it from wilderness to city park. Everything we cut was widely scattered in open areas so there would be no concentrations of fuel near the line. The Strike Team Leader reminded us that if we did not hold Hellroaring at the creek, the next (and last) line of defense would be the highway. And that's tacky.

By noon we were ready for the hose lay. With the aid of a New Mexico crew that had just arrived, we began packing 19,000 feet—over three miles—of one-and one-half-inch and one-inch fire hose through the woods. We deployed it along the camp side of the creek for the entire length of the line, installing a gated wye, an attack line, and a nozzle every 200 feet. If any spot fires ignited on our side of the perimeter, we'd nail them with water. The creek was low, but there was plenty of volume for our three portable pumps. By Western standards we were water-rich, and a "water show" is the kind of firefighting that folks from Minnesota and Wisconsin understand best.

My job was to scout 4,000 feet of the lay, hiking cross-country through tangled, jungle-like forest. I had to make a snap decision about every 100 feet. Should the hose go under or around a deadfall? Follow the crest or the base of a slope? I had to keep the amount of hose (and hence friction loss) to a minimum, while covering the maximum amount of territory. I marked the route with orange engineer's tape, rushing to stay ahead of the hose-haulers. The New Mexicans worked like demons, shouldering 8,000 feet of hose in less than two hours. Like us, they'd been out for weeks, and were acclimated to the grind.

Unfortunately, one of my quick decisions was wrong, and I had them lay the last 800 feet of trunkline too far from the creek. My profuse apologies were genially accepted, mainly because I succeeded in shifting the blame onto Overhead. Liability, after all, is one of the reasons foremen exist. The New Mexicans and I shared a tin of snuff, sadly clucking over our lot in life, until members of our crew joined us and we re-routed the hose.

On the way back to camp I almost stepped in a magnificent heap of bear scat that looked like processed tomatoes—red and seedy. It was huge and *fresh*. Another omen?

The backburn was scheduled for the next afternoon, so we spent the morning dressing up our ladder fuel work and testing the pumps and hose. By noon my lower back began to hurt. I had stepped in a marmot hole early on and slightly twisted it but not seriously I thought. At first it was just one more ache. Since we had started on the Hunter Fire I had endured a hyper-extended knee (another marmot hole), two minor burns, a bruised thigh, one day of smoke headaches (that is, carbon monoxide poisoning), a day and one half of diarrhea (always a treat in remote country), a badly blistered thumb, and near-constant sinus blockage. However, the back pain waxed ever more dominant until by 3:00 PM I was working on my knees, hacking away at low tree limbs and worrying about the future. It was possible to perform this relatively light work, but there was no way I could build handline with such pain—I wouldn't last an hour.

By 4:00 PM our defenses were tight, but the wind was wrong, and the Storm Creek Fire was lashing in from the east. Shortly before sunset an urgent radio message ordered us to "fall back into safety zones," but for us it was moot. Our camp *was* our safety zone, and its very boundary was the proposed fireline. There was speculation that Hellroaring, Storm Creek, and a fire to the south were going to merge, and that our backburn would be irrelevant unless it could be done soon—within twelve to thirty-six hours.

We had confidence in our hose lay, but we were not to discover how it worked out. Next morning, in the company of two other crews, we were bussed to Gardiner, Montana, about twenty miles northwest. It was essentially a day off, and I was supremely relieved. Maybe it would be enough of a break for my back to straighten out. I had told Schack about the pain—it's stupid and irresponsible to hide or deny an injury—and he was prepared to demobe me if necessary.

At the local ranger station, a bear expert briefed us on the do's and don'ts of living in grizzly country. Our new assignment was on another division of Hellroaring, this time deep inside the Absaroka Beartooth Wilderness. Our goal was the preservation of grizzly habitat, and while the expert outwardly stressed our safety, the message between the lines was clear: firefighters are expendable, the remaining grizzlies are not. We would be cautious about our food and behavior, not only because it might keep us alive, but, more important (or so it seemed), because it would help shield grizzlies from familiarity with humans. When bears grow accustomed to, and hence contemptuous of people, acquiring a taste for goodies such as sandwiches, candy, and garbage, their execution as "troublemakers" often follows. If grizzlies are to escape extinction, co-existence with humans must be minimized.

The expert emphasized that we should never surprise a grizzly. A startled black bear might run away, but a startled grizz would almost always attack—the simple reflex of an extremely aggressive giant with no natural enemies. He mentioned that, when he was working in grizzly habitat, he carried a baseball bat and periodically banged it against tree trunks to advise any bears of his approach. If given sufficient warning, grizzlies would often veer away from human contact. But it was a real possibility we might face a bear charge. What should we do? There were two basic options: 1) we could, he said, climb a tree. This brought forth snickers and hoots. We had been in this lodgepole pine country for two weeks now, and I had yet to see a tree I could climb. The first trustworthy limbs were typically thirty to forty feet off the ground. 2) We could curl up into a submissive, unthreatening fetal position and hope for the best; some people have survived such an encounter with only minor injuries, though others have been severely mauled or killed.

A firefighter raised his hand and was acknowledged.

"What about throwing a lit fusee at a charging bear?"

This gave the expert pause. "Wellll . . . that might scare it . . . but I don't really know."

Then another firefighter spoke up and said he had once seen a grizzly batting around a burning fusee as if it were a fascinating toy. Okay.

The expert also mentioned that we should never run from a bear because that was an excellent way to encourage a charge, and besides, they can sprint at up to thirty miles per hour. But he added, grinning, there might be one exception, and then tried to lighten up an otherwise grim session with a bear joke: Two firefighters are being charged by a huge grizzly. One drops his pack, jerks off his boots, and slips on a pair of Nikes. His buddy says, "Hey! we're not supposed to try to outrun them, remember." As the first firefighter hurries away he yells over his shoulder: "I don't have to outrun the bear, I just have to outrun *you!*"

Other morale-boosters at the Gardiner station included a T-shirt featuring a bear appreciatively licking a human femur. The caption read: "Send more firefighters; the last ones were delicious!" And there was a Far Side cartoon on the bulletin board showing a couple of people in sleeping bags; a grizzly has just parted some foliage to gaze down on them. "Oh goody!" the bear exclaims, "burritos!"

Our new home was to be the Beaver Creek spike camp. We would be lifted there by the next available Chinook helicopter, but, in the meantime, we were sent to a youth camp at Mammoth Springs where we were allowed to take showers, and sleep on beds under a roof. The roof was okay, but several of us opted to spread our bags on the floor. Once you're accustomed to sleeping on the ground, a bed is too soft. We rested well, interrupted only by Westby's sleep talking. A half-dozen times during the night he shouted out in a dream, issuing brusque commands for the laying of hose. When we kidded him in the morning, he retorted that since he had worked so hard, Schack should record that night on his time sheet.

We lazed around for most of the next day, awaiting a tardy Chinook. It was a lucky break for me. My back pain eased considerably after two easy days. There were newspapers and a TV, and we caught up on the controversy engendered by the Yellowstone blazes.

For several decades the park had rigorous fire protection. As a result, heavy fuels—deadfalls, overmature stands, thick brush—had accumulated, and now when a fire gets cooking it's more likely to crown out and race off on long, destructive runs. Wildfire—via lightning strikes—is a natural facet of the ecosystem, and periodic fires not only cut down on heavy fuels, but help check the spread of forest diseases, and for some species such as lodgepole pine, provide a natural means of regeneration.

So about twenty years before, the Park Service decided that natural fires should be allowed to burn, as long as they didn't endanger human life or property. There was wide support for the "let-burn" policy, but now the critics were saying that there hadn't been enough flexibility. It had been widely predicted that 1988 was going to be a dry year, so why didn't the Park Service jump on the fires immediately, leaving "let-burn" for a safer season? Good question. Still, some researchers believed that the 1988 fires were the apex of a two- to three-century cycle, an epic rejuvenation of the forest and not a disaster. Our Strike Team Leader, a wildlife biologist in the real world, said he expected a lot of fresh elk pasture the following spring. His chief concern was that erosion of burnt slopes would cause a silting problem in some streams, but he didn't believe it would be devastating. In fact, we even heard a defense of shallower streams: another wildlife specialist believed the Yellowstone waters were too cold for good trout habitat, and a deposit of silt would help to raise their average temperature.

There was no question that local merchants and Park concessionaires lost money, and they were among the harshest critics of the Park Service and its policies. It got mean. One newspaper I saw at Gardiner ran an editorial cartoon that pilloried Yellowstone Superintendent Robert Barbee. It showed a row of charred Smokey Bear toys and was captioned "Barbee Dolls." (Ironically, the next year would see a significant increase in tourism and profits as Americans flocked to the Park to view what the fires had done—proving again the old dictum, "there's no such thing as bad publicity." Exaggerated news reports and hysterical political attacks led citizens to believe that Yellowstone was all but destroyed, and many were surprised to see it wasn't true.) Generally, the fires spelled rejuvenation not catastrophe.

Besides, the Yellowstone fires weren't the biggest blazes in the nation that year. Alaskan fires burned 2,213,000 acres, but, because of the attention lavished on Yellowstone, almost no one heard of them. Al Andrews, my buddy from Hiawatha-3 and the Silver Complex, was on a Class I crew (the Redmond Hot Shots) in Alaska for a large portion of the season and later told me he was miffed that their firefighting efforts had been all but ignored due to the Yellowstone hoopla.

For us, though, it was heady stuff to be the focus of sustained international news coverage—to be a part of unfolding history and realizing that Yellowstone '88 wouldn't soon be forgotten. And the outside world was getting more than wire reports. I phoned home from the youth camp, and Pam reported that the sky of northeastern Minnesota was hazy with Yellowstone smoke. We were connected not only by a voice link, but our nostrils were filled with the same odor—the smell of money, I reminded her.

Our next day waxed tedious, but, finally, an hour before sunset, we were driven to a field north of Gardiner, and one crew at a time climbed aboard the twin-rotored Chinook. It was a military aircraft manned by Army personnel, and it amazed me that such an ugly, ungainly beast could fly. Tom had spent a good deal of time in helicopters while in the Marine Corps, and he hated them. Apparently there had been a mishap that hit a little too close to home, and he was vocal about his distrust of the machines and their pilots—especially military ships. When we had missed out on that helicopter ride back at the Hunter, he had been visibly relieved, and, when we heard a Chinook was coming to Gardiner for us, I teased him incessantly about making out his last will and testament.

After we had settled into our seats and buckled up, I saw Tom was just across the aisle, obviously nervous. I flashed him a grin and made a rotor motion with my arm; he grimaced and gave me the finger.

The Chinook pounded aloft in a cloud of dust, and we lumbered over wooded mountains, engulfed in the ship's roar. Sundown lent the smoky haze a purplish cast, and the high country ridges undulated off to the horizon. There were no roads.

We landed in a meadow bordered by blackened hills. It was a mile hike to the camp, and wranglers leading a thirteen-mule packtrain arrived to pick up most of our gear. About a hundred firefighters were working out of Beaver Creek spike, and all provisions were stored on a platform set on twenty-foot poles. All night there was a sentinel on watch—sitting by a fire with a rifle across his knees. Welcome to grizzly country.

There were a lot of MREs (Meals, Ready to Eat) in camp, the notorious combat rations of the U.S. military. Some maintain that "ready to eat" is a misnomer, especially the "eat," and it's true that one is instantly wary of a packet labeled "Not For In-Flight/Pre-Flight Use." Fortunately that proscription applies only to a couple of the meals—those with a "bean component"—and in my opinion most MREs are palatable, even guardedly good. Sometimes it depends on how hungry you are. (The Chicken á la King entree is excellent anytime.) MREs are convenient fireline food. They can be consumed cold or warm (heated in an armpit, say), and a plastic spoon is included. Besides a main course and dessert (I recommend the Maple Nut Cake patty), each packet contains coffee, cream, sugar, salt, chewing gum, matches, and, in military parlance, "Paper, Toilet." The latter is particularly apropos if you've drawn a meal with a "bean component." I never heard of anyone who got constipated on MREs.

There was already a seven-mile, sixteen-pump hose lay at Beaver Creek and vicinity, and next day we worked at improving the position, chopping ladder fuels and hauling cut logs across the line. Eventually, our principle mission was to ignite a backburn off that line. It was beautiful territory and pleasant duty—useful, steady work that wasn't too grueling—easier than building handline. As far as I was concerned, this whole tour had been blessed in that we had had important (if often difficult) assignments. Unlike the missions at the Silver Complex, Overhead wasn't merely trying to keep us busy so they could hang on to us as a reserve; we were in the big middle of the action and treated as a competent, valued asset.

But our Squad-3 Leader—I'll call him Horst—was unhappy. What had begun as occasional griping (we all do it), had evolved into nearly constant bitching about almost everything. There was little his criticism (often sarcastic) didn't encompass, and if I had commented on the pretty blue sky, I wouldn't have been surprised if he had retorted that the sky appeared a bit ugly, actually, and anyone could see it wasn't at all blue.

That afternoon Horst started complaining about what shitty duty we had had and were having. I was incredulous, and, for me, his disagreeable nature finally attained critical mass. It was especially galling that he was a squad leader, a chief function of which is to bolster the sometimes shaky morale of a fire crew—people stressed and far from home. A squad leader should be a viewer and promoter of the bright side, not the most relentless whiner of all.

I was still suffering some back pain, and that probably shortened my fuse. I blew up, regretting it almost instantly, but didn't shut up until I had loudly and acidly informed Horst "I am sick of your whining!" and preached that if we came out on Western fire for the next fifty years, we weren't likely to pull better assignments, and that he needed to quit being "such a fucking crybaby!" Ah, well. I thought for a moment he was going to fight me—particularly after that last barb, but he yelled something back and stalked off. We didn't speak for the rest of the day.

That night Schack beckoned me aside and asked what happened. Word had filtered back to him that Horst and I had been head-to-head for a few moments. I told my story, apologized for losing my cool, and promised it wouldn't happen again. Schack revealed that others had mentioned Horst's "attitude problem" to him. I said I hoped it would blow over, and that I would do my best to make peace. Schack agreed we were having a good tour, and stressed that we needed to be cohesive and alert the next day. The wind was forecast to be favorable for the big backburn.

It was, and so on the afternoon of September 7, with our crew and two others as backup, the Lolo Hot Shots hurried along the line with drip torches, setting the forest afire. A drip torch is a heavy metal container that holds about a gallon of a fuel oil/gasoline mix. It has a spout with a wick, and when lit, you can tip the torch at various angles to release either drops, or a small stream of flaming liquid. You can create a line of fire as quickly as you can walk.

We were spread out on the handline with the hoselay, two people at each nozzle, and lines charged with water. Overhead, a helicopter made several low sorties, dropping small incendiary devices known as "ping pong balls" further from the line between us and Hellroaring, which was about a half-mile away. The plastic spheres, which do look exactly like table tennis balls, are filled with potassium permanganate. Just before they tumble out of the ship they are automatically injected with a small dose of ethylene glycol (anti-freeze). An exothermic chemical reaction generates enough heat to ignite grass and brush, and a vast area can be sown with these hellish seeds very quickly. But control can be tricky, and the first two balls struck the ground on the wrong side of the line. A nearby nozzleman washed them away immediately and no harm was done, but it made us jumpier. We had seven safety zones mapped out behind us, with trails marked by blue ribbons leading directly to each. They were flat, grassy meadows—some marshy—and, if forced to abandon the line, we figured to fire the meadows with fusees and plant our fire shelters in the black. Some folks were convinced we'd end up doing it.

To fill any gaps in the ignition pattern, the Hot Shots fired charges from a flare gun. In a few minutes we were watching honest-to-god crown fire howl through pine trees only 200 yards away. I saw a mule deer leap out of the smoke and bolt for safety. The fire was so suddenly furious that exploding trees seemed to compete for immolation, with writhing pillars of flame shouldering into the sky like cyclones. We could feel the heat on our faces from two football fields away, and the roaring and crackling was storm-like—Biblical in its terrifying grandeur. We had unleashed an unstoppable monster of such power that I felt the hair rise on my neck. *Safety zones,* I reminded myself—blue ribbons lead to the safety zones.

Our job was to follow the Hot Shots as they passed through our sector, using the hose to keep the backburn at bay. We wanted the fire to burn well without crossing the line. If a tree within twenty-five feet of the line began to torch out, we would hit the base with a brief hose burst to cool it and lay it down, but not extinguish it. Tension increased. The Hot Shots and the helicopter were lighting 9,000 acres more or less at once, and, if the wind switched, we could be in deep trouble instantly. Our water source was a shallow creek and was definitely limited.

For two hours after ignition, we bumped up the line from nozzle to nozzle, knocking down big fire and dispatching periodic patrols out behind us to make sure nothing had drifted over. It's called "hotline" work, and by the end of the shift we had dirty faces, red eyes, and runny noses. When the wind died, smoke settled over us in a poisonous pall, and the burn was a mad desert of flaming deadfalls and collapsing trees.

I was detailed to "cruise the burn" with a couple rolls of orange flagging and tie ribbons around the trunks of any snags I thought should be felled immediately. A professional saw team was bumping up the line from camp. I found a huge old pine almost burned off at the base and gingerly cinched a ribbon to a low branch. That tree would topple soon. Moose was patrolling the line in the vicinity and assured me the snag was going to drop in twenty-six minutes. I bet him it would take forty-five. We synchronized our watches. I moved off to hunt more hazard trees, and a while later I heard a tremendous crash. Moose belted out a string of bloodcurdling whoops. I glanced at my watch: exactly twenty-six minutes! I yelled an acknowledgement of his triumph (and incredible luck), then saw the crew boss of Superior-5 hustling down the line toward Moose. He thought someone had been crushed by the falling snag. He said later that Moose needed to hone his whoops; they sounded too much like screams, especially when preceded by the thunder of an impacting trunk.

It was a tense shift, but except for a minor "slopover"—less than one acre burned—the line held, and two hours after dark we trudged back into camp for late supper and early bed.

At dawn we began mopping up, using handtools and water to extinguish all hot spots within fifty feet of the line. My lower back rebelled again, and I spent the afternoon literally on my knees, digging out heat with my pulaski and occasionally shuffling from hot spot to hot spot on all fours. The Strike Team Leader saw me and thought it was just aggressive technique. He told me to keep up the good work. By the end of the shift my back felt better, but my knees were stiff. No free lunch.

The day after we tried to mop in 100 feet, but the grizzlies had other plans. In the morning we saw huge paw and claw prints in the dust, and the Strike Team Leader said it was a "fairly small" grizzly. What?—they were the biggest bear tracks I'd ever seen—like a Hollywood exaggeration in a B movie. When we got to the first pump station we found the plastic holding tank ripped to shreds, and a jug of Gatorade left floating in the tank had been torn open and consumed. It was the same at the next two stations. The bear had ambled straight down the line, hitting one tank after another, guzzling Gatorade. There was sloppy, diarrhea-like scat amid the tracks, and the Strike Team Leader figured the Gatorade was giving the bear the runs. At one of the stations, we saw someone had screwed up and left six Milky Way candy bars on the ground. To our amazement we could see the bear had swiped at the bars, but not eaten them. Someone ventured a poor joke: "Maybe it wants fresh meat before it has dessert."

In early afternoon we were hiking down the line toward a new sector, Westby in the lead. Schack was back at camp working on some logistical matters. Suddenly Westby halted dead in his tracks and started backpedaling. I bumped into the firefighter in front of me, who'd just bumped into Westby. In a loud, hoarse whisper our leader said, "Grizzly!" (He told us later he'd seen a huge silver tip shamble across the line about twenty yards ahead. No one else saw it.)

There was a general backwards surge, people half-turning to hustle back the way we had come. Westby keyed the mike of his radio, but for a moment he was aghast, and all they heard back at camp and across the fireground was the huffing and bustle of a retreating fire crew. Listeners were puzzled until Westby finally caught his breath and blurted out the bear news. There was, we heard, universal laughter.

I laughed myself when I turned to see that at Westby's rasp of "Grizzly!" Tom had shinnied several feet up a lodgepole trunk, web gear and all.

Four hours later, when a pair of bears treed two pump operators further down the line, we were already withdrawing. Our crew was scheduled to move on anyway, but Beaver Creek was soon closed and the fireline abandoned. Grizzly habitat had been preserved, and with snow in the forecast, bears on the prowl, (and too much Gatorade stocked in camp), it seemed pointless to linger.

There were no Chinooks available, so we shuttled out in a smaller Bell 204 helicopter, four and five people at a time. It was a spectacular ride. To the south were roiling clouds from the North Fork and Wolf Lake fires. Dense, gray-black columns churned beneath a fire-generated thunderhead with a sunlit crest reaching up 30,000 feet and arching overhead. Deep within a veil of smoke we could make out the black shadows of mountains fringed with dark orange walls of flame. Holocaust. The North Fork had gobbled 56,000 acres in *one* day.

To the north was an oasis of blue sky dotted with puffs of cumulous cloud. Afternoon sunshine dappled green valleys and ridges, and the mountains rippled off into the indigo distance—to infinity it seemed. Looking from south to north was like having windows on different planets.

In the seat across, one of my comrades had his eyes glued to the cataclysm in the south. Despite all we had seen in the last three weeks, his face had the awed expression of a kid at his first circus. There is fire, and there is firestorm; we were viewing the latter. It's a good thing for a firefighter to see—from faraway.

I was seated behind and to the right of the pilot and was impressed by his skill. We had been banking around peaks and skirting craggy escarpments, and it was obvious the man possessed a certain aerial panache. I was curious to see his face—get an idea of his age. Was he a product of Vietnam, perhaps? I was facing the tail of the ship, so I leaned around toward the cockpit canopy, straining against the seat belt. In front the sky was half-and-half—smoke and clean blue. A thickly-wooded ridge loomed ahead, and we appeared to be below the crest. I craned my neck, trying to see the pilot's features. I froze.

He had the cyclic stick jammed between his knees, one hand vaguely hovering near the collective control as he earnestly fiddled with an Elvis Presley cassette. Apparently he was having trouble shoving it into the tape deck. The ridge seemed quite near. I quickly turned around, grinning at my colleagues. This was better for a firefighter not to see.

By late afternoon we were aboard one of the last buses to leave Gardiner. A roadblock went up behind us. The town was crowded with fire trucks and hoselays, with structural firefighters preparing to battle for buildings if necessary. Fire was reported near Mammoth Hot Springs.

We rode a few miles to the banks of the Yellowstone River, where a caterer had set up shop. After dinner we spread our sleeping bags out on the gravel of a wayside rest and watched the air show. In the foreground, over the river, we observed the local magpies. In the distance, in front of massive ramparts of dark smoke, we watched air tankers swooping low over the ridges. After sundown we could see a dull orange glow along 270 degrees of horizon. We were three-quarters surrounded by fire, and it seemed as if the globe itself were ablaze.

✳ ✳ ✳

3.

In the morning we heard our tour of duty was over—at least the fire-line portion. But as we were bussed thirty-five miles north to Chico Hot Springs for R & R, no one expected some of us were yet to face danger.

After twenty-one days out (nineteen of them on the line) the resort and motel were a fantasy come true. The local hot springs had been incorporated into a swimming pool, and at one end the soothing water was ejected beneath the surface in Jacuzzi-like jets. It was heaven on my abused back, and, as we blissfully wallowed and floated in the magnificent pool, snowflakes began to drift in. It was the beginning of the end for the Yellowstone fires. The next day saw several inches accumulation.

Not only did the Federal government feed us at Chico's four-star restaurant, but there was also a picturesque saloon with live music. That night it was jammed with Minnesota firefighters.

I was glad my knife was sharp, or I would never have gotten my initials into that bartop. Carving, though, wasn't the real challenge—it was finding room to work. The yellowed-wood expanse was packed with names, dates, arrowed-hearts and other hieroglyphics. Hundreds of patrons had beaten me to this tableau, inspired by the opportunity to legally deface a bar.

I had never been invited to vandalism before, but then this was a remote Montana tavern, an outpost in the semi-wild West. There was a dog snoozing under the pool table and mountains outside the door. I was 800 miles from home, but I knew half the people in the joint by name. The oddness of the situation didn't hit me until I had sipped two Mooseheads and eased under the influence of a warm buzz, that homey state where mellow felicity garnishes a vague feeling of goodwill toward men.

The faces around me were now utterly familiar, though I had known them for less than a month. We had shared danger, hardship, and even some triumph. We had heard everyone's jokes, guzzled from buddies' canteens, smelled each other's gas. We had been crammed together inside helicopters, Army trucks, and Bear Cats. We knew the nose-pickers, the snorers, the sleep-talkers, the snuff-spitters. We had been stressed and re-stressed, taxed and abused, and I knew more about the character of these people than of some folks back home that I had known for years. It's tough to hide yourself out in the bush, depending on other people to watch your ass (and vice versa), fighting a fire that would willingly eat your bones like so many crackling pine boughs.

Most of these guys I liked, others I didn't; but that night, after twenty-one days on the line and two beers, I loved them all—my comrades-in-arms, our happy band of brothers. It's the kind of love mentioned in the Bible, springing from "... wine that maketh glad the heart of man." (Psalms)

But there was also a core of genuine fellowship, a sense of having survived together. This was readily demonstrated in the negative. On Day-2 and on Day-4 we lost people—both had to be evacuated for injuries. Aside from Schackman (who had to fill out accident reports), and their respective squad leaders, I doubt there were four others who remembered their names. They were casualties—ancient history. On the fireline a week is a month, three weeks a season. The only people who count are those in the thick of it with you *now*, whether sucking smoke or drinking beer. The "outside world" is just that—out and faraway, briefly glimpsed through news clippings on a fire camp bulletin board. The fire, the crew, perhaps the strike team, are the axis. The past is the last shift, the future the next one, and only today matters. That's why a tour of fire duty seems so long; not because it's unpleasant, but because each pregnant day is a new era.

Anyway, my carving didn't do that rugged reliquary justice. Too many cowboys had spent too much time with finely-honed Bucks and Gerbers, lusting for a touch of artistry. My chief purpose was temporary distraction. Horst was talking. I was studiously not listening, bent over my work. The expression of my love was that I didn't jump down his throat as I had out on the line. Soon the lecture ended and he drifted off. His saving grace was that he knew fire and worked like an animal. He had pissed off some people, but when you're building handline in front of flames, it's how well you wield your tool *now* that registers; nobody gives a damn about your personality. The fireground is a meritocracy.

With my "PL" permanently, if sloppily engraved, I turned my attention to Fass. Here was a rookie who had blossomed. If he had a fault as a firefighter it was that he was too gung ho, pushed himself too hard. Above Slough Creek he had dug line in a virtual frenzy—energized by youth and adventure. Three times Schack told him, "Pace yourself, pace yourself; don't burn out." But Fass couldn't help it, he was high and flying. Finally Sean suggested to Schack that he replace Fass's pulaski with a shovel. It was a brilliant idea. Fass was crestfallen—you just can't be a berserker with a #2 shovel—it automatically slowed him to a reasonable level of effort. No doubt time and injuries will temper his zeal. He had already telephoned home to discuss his doing another tour. He'd found a niche, at least for now. Back home he was a sales clerk, and fire duty beat that all to hell.

He was staring at the wide-screen television behind the bar, the only blemish in an otherwise perfect establishment. I would have preferred a long mirror, the kind of entertainment device that was once so popular in taverns. Not only could I check on the course of my own mutation, but I could easily track the progress of my fellow travelers, the subtle (or blatant) evolution of disputes, seductions, stupors, practical jokes, compacts, orations, withdrawals, and flowerings the full length of the bar. In the looking glass was authenticity; the inevitable atavism gained a curious potency. There's a critical difference between touchable decadence and the electromagnetic, photon haze-daze that emanates from TV and infects the psyche like an overdose of soma. If we must slouch toward perdition, we should go arm-in-arm, awake, and not under the influence of an electronic medium, isolated and individually seared by cathode rays. Far better to scan the mirror than stare at the screen. Go ask Alice.

But that evening the movie was "Platoon," and Fass was transfixed. Once or twice I heard him intone, "Holy shit." He was of that post-draft cohort that graduated from high school in the mid to late 1970s, whose older brothers went to war, fulfilling their male destinies, and, if they weren't killed, paralyzed, or driven mad, spiced their lives with the seasoning of the universal soldier.

Firefighting was Fass's Vietnam, a rite-of-passage. The fireground is only a reflection of the battleground, hardly its equivalent, but such things are relative. Firefighting is vastly more potent say, than freshman year at junior college, or slipping gut-bombs into plastic foam boxes at Hardee's.

As the movie ended in an orgy of violence, with Charlie Sheen extending a clenched-fist salute from an ascending helicopter, I punched Fass on the shoulder and ordered him another beer. I almost said something stupid like, "You did a great job on the fireline, man," but realized in the nick of time that he was now a veteran too, and that such a compliment, however sincere, would be condescending. It was understood that we were all good, especially tonight. My punch was a love tap, a macho sweet-nothing between equals, and Fass didn't question its source.

Unfortunately, our buddy Bear had already called it a night, or we could have solicited his reaction to "Platoon." He had spent several years in the U.S. Army Special Forces, and had killed six men with his M-16—not in war, but while guarding an ammo dump in Georgia. We had listened, astonished, as he detailed the gruesome and disturbingly regular dramas that surround the safekeeping of Army ordnance. But then "normal" contraband, like pot or cocaine, has a fraction of the appeal of live ammunition. Even holy rollers play with guns, and there are apparently a lot of folks out there—black marketeers, terrorists, run-of-the-mill whackos—who would love to stock up on mortar rounds, grenades, and machine gun belts. Bear seemed bemused that he had had the opportunity to waste a half dozen of them.

One night he had faced a pistol-wielding intruder who had already shot another guard. Being new to the detail, Bear had nervously switched his rifle into the full-auto mode and fired a twenty-seven-round burst. He hit the intruder twenty-six times, "all in the vitals." Though the standing order at the ammo dump was "shoot to kill," the Army hassled him for three weeks with the question: "What happened to the twenty-seventh bullet?" Well, who the hell knew, or cared? Bear finally blew up at the panel of officer-inquisitors, obscenely interrogating them about the nature of their intelligence and experience. He was rewarded with time in the stockade.

Actually, he was quiet of demeanor, though he did provide the best one-liner of the tour—when we were airlifted into Beaver Creek spike via the Chinook. While in the service Bear had parachuted or rappelled out of Chinooks several hundred times. As we trudged down the rear ramp of the helicoper Bear flattened his face into mock amazement and quipped, "Hey, I didn't know these things could land." Never before had he actually walked out of a Chinook like a gentleman.

But of course we were a civilized crew. Oh, sure, we bitched, cussed, told dirty jokes, and often lived as close to the ground as marmots, but that's all fire crew boiler plate, and we were cleaner than many. Our refinement was rooted in discipline, in the fact that we were invariably where we were supposed to be, when we were supposed to be there, doing what we had been assigned in a professional manner. It's not that Schack was a crusty sergeant-major type with a whip and a taste for stripes; it's that early on he managed to fashion us into a family/team.

Imagine the challenge. You arrive at a staging area (in our case the Duluth National Guard Armory) after an emergency call and a long drive. You're assigned the responsibility for nineteen other humans, many of whom you don't know. All are *supposed* to possess at least an official minimum of knowledge and physical fitness, but there are usually a few who have no business on a fire crew. You try to spot them early.

You must organize the rabble into squads and choose three squad leaders—a weighty decision. The quality of your lieutenants can ease the burden of command or drive you to the brink of homicide. Which of these strangers has the right stuff? Or, among the people you know, who are you going to offend by *not* annointing them as leadership material, thereby creating your first morale problem immediately?

In a few hectic hours you must meet everyone and actually remember their names; make sure they have all the necessary gear and, when they don't, procure it, signing it out of Supply in *your* name; see that all crew members and their baggage are weighed and meet the restrictions; fill out twenty federal time sheets, intricate documents that are a cross between an algebra exam and a 1040 form; deal with the inevitable screw-ups; and, most critical, deliver a pep talk/sermon/manifesto that displays your competence and authority, inspires confidence and esprit de corps, and makes sense. Then you board a plane and fly directly to some of the most hazardous locales on the planet. Little wonder that many crew bosses are ever hoping for elevation to more congenial posts—like fire behavior technician or public information officer.

But Schack got a handle on it early, molding us into a responsive, fairly efficient unit without generating ill will. I wasn't sure how he did it, and maybe he wasn't either, but at least two factors stick out: he usually had a good reason for having us do something, and he practiced what he preached. Only once did he raise his voice in anger, then later apologized. He looked after us and we responded, quickly gaining a reputation as a "good crew," and thereby earning better, that is, more dangerous assignments. Competence is a two-edged sword.

Our anabasis had begun that night in Shadow Mountain in front of the Hunter. It's a story that'll grow fat with retelling, and we began that evening when Schack arrived at the bar and bought a round. His confidence and control had guided us through that harrowing shift, and when we raised a toast to our burgeoning sense of prowess, we were really toasting him. Since we were going home the next day, he could almost relax. Almost.

But sometimes, compared to R & R, the fireline's a piece of cake. On the line you're tense, alert, and primed for danger; you expect the worst. On R & R, after days or weeks of toil and pain, you're determined to have fun, expecting the best; but a single-minded quest for recreation and rest almost never leads to either. The standard perils include: locals looking for trouble, firefighters looking for trouble, overzealous peace officers, and impaired judgement due to alcohol consumption plus the dizziness of being safe, comfortable, and unscheduled. You feel freer and more appreciated than you really are.

I knew we didn't have any idiots on the crew, and nobody appeared to be pounding down drinks in a deliberate blast-off to oblivion, but I could see a storm brewing at the pool table.

Tom and Moose were on a roll. They had teamed up to challenge all comers in eightball, and they were apparently invincible. Their streak of victories was particularly galling to their opponents because Moose and Tom were drunk. I could see Tom wavering a bit, taking extra time to focus on the cue ball and line up his shots. Every now and then he'd cock an eyebrow and favor me with a crooked grin, as if to say, "Can you believe this, man?"

I knew Tom sported that ex-Marine wild streak that was coaxed to the surface by booze. I decided I should play guardian angel for the rest of the evening and try to steer him away from trouble.

What made me nervous was the way four local cowboys—complete with ten-gallon hats, shit-kickers, and Marlboros—were losing at pool. Those guys were good (and still mostly sober), but Tom and Moose kept acing them out with nifty bank shots and cross-corner strikes. And they'd laugh when they won, irritating hoots made grating by the ragged cheeriness of intoxication. They weren't mocking the cowboys; they were just happy with their game, but the good old boys were losing patience with the ill fortune that had pitted them against a pair of flashy, out-of-town drunks. And besides, losers fed the quarters into the slots.

At this point I was distracted by the dog. The medium-sized mutt had dashed out from under the pool table and attacked Lurch out on the dance floor. Despite his six-foot-six, 240-pound bulk, Lurch was lightly prancing around the floor, whirling and twirling with a woman who seemed to enjoy his style. The dog cut in, nipping at his heels while it dodged the surrounding dancers.

A cowboy next to me snorted and said, "Hey, the dog's after the big bull." He explained that the mutt was a blue heeler. They were employed to herd cattle (or was it sheep?), and they kept their charges in line by snapping at their "heels." I assumed the "blue" was derived from "black and blue." The man may have been joshing me, but it was a good story, and sure enough, the dog herded Lurch and a couple of others back to the center of the floor and then returned to the pool table.

When I re-focused on Tom, he was hammering a low-ball into a side pocket. His new adversary was one of "us"—not a member of our crew, but from another Minnesota unit. I'll call him Chip. I breathed a sigh of relief; Tom and Moose had dispatched the locals without provoking mayhem. But as I watched the game unfold I saw Chip's face begin to darken. He was being handily beaten and was not amused.

Tom had won too many games, he was definitely swaggering. Chip muffed a shot and Tom sidled up and spoke into his ear. Chip exploded. He dropped his cue and lashed out. Tom jumped aside and raised his fists. I flew out of my chair as Chip was viciously lunging for Tom's midsection. Chip was bear-hugged from behind just as I grasped Tom's shoulders and swung him out of the fray. Chip had a knife.

It's curious how an inanimate object can expand to fill a room, can have a presence that's almost lifelike. I never even saw the blade and thought that the men who had collared Chip so zealously were surely overreacting to a mere barroom spat. My chief concern was that Tom and Chip didn't break any furniture and get us all kicked out.

But then I felt the sudden pressure increase, the sense of urgency that coursed through the tavern like a sine wave on a scope. The buzzing, even slate of conversation broke into shards of hoarse whispering.

Tom shook out of my grip and said he was okay—meaning he wasn't going to pursue the matter. Chip was locked in the middle of an intense huddle that included his crew boss. He probably lost that knife for good and will never be on another fire crew. Or so one hopes. One of the cowboys was grinning, happy about something. Tom gulped the last of a drink and left.

Suddenly I couldn't stand the pall of cigarette smoke. I had been breathing the cloud all night—hell, we had been inhaling smoke for three weeks. But the flash of violence had broken a spell; I needed fresh air.

Outside, the mountain night had an edge of approaching autumn, the bracing aroma of frost. We had been sleeping in the dirt under the open sky, and I liked it. I wasn't excited about going to bed in the motel; I had grown accustomed to stars and chilly dawns. But I had to face it; our tour was over. Tomorrow we would board a plane somewhere and fly to Duluth. From there we would scatter to homes spread across two states. We had been buddies and brothers in the midst of fire, but it was likely I would never see most of these people again. The crew, in fact, was dying. The family would cease to exist, and I grieved.

The night in the bar was our wake, our last "shift." On the flight home we would start to break apart, start thinking about the "normal" world and all our routine obligations. In Duluth our crew would live in name only, in black ink on time sheets and manifests. Our final handshakes would leave us hollow—we'd all be casualties, and in time the names would fade.

But I had been there before, and I knew the flip side: there would always be another fire, always another crew. There'd be another *now,* or at least the hope of it.

I took a piss out in the grass, then went to the motel and slipped into a soft, clean bed. I didn't sleep worth a damn.

"The sky, it seemed, was filled with slurry, the earth with greenbacks." — Stephen Pyne, *Fire in America*

Red Top

About ten months later, in July 1989, at a spike camp in Idaho, I was awakened by a hacking gurgling cough. I sat up in my sleeping bag and saw Harry sprinting toward the medical tent. He was spitting blood. I was concerned, but there was no need to rise. The camp paramedic and our crew boss Roger Nelson would handle it. I could see Roger was already out of his bag and pulling on his pants. I went back to sleep.

It was our seventh day on the Whangdoodle Fire, but not our first blood. Only the day before Doug had stabbed himself in the thigh while cutting plastic bands off coiled hose with his belt knife. Our crew EMT tended to the wound—nothing serious—but it was a reminder of how routine activity could snap and bite.

It is routine, of course, that's most dangerous. In the early stages of a fire, when things are popping and chaos reigns, people are heads-up and primed. More than anything else, keenness of mind is what keeps a firefighter alive and healthy. For instance, at Yellowstone approximately 10,000 firefighters battled some of the worst fires of the century all summer, and no one was killed until October, when snow had muted the blazes and the operation was well into the mop-up stage. Accidents happen no matter what, but it's easier to let your guard slip when monster flames are no longer running amok.

However, we witnessed a notable exception on our first shift at the Whangdoodle. (Whangdoodle was named after a local creek, but to our ears it had a decidedly Saturday-morning, candy bar-commercial ring to it, and we started calling the incident The Smurf Fire, and sometimes, provoked by Overhead antics, The Mickey Mouse Fire.) Our crew—Minnesota-2—was deployed along a fresh dozer line, reinforcing the cut by clearing extraneous brush and digging out bear grass, when the fire blew out of a draw and threatened to overrun the entire operation. With the roar of headfire in our ears, we retreated down the lee side of the mountain to a safety zone—in this case, a meadow adjacent to the main road. Two other crews joined us and we gathered on the southern aspect of a small rise to gawk at the air show. A pair of DC-6 air tankers were executing repeated sorties, lumbering over the ridgetops, in and out of smoke, until they dropped their loads and banked away, engines howling. The fire was at the nearest crest, barely a quarter-mile away, and a pink mist of retardant drifted down and settled over the far side of the meadow.

As we watched, a jeep pulled up, and a member of the Overhead Team hopped out and gave us a perfunctory wave. On the back of his orange vest was stenciled "Safety Officer." Here was a powerful man—able to veto any order, tactic, or idea he deemed unsafe. (Or at least *inordinately* unsafe; just attending a big fire is hazardous to your health.) I assumed he would stroll over to chat, ask crew bosses about conditions up on the mountain, but instead he ambled off toward the near crest, uphill into brush spattered with red drops of slurry. Someone asked aloud, "Where the hell is he going?" and speculated on the comic possibilities. Then much to our alarm and delight, it actually happened.

One of the air tankers swooped in, further downslope than before. The sound of its approach was masked by the ridge, and, when it surged over the trees and into his awareness, the Safety Officer had no time to react. The plane unleashed a wave of retardant. The main body of the drop missed him, but for several seconds he crouched in a heavy downpour of slurry. When he stood he was actually dripping—dyed red, literally from head to toe. And the embarrassing shower had been taken in full view of sixty firefighters, who were now making a poorly concealed attempt to keep from weeping with laughter. A safety officer!

He could have slunk off or yelled at us, but the guy was cool. He strode directly to our position, then grinned as he wagged a finger like a reproving schoolmarm. "Did you see that demonstration?" he chided. "Well, don't ever get yourself into that fix!" We roared. He had courageously saved as much face as possible under the circumstances.

Harry's blood-spitting wasn't as serious as it seemed. He was hustled down the mountain to a hospital in town, but rejoined us next day. His sinus and nasal membranes had simply dried out to the point of extreme, bleeding irritation, and blood dribbled down his throat to choke him awake. The doctor gave him a non-prescription nasal mist (not a decongestant) called Ocean, to re-moisturize the afflicted passages, and Harry raved about its miraculous powers. I tried a shot and it was like nectar for the nose—almost instant relief from the ravages caused by smoke, dust, and low humidity. I now keep a bottle stashed in my red pack, and laud its virtues to rookies. Lord knows there's little that's more efficacious than good drugs for easing you through a fire tour.

I also preach readiness, and only half-jokingly assert that three items should have priority in your packing: socks, underwear, and Ocean. (And probably your favorite over-the-counter pain killer.) It's difficult to predict when we'll be abruptly invited to a staging area with all our gear, and it's less stressful if our stuff is pre-packed. This trip to the Whangdoodle, though, had been a little different. I knew before the dispatcher even phoned that I was booked.

I was sitting on my living room floor, watching the 10:00 PM news with my father-in-law, when it was reported that over 200 fires had been ignited by lightning in Idaho. "Well," I told him, "I better get my act together." I inventoried my gear and collected it into a pile in the bedroom. (I preach pre-packing, but hardly ever get it done myself.) I slept lightly, restless with anticipation. The phone call came at 3:00 AM, and by that hour the next day I was sleeping on the lawn at BIFC.

The Boise Interagency Fire Center (BIFC—"Biffcee") is a cross between the Pentagon and a summer camp. Established in 1965 by the US Forest Service, Bureau of Land Management, Bureau of Indian Affairs, National Park Service, and US Fish & Wildlife Service, it's an operations nerve center and a fire analysis/information source for major incidents all across the West. The complex is adjacent to the Boise, Idaho, airport, and includes a smokejumper school, a massive fire cache, and several acres of open lawn to accommodate crews in transit. Small pavilions are erected to provide shade, but firefighters sleep on the ground. As you march from the tarmac to the BIFC gate, you're greeted by a large circle-and-slash sign that reads: NO WHINERS!

But who would whine at BIFC? For crews it means lots of good food, showers, movies, and volleyball. Though a wise crew boss will discourage the latter if his outfit is on the way to a fire. Aggressively engaged volleyball, charged with crew and/or regional pride, can be more threatening to ankles and knees (and faces) than the fireground. What's inspiring is that while you're waiting at BIFC to be deployed to a fire or routed home, you're guaranteed eight hours pay per day, so it's possible to be financially rewarded for your serve, spike, or bump. For most of us, it'll be our only brush with "professional" sports.

To say we slept at BIFC is exaggeration. We laid out our pads and sleeping bags only a few hundred yards from the runway, and the light, noise, and stink of a jet port are hardly soporific. Inserting earplugs, we did lie down and rest, and I dozed off intermittently until the blessed call for breakfast.

As our five crews out of Minnesota boarded school buses shortly after daybreak, we were each handed a memo outlining standards of behavior for our stay in the Payette National Forest. A communal groan arose in our bus. The gist was: There had been firefighter behavior problems in the past, particularly when crews were in the town of McCall, and an era of toleration had ended. Miscreants were subject to "immediate release from the fire to your home unit with a strong recommendation for the appropriate disciplinary action" or "arrest by the local law enforcement." The ominous thing wasn't the content of the memo, but rather that it had been prepared and distributed in the first place. This wasn't common practice and didn't bode well for the future.

After a long, scenic ride up Highway 55, we arrived mid-afternoon at a forest meadow along the bank of the Secesh River, not far from the old gold mining settlement of Warren. This would be the site of the Steamboat Complex fire camp, and we were the first crew to arrive. They put us to work, and within the hour our crew suffered its first casualty. While helping to drive stakes for some large, military-style tents, one of our people smashed an index finger with a hammer. It wasn't an incapacitating blow, but it certainly struck a sour note. Often it's the accumulation of minor mishaps that finally puts you out of the game, and the loss of a firefighter hurts the entire crew. It not only increases the work load for everyone, but jacks a crew one notch closer to being considered officially ineffective, and hence demobed—thus costing all crew members lost wages. I felt for the man's pain but was also irritated that he had hurt himself on day one—with a thoroughly unglamorous, Three-Stooges kind of injury. I hoped he wasn't establishing a pattern.

Next morning we suffered an embarrassment. Understand that on most big fires a crew without a chain saw is like a bridegroom without an erection—a potential disappointment to everyone. Since it's often difficult to acquire a saw from the supply unit at the incident, it's wise for a crew to pack its own. The State of Minnesota had issued us a saw kit in Duluth, and we were much pleased until we opened the crate. The fire cache folks had graciously provided us an ancient, morbific-sounding Echo with a sixteen-inch bar. Just as we were pulling it out of the box, the Globe Hot Shots were marching past and one of them grinned, nodding dismissively at the tiny Echo.

"What're ya plannin' to do," he rasped, "trim a hedge?"

Prick! We noticed he had a Stihl 064 with a twenty-four-inch bar riding on his shoulder, and we hated his guts. It's been my experience that hotshot crews have a hard time dealing gracefully with the notion that they're supposed to be elite.

In any case, we managed (miraculously) to requisition a brand new saw from Supply the next day. In handing it over, the man quipped, "I know you requested a chain saw, but all I could find was a Homelite." We snorted appreciatively. On the third start-up the recoil malfunctioned and our sawyer had to field strip the saw before it had consumed the first tank of gas. It's sad, but true—compared to some of its foreign cousins like Stihl or Husqvarna, the Homelite is junk. (And not substantial enough to make a decent boat anchor.)

That first shift, as mentioned, we were run off the mountain. Next morning we were teamed up with the Globe Hot Shots (joking with them about retiring our hedge trimmer) to fell snags and build handline around some small spot fires. It was a grueling day of digging, scraping, and hauling bucked trees, and, after twelve hours, we hiked up to Drop Point 6. A bulldozer had plowed away about an acre of the forest floor, exposing a patch of sand and gravel that was now our spike camp.

Overhead had seen fit to designate us as being on "coyote spike." Picture a mangy, scraggly animal that's endured a hard, lean winter—or perhaps Wiley Coyote just after he crawls out from under a boulder that's clobbered him from the top of a cliff. Because "coyote spike" meant that for the next five days, we were only allowed what we could carry in our day packs. (I had my personal medications, a sweatshirt, longjohns, one extra set of socks and underwear, and a paperback novel.) Our red packs, containing such decadent luxuries as sleeping bags and foam ground pads, were piled up under a tarp back at base camp. Their whole purpose, of course, is to be portable enough to accompany us on spike-outs, and five-ton military trucks (by no means fully loaded) were regularly rumbling directly past our "camp." Nevertheless, Overhead claimed they didn't have the transportation resources to reunite us with our red packs. Nobody was buying it. Our strike team leader, a native of Arizona, shrugged and mumbled, "This is Idaho. What do you expect? I try to avoid this area whenever I possibly can." He had obviously failed this time.

We were supplied with one paper sleeping bag apiece, and we laid these over sheets of polyethylene directly on the ground. Before nightfall, we tried to root out as many rocks as possible, using pulaskis and mcleods to smooth out some sleeping areas. The site had been partially burned over during the first day's blowout, and Jon Luepke, our principal sawyer, felled two charred snags that were making everyone nervous. There was no decorum in being squashed in your sleep at such a garden spot.

Sleep didn't come easily on our first long night of coyote spike. We were weary, but sleeping in the dirt requires acclimation. After some fitful rest I awoke in predawn darkness, thoroughly chilled. The thin paper bag wasn't enough insulation against the heat-sapping sink of bare ground. Later that day I found a body-size chunk of cardboard, and was genuinely joyful. Here was some decent insulation! Now I know how a bag lady feels. That cardboard was precious, and I clutched it to my breast like a heavenly gift, laughing with pleasure. I could easily have sold it to any of my envious comrades. Fortunately, as the operation unfolded, an increasing quantity of tools and supplies arrived at the drop point in cardboard cartons, and soon there was enough for all. Harry used a long box as a complete unit, climbing inside at night like a vampire into a coffin, and pulling a tarp over the top. Our camp soon resembled a particularly nasty hangout for the homeless.

That first morning out of coyote spike began innocuously. Our crew spread out through a rugged tract of unburned forest in search of spot fires across the line. It's called "sweeping" or "gridding," and it sounds simple enough. You line out in the woods at roughly twenty- to thirty-foot intervals and walk slowly forward, scanning and sniffing for smoke. (Small smokes are usually easier to smell than to see.) The idea is to establish one fire-fighter as an anchor on the line, with everyone else keying off the person to their right (or left, if you're heading in the opposite direction). Depending on the thickness of the foliage, a single crew may be spread out for 300 to 600 feet. Commands to "go" "stop" "bump left" "bump right" are passed down the line via hearty shouts. It's basically run like a great game of "Simon Says." But in rough, unfamiliar terrain, and especially at night, I've seen crews get so fouled up and disoriented that "sweeping" deteriorates to groping/cursing/creeping.

Nevertheless, Minnesota-2 was one of the best gridding outfits I had been on, and, with a minimum of irritation, we thoroughly scouted a half-mile of line by noon, halting periodically to extinguish and isolate several "duffers"—smoldering patches of needle and leaf litter that were time bombs waiting for wind.

Our squad found a huge, smoking pine stump that had apparently been struck by lightning. It was at the base of a narrow drainage, and there was a vernal pool (a puddle, actually) nearby. While one firefighter hacked at the stump with a pulaski, the rest of us used our hardhats to shuttle muddy water from the puddle and dump it on the exposed heat. So much for the glamour of fire suppression. There were several duffers in the immediate area, and the subsequent line building was tough going through matted roots. It appeared we might kill the rest of the shift in that spot, when we heard the Division Supervisor page Roger over the radio and request that he cut loose a squad and send them up the line.

I believe Roger sent our squad because Bill Julson was our squad leader. In my opinion he was among the best, and Roger obviously had a lot of confidence in his abilities. I first met Bill when we were dispatched together to battle a rash of peat fires in north central Minnesota two years before. We spent seven punishing days manhandling hose lays and peat nozzles in sub-freezing November weather (interspersed with a couple of initial attacks on grass fires), and grew to appreciate each other's *joi de vivre* in the face of standard fireground suffering. At staging in Duluth, Bill reminded me of our "venison score" at the peat fires. We had been driving back to the station from a grass fire when we saw a doe bolt from the ditch into the path of a car ahead. There was a spray of glass from a headlight, and the deer collapsed onto the highway. The car never slowed down. We were amazed and speculated that the driver had seen our DNR truck in his rearview mirror and either thought he'd be in some kind of trouble for hitting a deer or figured (more likely) that, as state employees, we should handle the mess. We pulled over next to the fallen doe, which had been struck in the head and was now flopping pathetically across the centerline and bleeding profusely. She was dying, and it was a sad spectacle, but we didn't see why the ravens should get this fresh meat. One of our firefighters quickly and neatly slit her throat with his pocketknife, and we lifted the carcass into the back of the truck. I registered the deer with the local sheriff, then we field dressed it in the woods outside town, and hung the carcass in the garage at the forestry station. As it happened, one of the local smoke-chasers was a professional butcher, and the next day he processed the deer so expertly that we never found so much as one hair in the meat. At the end of our tour I hauled home forty pounds of venison. Ironically, it was deer season, and I don't hunt. I offered Bill some of the booty, but he was too proud to "pack home a roadkill," and I replied with something endearing like "up yours!"

Bill's a full-time DNR forestry technician who's seen a lot of fire. He spent some time on a hot shot crew, and thrives on fire action. He has an aptitude for non-oppressive leadership, and our squad, impressed by his competence and cheered by his natural bent for comedy, was clearly the most efficient of that crew. I thought it apropos that we were designated Squad #1.

In contrast, the Squad #2 leader, though also a full-time DNR forester, seemed to have trouble convincing five people to walk in a straight line. He was the first to start whining about going home (before a week was up—unforgivable!), and, as the days passed, his people were lagging and bitching. If not for an extremely well-conditioned and experienced casual in their midst, they may have evolved into an embarrassment. Later in the tour, Jon, who was on Squad #1, spent most of a day doing chain saw chores with Squad #2, and when he returned to us, he strode over to Bill and dropped to his knees. Grasping him around the waist he fervently cried, "Oh Bill! Thank God, I'm on your squad!"

After the radio call from Roger we cheerfully turned our line-building over to another squad, and humped for nearly a mile, trudging up steep grades through loose dirt, and approaching ever nearer to a major smoke column. The Division Supe was at the point, trailing a D-7 Cat as it punched new line on the flank of the fire. The dozer was cutting rapidly through sandy soil, shoving aside fir and hemlock on a jagged series of ridges. We assumed the Supe would assign us as back-up for the dozer—cleaning up hot spots near the line as the operation closed in on the head.

But when we finally reached him, he pointed away from the line, far off across the next drainage to a pencil-thin plume of smoke rising from the trees. It was a separate fire—either a spot, or a distinct lightning strike and was definitely a serious threat to our flank. He turned to Bill and said, "I'd guess that's about a quarter-acre. I want you to go in there and take care of it before dark." He paused, and one of his eyebrows arched skeptically. "Do you think you can find it?"

Well, if he had his doubts, then why did he call us? One of these days we'll get some respect. I suppose. But in 1989 we were still "just" an Eastern crew on a Western fire—in Idaho, no less, that most insular of fire fiefdoms—and, regardless of our qualifications, we were tacitly considered second class. No matter that we had zero greenhorns on the crew: all had fire experience in Minnesota, most had been on Western fires before, and some had been firefighters for a decade or longer; a few had more Western fire experience than many Westerners.

Without sarcasm Bill replied, "You bet. No problem," and pulled a compass out of his shirt pocket. What he'd really wanted to say was: "No problem, dipshit. The State of Minnesota has been aware of this compass development for some time now."

As Bill took a bearing on the smoke, the Division Supe asked, "You guys got food and water?"

What do you think, dipshit?

"Affirmative."

Bill got a fix on the plume, and we set out immediately. We had to drop into the drainage and scale the other side to reach the fire—cross-country through dense woods, and we lost sight of the smoke immediately. Bill was glued to the compass, and I brought up the rear with a roll of flagging, tying fluorescent green ribbons to trunks and branches as we snaked through the "jungle." There were numerous deadfalls, and even a stretch of swamp where we churned up a trail of mud. In the ambient dryness it was actually refreshing.

As the raven flies, we had estimated the fire to be about three-eighths mile from the dozer line, but by the time we traversed the drainage, found the best route through the woods, and climbed the opposite slope, we had gone close to a mile. We heard the fire before we saw it, and it sounded more wicked than the distant plume had suggested. There was the angry snapping that indicated open burning, and, as we neared the crest of the ridge, we heard the roar of a torching conifer. We exchanged nervous glances and hurried forward to find about five blackened acres of grass, brush, and deadfalls. Several "jackpots" of fuel were burning fiercely, and surface fire was alternately creeping and running along the forest floor as the breeze waxed and waned. I could see at least a dozen standing snags blazing within and without, spewing sparks and embers. It was a mess, potentially explosive. There were a half-dozen spot fires on the windward side of the burn, and it was far more than the Division Supe had guessed—and certainly more than we seven firefighters were going to dig a line around before dark.

Bill decided we needed some air drops to cool things down, and he was trying to squeeze through the radio traffic to the Division Supe when a lead plane blasted by at treetop level, directly overhead. It was a twin-engine Cessna, and the sudden racket made us jump. We scattered like a covey of flushed grouse, hustling downslope and away from the flight path. I crouched behind a massive log, and in moments a DC-6 thundered over, and retardant rained through the forest canopy, hissing and whooshing as it slopped onto flames. Everyone was lightly spattered with slurry, and we figured there would be another drop, so we regrouped and began contouring west, away from the main burn. We had gone about two chains when the lead plane zoomed in—again directly overhead. We hurried further downslope and once more were splattered with retardant as the tanker roared by. We laughed. It seemed like we were the target. As soon as the plane banked away, we descended halfway back to the swamp and waited while a second air tanker joined the fray and four more slurry drops pounded the crest of the ridge. After several minutes, we climbed back up through the slippery, red-painted brush and found the retardant had dampened the fire considerably. It was still hot, but no longer on the verge of blow-up.

When Bill finally connected with the Division Supe and offered a size-up of the situation, the man asked, "Are you behind me on this dozer line?" We guffawed. The Supe had clearly misplaced us already. That explained the air drops on our heads. Once Bill got it straightened out as to our identity, location, and purpose, the Supe requested that we spend the night building line and patrolling. He'd see that sleeping bags and extra rations were sling-loaded in via helicopter. We heard Roger call the Supe to offer the rest of Minnesota-2 for the night shift. It sounded fine—great hours and good duty—but a few minutes later the Supe suddenly changed his mind. Our squad was to do what we could until the end of that shift, and then tie in with our crew back on the dozer line and head up to the spike camp for the night. I imagine the Supe came to his senses with a start, instantly repenting of so rashly treating an Eastern crew as if they knew what they were doing. In any case, Squad #1 dug line for a couple of hours where we determined it was needed most, then followed our ribbons out.

Back at the dozer line, we enjoyed a panoramic view of the drainage, and saw the ridge where we had been working was stained red. The slurry was so thick it looked as if the trees had been spray-painted by the overly-ambitious Christos, in an avant-garde attempt at jumbo-scale abstract art. So we gave the work a title: Red Top. The hope was that we would be sent back in the morning to finish the job. Red Top should be ours.

A half-hour later, as we humped a steep mountain trail toward camp, a Jet Ranger helicopter swung into view and hovered loudly overhead, sliding along to the south about a hundred feet above the canopy. We were aware of it, but not particularly interested—we were accustomed to the air show by now. Then the noise quit. *That* caught our attention. The raucous beating of rotors had abruptly cut out. We stopped in our tracks and looked up. The helicopter was gone; just like that. We clustered around Roger and his radio. In a moment it crackled to life:

The Strike Team Leader to the Division Supe: "Yeah, Ralph. I think a chopper just went down."

Division Supe: "Ten-four, Tom. We'll check it out."

The tone of this exchange was in the "calm command mode," the voices carefully modulated to an even, unrushed beat that conveys an air of efficient boredom—no matter what brand of craziness is going down.

About two minutes later the pilot of the vanished helicopter came on the air. He couldn't quite stifle a tremor: "Yeah, th-that's a-affirmative, Ralph. We had a *very* hard landing."

Actually, as we saw the next day, his ship was totally destroyed. A tail-rotor failure had sent it spinning into a huge fir, which broke it in two before it tumbled to earth. (The tree survived.) There were still aircraft parts hung up in the branches, and what was left of the fuselage looked like a crushed beer can. By some quirk, the pilot and his single passenger had walked away. But it hadn't crashed. It had merely endured a "very hard landing." And if the pilot had waited another minute to get on the radio, he probably could've calmed his voice into sleepy nonchalance. Some might write it off as pure machismo, but I understood this bravado. How else should the pilot react? Especially if he intended to fly again. "A very hard landing" didn't sound all that terrible.

Still, the sight of the wreckage was sobering, and if the "landing" had occurred a few minutes earlier, some of us grunts may have been ripped with shrapnel from disintegrating rotors; we had just walked within yards of the crash site. That would've been the ultimate bad joke—slaughtered by a helicopter while minding your own business on the ground. We could have said: "We had a *very* hard shift."

I didn't realize until later that this ship was One-Three-Juliet, a Jet Ranger that had been on fire duty in northeastern Minnesota the year before. In fact, I had worked at least three fires with 13J. The most memorable had been a ferocious grass/brush blaze within the city limits of Hibbing. My engine was first on the scene, and we plunged through dense smoke to the head of the fire. A gusty west wind and tinder-dry fuels were generating fifteen-foot flames, and houses were in their path. I drove into the smoldering black behind the head, and we attacked it from the rear with our hoseline and pump cans. Three times I dropped to the ground gagging, sucking in the relatively clear air at dirt level. Reinforcements arrived, including 13J, but the only convenient spot to land the ship so the Bambi bucket could be attached was near the right flank of the fire, which was moving so fast that the pilot declined to touch down, afraid 13J would be overrun, or the helitack crew trapped on the ground. Some considered the pilot overly cautious, but the crumpled wreck before us at the Whangdoodle was eloquent testimony to the potential hazards of fireground aviation.

Actually, it was two years later when I made the connection between this crash and the Jet Ranger I had worked with in Minnesota. In the summer of 1991 I was a member of a helicopter crew in Idaho's Nez Perce National Forest (more on that later). I was in a tavern in Dixie, Idaho, one evening, drinking beer and swapping stories with a helicopter foreman from Washington state.

"Yeah," she said, "the ship I had on the Whangdoodle augured in."

"Really?" I replied. "I saw the wreckage—nearly came down on top of us."

"No kidding?" We chuckled at the link in our personal lore. "Yeah," she went on, "poor 13J; it was a fine ship."

"Did you say '13J'?"

"Affirm."

And so my experience of that helicopter came full circle; the fireground encompasses a relatively small community.

Next morning our entire crew was dispatched to Red Top, and there was general rejoicing. We basically had our own fire—a clear-cut mission with little or no interference from Overhead, and plenty of useful work to keep us engaged and lend purpose to our lives. Sometimes, on big project fires, the impulse of the incident commander is to order too many firefighters, and it's easy for a crew to be shunted aside into some marginally significant patrol duty or cold trailing, and be essentially forgotten—not unlike our experience at the Silver Complex in '87. Such shifts can become excruciatingly long, and morale appallingly low. A helicopter crashing on your head would almost be a relief.

But there was little danger of boredom on Red Top. The fire had spread to about ten acres overnight, and we hit it hard immediately. The Division Supe sent a dozer up to push in a line, and we spent the day felling snags, lining isolated spot fires outside the dozer line and using dirt to extinguish the jackpots. No water was available. We also worked hard at trimming the ladder fuels, and while I was hacking the lower limbs off a fir, a dead branch was jarred loose from higher up and tumbled onto my head. Fortunately this one wasn't of the "widow-maker" quality. Despite my hardhat, however, the branch somehow managed to cut the bridge of my nose. (Some would say because it's too big a target.) There was blood, but it was the kind of minor injury I would probably ignore at home. Out on the line, though, I hate to take healing for granted. Even a small laceration can become infected, and it might cost me hours and wages. So I had our crew EMT dress it up just to be on the safe side, and, naturally, it made him feel valuable to play the angel of mercy. It's wise to keep the morale of your medics high.

By the end of the shift, our line around Red Top was secure, and next morning we were instructed to do a one-hundred percent mop-up—make the whole ten acres cold. Around noon the Division Supe hiked in to inspect our work, and, though pleased, decided to call in another crew to give us a hand. About two hours later a New Mexico contingent trudged up to Red Top. They looked sullen. All were Mescalero Apaches, except for their Caucasian crew boss, and I was the first member of Minnesota-2 the boss happened to encounter. After his people deployed, bitching, into the burn, he confessed: "I'm losing control of this crew."

It seems they were about a mile away when the Supe summoned them to Red Top, and on the march over they had passed an Alaskan crew that was taking a lunch break on the line. The Alaskans were all Indian females (except for a white male crew boss), and as the Mescaleros walked by, a couple of the women had suggestively fondled their own breasts and called out: "We want Mexican babies!" It had been difficult, reported the crew boss, to keep his people moving along, and they were not happy to be far away on old Red Top. He mournfully shook his head. "I'm going to have trouble." But he couldn't stifle a lopsided grin. "And why," he went on, "didn't they want Caucasian babies?"

Nevertheless, his crew worked diligently for the rest of the shift, and we exchanged some friendly banter about the drudgery of dry-mopping. However, a week later we heard via the fireground grapevine that the New Mexicans had been shipped home after a knife fight broke out between some of its members. Or so the story went. In any case, after they left Red Top, we didn't see them again.

However, we did have a rotten apple of our own. Mike was one of the grunts recruited through the Job Service in 1988, and dispatched out West after a crash course in firefighting. Therefore, he was "on the list" and was called to join us in 1989. The Job Service recruitment drive produced a few good hands, but Mike wasn't one of them.

What first annoyed me was that, even after a week, he still hadn't learned the names of all his colleagues. I made it a point to know all first names, at least, by the second day. Not only does it aid comradeship and morale, but if someone is about to be nailed by a snag, or otherwise threatened, it's more helpful to be able to shout, "Bob! Look out!" rather than "Hey! You!" Not knowing a mere nineteen names after a full seven days indicated to me that Mike was either lazy or self-centered, or both.

But what turned the crew against him was his gross dereliction of duty. For several days the contingent of native Alaskan women was based out of the same spike camp, and Mike hit it off with one of them. Their relationship evolved to the point where they were slipping off into the woods after supper, sleeping bags in hand. Aside from one of our people who was a Mormon, I don't think anyone considered this fire-camp tryst morally objectionable per se. A few hinted they found the racial mix repugnant, but the basic reaction was bemusement mixed with distaste—not at two consenting adults having sex, but at two firefighters copulating out in the bushes. There was a sharp sense this was inappropriate fireground behavior; it was definitely unprofessional.

But Mike would have probably been the first to argue he wasn't a pro, and this was demonstrated conclusively the morning he told Roger he was sick and requested to be left in camp for the day. Roger, of course, consented but was suspicious. He told Mike he was to stay in our crew area and rest, and then asked one of the camp security people to keep an eye on him. No sooner had we been bussed off to the line, than Mike hooked up with his lover, who had apparently made a similar arrangement with her crew boss, and they ambled off together with their sleeping bags for a day of play. Roger was duly informed by security and refused to tally the eight hours pay Mike would have received if he had really been ill. Mike had the gall to complain bitterly, and I saw several of the crew regard him with looks usually reserved for dog shit clogging your Vibram soles.

But even a day of shirking may have been forgiven if Mike had chosen to redeem himself out on the line. Instead, he managed to remove all doubt of his crass immaturity. A few days later his squad was hiking up a steep mountainside, and as a prank, Mike reached up with the head of his pulaski and snagged the boot of the man ahead, tripping him. On a slope! Brett whirled around in justified rage and, if not for the quick intervention of the Strike Team Leader who happened to be nearby, would have assaulted Mike then and there. Violence wasn't the smartest reaction, perhaps, but Brett would never have been convicted by a jury of his peers. Roger reported the incident to Overhead, who assured him they'd see that Mike never got on a fire crew again.

Unfortunately, with the help of the Mescaleros, we had prematurely wrapped up our secluded, pleasant Red Top gig (or so we figured), and the following shift found us back in the mainstream of the operation. The next week and a half was a roller coaster ride between good and evil.

First, we were driven out of the division by another blow-up, and the crew was temporarily split by the fire, waiting out air strikes in separate safety zones. Ours was a rock slide just below the headfire, and we enjoyed a front row seat to an awesome display of fifty-foot flames and exploding trees. The Division Supe joined us, perched high on a boulder clutching his radio and directing the air attack. The first tanker angled in very low—we could have counted rivets on the fuselage—and, just as it loomed into view, the Supe, an otherwise very businesslike guy, raised an arm skyward, and in a perfect imitation of a well-known midget he called out: "De plane! De plane!"

Later, while building line one hot afternoon, someone bumped a wasps' nest, and two firefighters were instantly stung. Since we had to keep working in the area, I used a lit fusee as a blowtorch to fry the nest, and only got stung once in the process. On another occasion, Harry stepped on a ground nest, and, when he jumped aside, slapping at his face after being stung on the cheek, his eyeglasses were brushed off and landed exactly on the nest. Angry wasps swarmed around them in a cloud. Now what? We waited until the hubbub died down a little, and then with two people throwing dirt as a covering barrage, another dashed in to snatch the glasses. (He was only stung once.) Harry subsequently smeared toothpaste all over his cheek—claimed it soothed the sting and drew out the poison. Unfortunately his toothpaste was of the gel type, and he walked around for a day with a blue-green smear of gunk on his face. We encountered another crew that shift, but, though some stared, no one was rude enough to ask why our guy didn't wipe the snot off his cheek.

One evening a thunderstorm burgeoned out of nowhere and dumped enough rain to form puddles at our spike camp. We slept in them. It sprinkled off and on all night, and we pulled sheets of polyethylene over our sleeping bags, which then rendered the wet bags unbreatheable, and we sweated—soggy both inside and out. The temperature plummeted by morning and we all awoke freezing and miserable, afraid there had been enough rain to knock out the fire and send us home before our twenty-one-day tour was up. Fortunately the shower was isolated—sufficient to torture us for a night, but inadequate to extinguish the Whangdoodle.

One of the tragi-comic aspects of the operation was that every evening exhausted crews had to struggle up a long and extremely steep road to get back to camp. The road was entirely suitable for five-ton Army trucks, but none were ever dispatched—until three days after we left Red Top. Just as the crews on our division (there were eight or nine at that point) were preparing to hike out of the burn for the day, we heard the Strike Team Leader come on the division radio channel and announce for all to hear that a truck was being sent down the mountain. However, it was *only* for Minnesota-2. All other crews would hump it up as usual. We were shocked. This was not the kind of information that a strike team leader would normally broadcast for "public" consumption. If we were to be singled out for a pat on the head, then why didn't he arrange it between Roger and himself, person to person? But then, we thought, maybe it wasn't so much that Minnesota-2 was being rewarded, but that someone else was being punished. Our initial enthusiasm cooled rapidly. There was no advantage in having other crews despise us. Our "reward" seemed dubious at best.

So we were somewhat relieved when our ride turned out to be a curse in disguise. The five-ton truck sent for us had no canvas cover, and during the forty-five-minute drive down the mountain to the main camp (it was our turn for showers), we were pelted with icy rain. Following closely behind were two other five-tons—both with canvas covers snugly in place, and both loaded with handtools and garbage. The other crews later rode down to the main camp in heated school buses. With "rewards" like that, who needs chastizing?

But a couple days later, I experienced one of the high points of the tour. I was packing one of our chain saws as our squad cold-trailed and mopped up in Division H, and in early afternoon the Strike Team Leader pointed across a drainage at a plume of smoke. "Find that and put it out," he said. After a long, arduous hike, we came upon a huge fir. It was blackened and dead, but 120 feet tall, and still burning. Windblown embers spewed from its top, threatening to ignite spot fires beyond the control line. It had to come down. But the monster was forty-eight inches in diameter, and until then I'd never felled one more than twenty inches. Indeed, my official "Incident Qualification Card" (or "red card"—it's actually pink—a firefighter's wallet-sized credential) listed me as a FALB—Faller Class "B." As far as the Federal bureaucracy was concerned, I could only drop a tree that was in the "B" range, twenty-four inches or smaller. But there are two sets of rules: pre-fire and fire. When, as Kurt Vonnegut says, "the excrement hits the air conditioning," you just do what needs to be done.

I was intimidated by that fir. It was on the scale of *topography,* and the Homelite sounded tinny in the shadow of its bulk. I studied that tree like a contract, searching for the dendrologic fine print that would determine my tactics. Fortunately it had a slight lean that wasn't exactly counter to what I wanted at least in a general way. Thusly fortified, I launched into a wide undercut. With my swamper keeping an eye out for widow-makers and occasionally gesturing advice over the whine of the saw, I carved out a wedge the size of a coffee table top. The swamper knocked it free with his axe. I executed a dangerous "plunge cut," working the nose of the bar straight in to widen the notch, then started on the back cut, swinging from one side to the other. Before it was done, the twenty-four-inch bar of the saw was buried to the hilt. At the first creaking of heartwood, we scurried away like squirrels, neither of us completely trusting my work to tip the trunk in the right direction. When the tremendous burning fir hit the forest floor, the ground shook, raising a mist of ash and soot. The noise of its falling caused firefighters on the opposite flank of the drainage to stop and look around. It lay roughly where I had intended, and no one was maimed or killed. It was a sweet moment when the swamper slapped me on the back and said, "It wasn't pretty . . . but good enough."

During this period, we started rehabilitation work on some of the dozer lines. This consisted of seeding them with clover and then scattering brush and felling trees to protect the line from erosion. We were still sweeping for smokes occasionally, but the Whangdoodle was dying quickly, and the Strike Team Leader began to offer the promise of one beer for each smoke discovered—to be fulfilled if we ever got into McCall for R & R.

When we arrived at base camp for our weekly shower, we found this was not to be. We would get a day off and be bussed into town if we so desired, but it would be only to phone booths (stinking phone booths!) at the airport, so we could call home. All taverns were absolutely off limits. In fact, there was a little backwoods bar (named, inevitably, The Wagon Wheel) only a mile or so up the road from the base camp, and the Forest Service was paying the proprietor $200/day *not* to serve alcohol. Bill, Jon, and I wandered over there on our day off to sip pop and play pool, and we found the owner was ecstatic. He rarely made that kind of money, especially for not doing something. If there's ever another big fire in that area that can't be directly linked to lightning, the man would have to be a prime suspect. It was plain proof of the old adage that there's no disaster so severe that someone doesn't benefit.

As a result of this hardnosed R & R policy, a black market in contraband beer sprang up, with civilians from town smuggling cases out to the base camp and selling them for thirty-five dollars apiece. When people are treated like children, they act like children. But the camp was crawling with Forest Service and Park Service security people (I have met some normal, pleasant ones, but most, I think, are IRS rejects), and there was a crackdown. One night I saw three firefighters lying in front of the security tent, handcuffed and shackled in leg irons. They were drunk (the dingbats!) and a Forest Service dude with a .357 Magnum on his hip hovered over them, apparently on guard. An over-reaction to an over-reaction—and terribly funny if it hadn't been so absurd. Nevertheless, I suppose it did get the point across.

One point that never seems to get across is that new boots shouldn't be taken on a fire tour. This was demonstrated yet again by the guy on our crew who had smashed his finger on the first day. Before the middle of the tour, his fresh, unbroken boots had chafed his feet raw. The blisters blossomed to the brink of infection, and he was lucky he wasn't shipped home. He worked at the base camp for a week, doing light duty at Supply, and rejoined us out on the line for the last few shifts. Mountainous terrain is merciless, and new boots will generally break the feet before the feet break the leather. Anyone who shows up in Duluth sporting brand new boots shouldn't be allowed on the plane.

I could tell the Whangdoodle was winding down by the character of the radio traffic. One morning I was issued a chain saw, a radio, and one swamper, and dispatched to rehab a remote helispot. The site was a high point, featuring a spectacular vista of the Salmon River Range (plus three other major fires), the radio reception was excellent. I could monitor every conversation in two divisions, and the chatter was turning casual. At one point I heard an Alaskan crew boss nervously calling for a helicopter bucket drop near his position. He gave the coordinates, and I was able to pick out the smoke in question. It was far off down the valley, but from my vantage it did look potentially troublesome. Three times the crew boss got on the air, increasingly agitated, and apparently feeling that his request wasn't being responded to promptly enough. I could see what looked like a big Sikorsky headed his way, and after the crew boss' third transmission, a bored pilot finally came on the air.

"Oh, now, don't get your panties in a wad," he drawled, "won't be any fire shelters deployed out *here* today." Silence from the ground.

But I could picture all the people scattered through the Whangdoodle—snorting and hooting, and thinking twice now about calling for a helicopter. Of course only a pilot could get away with a transmission like that.

The year before, on a fire back in Minnesota, I radioed a request for a firefighter to hurry to my location with "an extra piss can." It was an unconscious use of slang, but when I returned to the station, the Area Forest Supervisor met me at the door. "The term," he said stonily, "is *pump* can." I'm no pilot.

That night, back at spike camp, I awoke at 3:00 AM to make a piss call (no pump involved). The northern half of the sky was blood-red—not with the glow of fire, but with the spectral, electromagnetic "flames" of the aurora borealis. The shimmering curtain was all the more vivid because of our 6,000-foot elevation, and the waves of light were as zestful as fireworks. After I returned to my bag I stared at the crimson apparition—framed by pitch black pine tops and girdled with bright stars, until I drifted off to sleep with the display in my eyes. Next morning I raved about the show and was chided by my comrades: "Why didn't you wake us!" Ha! The hypocrites! Rouse sleeping firefighters? One may as well poke sticks at hibernating grizzlies.

A couple days later, we were dispatched to the helibase, assigned standby for initial attack. If a new fire broke out, or there was trouble with an old one, we would be flown out and dropped off where needed. Two Army Blackhawk helicopters were parked out in the meadow, and we all lusted after a ride on one of those. They looked mean, fast, and exciting, and no matter where they took us, it would be better than rotting at the helibase.

We watched enviously as a Park Service crew from St. Croix National Scenic River lined up to board a Blackhawk, bound for some remote rehab in Division "H." They were in high spirits, but as they started to climb into the helicopter, the helitac foreman strode up to one of their crew members—a diminutive oriental woman barely taller than a shovel handle—and pulled her out of line. The crew boss came over, and a discussion ensued. We found out later that helitac hadn't liked the way the woman looked—she appeared pale and drowsy—and forbade her to board the ship. The crew boss resisted, figuring she was just a little weary, and the woman vouched for her wellness and argued for permission to accompany her crew. She probably didn't want to miss that copter ride. But helitac insisted and escorted the woman to the shade of a tree near us, where she watched her crew depart.

In moments she began to hyperventilate, and, by the time an EMT was rushed to her side a minute or so later, she was convulsing. The EMT summoned another firefighter and myself, and while the other guy supported her head and wiped her brow, I was directed to hold both her hands. She clutched me with surprising strength. The EMT took vitals and uttered a constant stream of soothing words until an ambulance arrived from the base camp with a defibrillator. They hooked her up and concluded she should be evacuated to a hospital in McCall via the other Blackhawk, The EMTs decided the thirty-five-mile ambulance ride would take too long.

So she got her helicopter ride after all. We strapped her onto a stretcher, and four of us carried her out to the gaping door of the Blackhawk. (I got to touch it at least.) In moments it lifted off with a grass-flattening burst of rotor wash and banked away to the south. The helitac foreman shook her head. "What would've happened," she said, "if I'd let her go with her crew?" I congratulated her. It had been a heads-up, professional call.

Minnesota-2 killed the rest of day on mere stand-by—napping, reading, or bored—and word filtered back next day that the woman was all right; she would rejoin her crew shortly. She'd been fighting a cold, it was reported, and had inadvertently overdosed on Sudafed. Or so the story went. Our guess had been some sort of allergic reaction. In any case, we appreciated the excitement—it was all we had that day.

On our final shift at the Whangdoodle Fire, we swung full circle. As an admirer of symmetry, I was mightily pleased when Overhead directed Roger to send one squad back up to Red Top to mount a last hunt for hot spots and lay the finishing touches on rehabbing the dozer line. The choice was obvious, and Bill happily led Squad #1 back to our private fire. The recent showers had rinsed some of the retardant off the trees, but the ridge still appeared distinctly red from a distance.

We laughed about our first afternoon on Red Top, forgotten by the Supe and playing hide and seek with slurry drops. We assiduously combed the burn, searching, sniffing and cold trailing with bare hands, but found no lingering heat. We cut more brush to shield the dozer scar, then took a leisurely lunch break near our original handline. We wallowed in a last opportunity to vociferously bitch about the Skittles. Every day without fail our sack lunches had contained a package of Skittles, a brand of candy loathed by everyone on our squad. Oh, sure, we ate them, but only because we ate everything—there's no such thing as too many calories on the fireground. But the stinking Skittles served as a focal point for good-natured (and some foul-natured) grumbling, and they came to symbolize whatever had irritated us about the operation. Jon wondered aloud: "Would a Whangdoodle eat Skittles?" Bill hit him in the head with one and replied, "No. They shit Skittles!"

But in many ways it had been a perfect tour. It was our nineteenth day out of Duluth, and by the time we arrived home we would make our twenty-one days. We were among the first outstate crews in, and we would be among the last to depart. We had worked all phases of the 7,000-acre fire—initial attack, mop-up, rehab. Our Strike Team Leader loved us (though he had a funny way of showing it), and the Division Supe finally figured out who we were and where he'd put us. In fact, a few days before, he had encountered us out in the middle of nowhere on a sweep, and we were shocked when he broke into a grin of recognition and said, "Ah, Minnesota-2. My friends." Well, good. He probably hadn't intended to kill us with those first tanker sorties on Red Top.

We waxed a bit nostalgic about Red Top and the Whangdoodle before we left. Bill said he was sorry our squad never got the chance to share a few beers on a decent day of R & R. It was a pity; we would have to make do with Skittles and one last lunch on Red Top. But all in all it had been a good gig.

On our way home, we were routed back through BIFC, and felt free to play volleyball. We put together an all-Minnesota team with members from our crew and a Superior National Forest crew, and thoroughly waxed all comers—Ohio, Maine, Tennessee, New Mexico. The scores were so lopsided that we finally decided—after fifteen straight victories—to disband our team for the sake of public relations. It was too bad our crew rating sheet didn't have a space for "volleyball," right next to "mop-up." Amazingly, no one was injured—other than wounds to pride.

It's a tradition among Minnesota crews to establish a betting pool when you're demobed. Everyone kicks in a buck and guesses the exact time our airliner's wheels will touch down at Duluth International. It means an extra twenty dollars or so for someone (though never me). Bill won the pot. It so happened he was the official timekeeper, so he was also heaped with character-building scorn.

That year saw the institution of a CSID—Critical Incident Stress Debriefing—for each crew that returned to Duluth from an outstate fire assignment. There was a fire official and a psychologist on hand to rap with us about easing back into "normal" life, and to record any complaints we had about how the incident had been handled.

Three crews went through the CSID before us, and as we filed into the debriefing room past the head table, I happened to glance at the psychologist's notepad. Near the top of the page, in all caps and underlined three times was: SKITTLES!! Excellent. I'd been skeptical of this debriefing process until I saw that. This was going to do some good after all.

The Malheur National Forest Tuberculosis Blues

1.

It wasn't an auspicious start. Minnesota-1 had just been bussed to the Duluth airport, anxious to board a 737, when some staging geek rushed up and announced that we must dump our sleeping bags. He was muttering about "not enough room in the cargo bay," and I knew it had to be bullshit. But he was insistent and overwrought, so reluctantly, and definitely against my better judgment, I zipped open my red pack and yanked out the bag.

"You can get paper sleeping bags out in Oregon," the man said. Oh, goody.

Meanwhile, the geek had locked himself out of the government van he was driving, so we left sixteen sleeping bags in a heap at the curb. (Four members of the crew—the smartest ones I guess—left their bags in their red packs, claiming private ownership.)

When we loaded our gear into the 737, there was more than enough space, of course, and we learned later that three members of a Wisconsin crew that boarded the plane first had sleeping bags lashed to the outside of their packs—long forbidden, as every firefighter should know—and somehow the order for them to leave *their* bags had been elevated to a general proscription for *all* of our (properly stowed) bags. No one knows how these things happen. When we got to the Malheur National Forest in east-central Oregon the next day, we were able to draw replacement bags (real ones) from Supply, but I was angry with myself for hours over allowing a guy who wasn't even going to the fire to convince me he was right when I knew he was full of it. It's wise to please Overhead, but *nobody* messes with your sleeping bag. It won't happen again.

We were the seventh crew to arrive at the Snowshoe Fire. Camp was just being established, and the officer greeting newcomers told us the fire had started the day before, displaying erratic and dangerous behavior. She pointed to a wall of smoke in the east—perhaps a mile distant—and assured us it obscured a small mountain range and some very wicked terrain. On Western fires it seems there's no other variety.

The camp was rising out of a huge dusty meadow—a desert plain ringed by wooded mountains. There were no trees within walking distance, and the afternoon temps had been in the mid to upper nineties for days, with no relief forecast. The grass was brown, the ground baked hard, and after an hour I felt marooned on the planet Mercury—far too close to the blazing noontime sun. The camp was as inspiring as a cookie sheet, and we couldn't wander. Barbed wire and a ditch denoted our bounds. The meadow had been a native American encampment in the good old days, and was supposedly rife with archaeological artifacts. The Forest Service didn't want firefighters stumbling around the site grubbing for arrowheads—as if anyone would have the energy.

While we helped the camp crew erect our crude, lean-to/tent—a tarp tied over a rough two-by-six frame—Craig Scherfenberg, our Crew Boss (Scherf, for short, especially on the radio) attended an official briefing to discover our role in the gig. He returned with a good news/bad news scenario. Good news: we were assigned to night shift, so we would be laboring in the cool evening air. Bad news: we would thus have to attempt sleep during the day—with only our pimpy tent as shelter from the merciless sun. And also, as fire camp veterans know, amidst the racket of generators, loudspeakers, truck engines, and camp construction. Fortunately, the meadow wasn't also the helibase. The thump of rotors may be music to some ears, but it's never a lullaby.

We passed the afternoon indulging in that brand of listless rest that only leaves you more tired, and at 1:00 PM, we boarded a bus for the fire. Well, almost. We were shunted to a campground—"staged" as it's called—where we waited for five hours. Initial attack was still evolving, so assignments were in a state of flux and no one was sure where we were needed most. But it was a good time for the crew to become further acquainted, swapping fire stories and an endless stream of jokes (mostly bad). Since we were Minnesota-1—the first crew of the Minnesota Department of Natural Resources to be dispatched outstate that year—most of us were hoary, fireground vets with about a century of accumulated experience. Of the twenty, only five had never worked a Western fire; fifteen of us were "casuals," and we had one woman.

Motivation was high, fueled by over a month of anticipation. Most had been contacted by dispatchers five weeks before, alerted to a "seventy percent chance" that we would be shipped to a fire in Arizona. I hung near the phone for an entire weekend, but no Minnesota crews were sent. It was a disappointment, but at least the false alarm had spurred me to have my gear in order. Priority One had been to transfer the entire contents of my underwear drawer to my red pack, and that's where the briefs remained—I just cycled them through the pack—permanent readiness. I even had to go to the pack every night for my toothbrush. I was basically camped out in the house. Of course there's a fine line between readiness and laziness; *un*packing is tedious, *re*packing a drag. Once packed, stay packed. (Or own *two* sets of everything.) So when the call came for the Malheur, I had to do little more than emit a joyous whoop and skip out the door. It was early August, and I had been primed since late June; so it was with most of the crew.

At around 11:00 PM the boss of Division E sent a bus, and, after a long, bumpy ride through smoke, we finally saw the fire. We were on the southern flank, with a dozer pushing line east toward the head. Our task was to secure the line, and the very first thing I did on the Snowshoe Fire was light a fusee. That, I thought, was a favorable omen. There were patches of unburned grass and brush up against the dozer trail, and we advanced along the line, burning them out. That's why I appreciate night shift. Since the humidity usually rises, and the wind usually tapers off, crews can more often directly engage the fire and/or ignite some fires of their own as a control tactic. What can I say? I've yet to meet a firefighter who didn't enjoy starting fires. Fire is power. Lighting them seems an almost primal, archetypal activity, and one can argue that for better and for worse, mankind's hegemony of the planet began with the ability to employ fire as a tool. As Aeschylus wrote, "You have it in a word: Prometheus founded all the arts of men." If wildland firefighting is one of those arts, then the fusee is its paint brush. I always carry at least three fusees in my field pack.

By 3:00 AM we'd torched all available fuel adjacent to our section of line, and we strung out for about a mile, patrolling and hunting for spots on the green side. We found one about twenty feet off the line, where the dozer had pushed some debris into a small pile. Apparently a smoldering chunk had been inadvertently snagged by the blade and partially buried. Jim and I smelled it before we saw it, and spent about twenty minutes digging out every vestige of heat. That alone was worth our pay for the night.

The last two hours of the shift dragged. What active fire remained in our sector was safely remote from the line, and our chief struggle was to stay awake. In the last forty-eight hours, I had had about six hours of honest-to-god sleep. At one point I sat down on the line to finish my lunch, and awoke with a start when the back of my head struck the ground. I decided to keep moving then, scanning the green side for smokes and staring at the waning gibbous moon. Besides, the temperature had dropped to near freezing, and I had to walk to stay warm.

We returned to camp at daybreak, waving at the dayshift crews as their buses and trucks left for the "front." There was a brief debate about skipping breakfast and heading directly for the sleeping bags before the sun started to climb, but most were too ravenous to pass the chow line. I pounded down a plateful of eggs, toast, and sausage—heedless of taste—just quickly taking on necessary fuel and easing the hunger pangs. As I crawled into my sleeping bag, the sun was an oval red-orange blob on the horizon, filtered by an inversion of smoke. The meadow was cold, the grass limned with frost. I shoved in a set of earplugs and was unconscious in minutes, but three hours later the whole crew was awake. Our tent was an oven, our bags clammy with sweat. It was two hours shy of noon, and already sleep was impossible. We frowned at each other, bleary-eyed, cursing the sun and wondering why in hell we had been so damned excited about heading to a Western fire. Nevertheless, I was still glad we weren't out on the line in such savage heat.

That evening we lost two people. Just as we were about to board a bus for Division E, an Overhead dude strode up and asked if we were Minnesota-1. Affirmative. How many of you, he asked, have helitak experience? Six raised their hands. I thought so, he said. (Minnesota has a reputation for aggressive air operations.) We need, he went on, a helispot manager; who's qualified? Tony, one of our Squad Leaders, was conscripted (happily, on his part) for air operations, and we never saw him again that tour. Scherf decided that Ross, an experienced smokechaser, should take Tony's radio, and he was thus consecrated as a new Squad Leader. Fireground commission. It meant an eighty-eight cent per hour raise and a mantle of responsibility.

Our other loss was Debbie. Less than two shifts into the tour, and already she had folded. The mood of the crew was a mix of sympathy and irritation. She simply couldn't function in the mountains. Just the short hike from the drop point up to the line—less than a mile—was too much, and she sat wheezing and coughing by the side of the trail. She was a smoker and overweight, and while no one places great stock in the step test, I couldn't believe she'd passed it. There are many outstanding female firefighters, but Debbie wasn't one of them. She had no business on the fireground, and Scherf was afraid he'd have to send her home. Fortunately, Overhead needed another clerk at camp, and she was able to fill that slot next day—and, we heard, garnered rave reviews for her work. Still, only two days out and we were cut to eighteen. It made me nervous. A couple routine injuries and we would be out of the game.

That night we were assigned to back up two dozers, but the Strike Team Leader discovered a three-acre spot fire early in the shift, and our crew was dispatched to handle it. One of the dozers gouged a line around the spot and Scherf had him clear a safety zone for us. The main fire was actually *below* our position, with plenty of fuel in between—a potentially deadly arrangement—and it was comforting to have an area we could easily reach to deploy fire shelters if necessary.

It was a hellish three acres. Heaps of cured logging slash, and a half-dozen lofty standing snags were burning fiercely—fanned by upslope winds at the start of the shift, and downslope breezes as the night cooled. Showers of sparks wafted almost continually over the line into dry brush and more slash, and we diligently hunted down any that still glowed on the ground, snuffing them with handtools or gloves.

One squad was detailed to cool a particularly hot area abutting the line; by throwing dirt and separating some of the burning logs they were able to approach from the windward side. It was here that Frank fell into the fire. He was shoving the end of a burning log, leaning into his shovel, when he tripped and pitched directly into three-to-four-foot flames. Fortunately he twisted, landing back-first instead of face-first, and leaped out of the inferno instantly. Leather and Nomex were his shield, and he wasn't so much as singed. But all witnesses were nonplussed, and after a moment of shocked silence—no one recalled ever seeing a firefighter actually tumble into a jackpot of flame—there was an outburst of speculative banter. Was Frank tired, and, therefore, a tad clumsy, or was he simply a natural clutz? Or would "hot-spot diving" now become a fireline fad and/or rite of passage? Of course anyone could do it in Nomex. How about naked? Would Frank like to be the first? And what about a point system to judge fire-diving form? The joke wore thin quickly, especially for Frank, but at least we had had a laugh and not a medical evac.

Speaking of jokes, that night we ran into the Liberty fire crew—as in Statue of Liberty. They were a conglomeration of Park Service people from New Jersey, who Bill Foss, one of our Squad Leaders, found wandering in the forest. Well, anyone can get lost, especially in the ambient confusion of the fireground, and Bill graciously led them to their assigned position. However, our squad was startled later that night. We were enjoying a break perched on an outcrop overlooking a valley, and on the far side of the drainage below we could see the main fire. There was no crowning, but it was vigorously ripping along the ground, torching trees by the dozen, and leaving bright pockets of flame in its wake. It was a middling fire at that point—inspiring, but not awesome. I was comparing it to other night fire scenes in my memory, from northeastern Minnesota to Yellowstone, when a squad from Liberty emerged from the darkness to join us.

We exchanged pleasantries, and then one of the older Liberty people laid a fatherly hand on the shoulder of a younger firefighter (half their crew appeared ready for the nursing home, and half for the eleventh grade) and said: "Well. Now you know what a forest fire looks like." It came out that this kid, and others on the crew, had never worked a fire before—of any kind. It was a fact that we, if not they, would soon bemoan. (Toward the end of the tour our crew was playing word games one day to ease a monotonous shift, and someone initiated a round of oxymorons. Some favorites were "military intelligence" and "casual sex," but the house was brought down by "Liberty firefighters.")

✳ ✳ ✳

2.

Next morning was a little cooler, and I slept for nearly four hours. I may have even gone longer except for the spiders. They appeared suddenly—in droves—scuttling outside and inside our bags, over feet and faces, and we literally slapped ourselves awake. The tiny arachnids were our constant tent companions from then on, the tempo of their intimate explorations rising with the heat, making the quest for sustained sleep even more futile.

Before we went on shift that afternoon, Bill Foss was drafted by Overhead as a Field Observer (a scout and fire mapper), and Scherf offered me Bill's position as Squad Leader. The King radio was duly passed on, and I was bumped up a pay grade to AD-III, that extra eighty-eight cents.

Most of the time a Squad Leader is a glorified grunt whose chief responsibility is ensuring that his five or six charges get on the right bus at the right time. That's not trivial—it's easy to lose people sometimes—but it's not exactly glamorous either. An effective classroom monitor in the sixth grade would probably get the hang of it.

Nevertheless, Squad Leaders can be critical to the character of the entire unit in more subtle ways—chiefly in the nurturing and maintenance of morale. A Squad Leader with a negative attitude (whining, bitching, hypercritical) can puncture everyone's mood in a hurry. That doesn't mean you must constantly be Merry Sunshine (recreational bitching garnished with wit is an art form, and can actually be a mood elevator), but you should be basically content with being on a fire, and able to treat general suffering with equanimity. It helps to view the operation as a rigorous camping trip, and yourself as a genial scoutmaster who just wants to see that the kids have a good time.

But occasionally a Squad Boss is bequeathed a more active leadership role. Such was my burden on my first shift at the head of a squad; and I ended up with the Liberty crew as well.

The Snowshoe Fire was mutating into a massive "water show." Within a week there would be over 250,000 feet of hose—fifty miles—deployed and operational. The basic plan: a 1,000-gallon drop tank was set up on a mountain road, serviced by a tank truck shuttling water from a creek in the valley. We set up a Mark-III centrifugal pump (the loudest contraption this side of a 747) and started stringing inch-and-one-half hose down a steep handline. Every 100 feet we installed a gated wye and came off the trunk line with a pair of one-inch attack lines and nozzles. The slope above the line was burning in patches, with some swaths of fire creeping downslope, and an occasional conifer exploding. Our crew was to deploy the hose and bump from wye to wye, extinguishing all fire within 100 feet of the line, and keep on extending. Ohio-1 would fall in behind, doing further suppression.

This portion of the Snowshoe had been extremely active that afternoon, and we were still in an initial attack mode.

My squad went first, our specific goal to lay hose down to another forest road at the base of the slope. The Liberty crew was down there somewhere, supposedly working their way up. Scherf scouted ahead, then made me the point man, leaving to my judgment how fast we could move—balancing suppression with hoseline advance.

It took about an hour to reach the lower road, and no other crew was in sight. We had also run out of hose, and there were some hot jackpots close to the line (in this case the line was the road). I radioed Scherf to outline the situation, and he had my squad spread out along the road as far as we could effectively reach, using handtools to knock down any flame we figured was too close to the line.

I was at the end of our deployment, briskly shoveling and scraping dirt onto flame, when two members of Liberty strolled up the road and paused to watch. It wasn't my place to give them orders, and I didn't think a request for assistance was necessary—my purpose must seem obvious. So I continued working for several more minutes until the line of fire edging for the road was knocked down. To my surprise they kept observing without comment (or movement) until I joined them on the roadway. I was too puzzled to be rude, and our subsequent small talk revealed they were indeed greenhorns, with only a vague notion of the overall mission. Well, everyone has to start somewhere, but hot line work on an 11,000-acre fire is probably not the best primer.

I was irritated. I wanted to make a good impression on my first shift as Squad Leader, and now I had to work with a crew that seemed to lack experience and self-starters. As often happens on the fireground, my initial modest mission of escorting five firefighters along a hoseline had casually evolved into defacto responsibility for completing the entire hoselay from the drop tank to the end of the lower road, and making sure said line was secure. Ross's squad had been pulled from the line to scout ahead of a dozer (there were so many confusing fingers of fire that the Dozer Boss needed help in designing his line), and Scherf had gradually taken on the duties of a Strike Team Leader, busily coordinating our advance with that of Ohio-1, and dealing with some water supply glitches. He had already made a favorable impression on the Division Supervisor, who was freely using Scherf's knowledge and experience to keep the operation tight.

Minnesota-1 had rapidly become a pivot. In two shifts we had gained a reputation as a "good crew"—an aggressive outfit that was willing to take the ball and run. (On our subsequent evaluation sheet the Division Supe mentioned Scherf's "attitude, desire, and overall bust-butt initiative" and averred that "the crew was [bar none] one of the best" he had worked with.) As a result, the operations of the Division began to revolve around us, and soon I was communicating directly with the Division Supe, which isn't standard operating procedure for a Squad Leader.

But then Dan Olson, of the Washington Department of Natural Resources, wasn't your standard-issue Division Supe. He wasn't awed by the organization, nor wowed by the hierarchy. The Incident Command System is a wonderful tool and can truly expedite action, but it can also become a stumbling block if individual authorities get hung up on personal power, or become rigidly locked into official channels and procedures. But Dan was a relatively free spirit who never lost sight of the fact that our primary goal was to fight fire (and not punch career tickets, kiss ass, properly arrange the paperwork, or make himself look good). To a casual observer it might seem difficult to lose sight of the fire on the fireground, but don't sell the bureaucracy short. Fortunately, Dan wasn't a bureaucrat.

That was made plain when he: 1) asked me (via radio), a lowly Squad Leader, what the situation on the lower road was, 2) actually listened to my report, and 3) wanted to know what I needed. More hose, more hose. When he said he would take care of it ASAP, I expected that within three hours or so (if we were lucky) I'd see the Liberty crew packing it in roll by roll. The radio traffic didn't sound encouraging—Dan was having trouble tracking down extra hose through the Supply people.

I was pleasantly astonished then, when a pair of headlights appeared far down the road about twenty minutes later. Dan got on the radio. "What's your location?" I told him. "Be right there with some hose," he chirped.

The backseat and cargo area of his Ford Bronco were crammed with hose and fittings. "You Leschak?" We shook hands and he grinned, looking from side to side in exaggerated furtiveness. "You seen the Safety Officer lately?" he queried.

Negative.

"Good. Hop aboard, and we'll get this hose deployed."

And so as the Division Supervisor drove (with authority) down the line, I clung to the tailgate and kicked off rolls of hose every hundred feet or so. At the end of the line he said, "We didn't do that. Right?" Right.

"Look," he went on, "it's critical that we have this road secured by daybreak. Help get this Liberty crew lined out, will you."

Great. Now I was a defacto Crew Boss. Dan roared off to fix some other problem.

So for the next hour I scuttled up and down that half-mile stretch of road like one of our chummy spiders, ramroding my squad and most of the Liberty crew, organizing and installing some 5,000 feet of inch-and-a-half and one-inch hose. I endured some whining from Liberty about how some of the rolls I had kicked off the Bronco weren't evenly spaced and they had to fill in the gaps by actually *carrying* hose (horrors!) I was tempted to snap, "That's what grunts are for!" but apologized for my miscalculations of distance instead. When we finally had the lay together and charged (from the Mark-III at the top of the line), I hiked from wye to wye to make sure they were all manned. One Liberty crew member was standing out in the black with a limp hose.

"Trouble?" I asked.

"No pressure."

I flashed my headlamp on the valve. Open. I followed the one-inch line as it snaked away from the wye toward the nozzle he had in his grasp, and there, not three steps from the valve, the hose was kinked. I strode over and kicked it straight. The line bucked to life.

"Now it's okay," the guy said. No kidding. I shook my head and moved on. Apparently the man had never even checked his hose. Liberty's stock wasn't rising. Unfortunately, an incompetent Eastern crew will probably send more reverberations through the Western fire hierarchy than a competent one will. That's just the way things seem to work.

We spent the rest of the night ferreting out all the heat we could find within 100 feet of the handline and road. The day shift would extend our attack lines further into the burn and begin heavy duty mop-up. I was exhausted, but the morning heat rose faster and higher than usual (to near 100 that afternoon), and I managed only brief, fitful sleep. Perhaps the lack of rest contributed to the shortness of temper that created my leadership blunder.

Our assignment was similar to the previous night's, but this time we worked *up*slope from the drop tank, and with Ohio-1 rather than the Liberty bunch. My squad was again at the point, and as we trudged up the mountain to our assigned section of line, Mike, an experienced smoke-chaser, wandered off on his own. It's a fundamental tenet of squad (and crew) operations always to stick together unless explicitly instructed otherwise. "Freelancing" is often both hazardous and inefficient. The greatest offense in being a loner on the fireground is that one may easily put other firefighters at risk when they waste time and energy and disrupt tactics because they're searching for the wandering freelancer.

The handline upslope was irregular, and Mike apparently decided to take shortcuts across some "switchbacks" and shoot directly for the crest of the ridge that was our eventual goal. Efficiency of travel wasn't, of course, our objective. We were to closely inspect the line all the way up, so a shortcut defeated the purpose. When I realized he had gone his own way, I called his name a few times, but there was no response. Once I actually glimpsed him, far ahead, but couldn't get his attention. I steamed. This was Mike's third Western tour, and he should certainly know better.

Twenty minutes later, when I met him at the crest, my smoldering anger was on the verge of open flame. Mike ran his own full-time business back home, and earlier he had told me he considered an outstate fire tour as a "paid vacation." That's not a bad attitude if it helps keep morale up, but solo sightseeing isn't part of the package.

He saw my anger from thirty feet away, and his welcoming grin faded. It was clear he didn't know why I was pissed, and that made it worse.

"Mike," I said, struggling to hold my voice even, "how many times have you been out West?"

That caught him off guard, and he looked puzzled. "This is my third."

We were face-to-face now, and acid seeped into my tone. "Then how come you're acting like a stinking rookie? Like you belong on the damn Liberty crew?"

There was a snicker from behind us, and my heart sank. In my irritated haste I hadn't noticed that Jim was right there, an unintended witness to this tongue lashing. Mike went red with anger and embarrassment. It was a mortal sin of command—humiliating a subordinate in public. But it was done, and I went on to assure Mike of the benefits of sticking together. Fortunately Jim didn't rub it in, but whatever warmth had developed between Mike and me was permanently cooled. On the other hand, he didn't wander off again.

The next night was our fifth, and for me that's usually the watershed shift. After five days, the fire camp seems like home, and it's strange to think you've known some of these utterly familiar crewmates for less than a week. After five days, the fire is normal life and going home requires readjustment.

We were back at the line of the previous night, shifting the entire hoseline further into the black so we could mop up another 300 to 500 feet. Before it got dark we spotted a black bear cub poking around near the line. Extreme caution was replaced by curiosity and cameras when it became obvious the cub was alone. It all but posed before finally ambling off into the woods.

Shortly after midnight, one of our squads heard some rustling where they had dumped their field packs, and discovered the bear cub trying to drag one off. It'd apparently caught a whiff of someone's lunch. They shooed the cub away.

Scherf mentioned the bear to Overhead, and during the next couple days some wildlife people hunted it down. Smokey Bear had recently died at the National Zoo (the second Smokey actually—the original having passed away in 1976), and the Feds were looking for a replacement. Here was a lone cub on a fire, hence a prime candidate. They used an apple laced with tranquilizer to nab the naive cub. Naturally we firefighters were rooting for the bear, and one day the shift plan cover had a drawing of a bear cub with glazed eyes who had just dropped a half-eaten apple. The caption read: "Just Say No."

But the cub didn't and was captured. We heard later, though, that there was already another Smokey candidate—from the original Smokey's home forest in New Mexico—and our little friend wasn't shipped to Washington, D.C.

The other attraction that night was the annual Perseid meteor shower. During breaks we tried to find openings in the forest canopy—preferably on a ridgeline so we could watch for shooting stars. It was an exceptionally clear night, with little smoke in our division, and the skyscape was spectacular. To be out all night under such vivid starlight, working in the depths of remote mountain forest makes me feel like a *creature,* like a denizen—a cognoscente of the wilds. The world seems more "real" at night, more closely attuned to the rest of the cosmos. The vast majority of humanity passes most of their nights asleep, and it feels special to be awake and mobile in the darkness, counting silent meteors, startling some invisible nocturnal animal, or listening attentively to an owl. After several days I noticed that many firefighters use their headlamps more sparingly, acclimated to night and less willing to spoil the dark with beams of electric light. Night shift on the fireground is seductive; darkness becomes friendly and soothing, like music for the eyes.

The next afternoon the Snowshoe Fire blew up. We were lounging around camp when someone called out, "Look at the mountain!" A new, gargantuan column of smoke was roiling furiously into the sky—like a thunderhead burgeoning over the horizon. Its base took on an orangish cast, lit by tremendous flames. A crowd of night-shifters gathered in front of the tents, gawking and cheerfully joking about "money bubbles." In a few minutes a long line formed in front of the laundry tent as people realized the fire had taken on fresh life, and our stint in Oregon was likely to be prolonged—having more clean underwear became urgent.

✳ ✳ ✳

3.

Later, just before we boarded our bus for the fire, I received a shock. We knew that additional Minnesota crews had arrived on the fire two days after we had, and I heard through the grapevine that my friend Razz was on Minnesota-2. But they were assigned to day shift, and, due to the logistics of daily transport, we never crossed paths. But as I was walking past the medical tent toward the chow line, I glanced into the open rear doors of a Suburban/cum ambulance, and there lay Razz—plastic tubes up his nostrils, sucking off an oxygen bottle.

"Whoa, Razz! What happened to you?"

He grinned weakly and waved, protesting that the tubes were overkill, and he now felt fine. Earlier in the day he had been pulled off the line when he complained of chest pains. Well, small wonder: he was working hard in smoke at unaccustomed high elevation while wearing a respirator mask. My theory was that his chest got sore from breathing harder than normal. But only the day before a Field Observer had keeled over dead at the morning briefing—massive heart attack. He collapsed in a tentful of firefighters, almost all of whom were CPR-certified, and received instant attention (an EMT was only a few steps away), but died anyway. I think Overhead was touchy about chest pains after that, and Razz said he was being shipped to a hospital in town for further examination. It was only the beginning of his sorrows, but more about that later.

After supper we bussed back up to Division E and deployed along the summit of a long ridge. Day shift had hastily installed a hoselay, and Scherf sent me to scout its length. I counted couplings as I hustled along, and soon the line began to drop downslope through tangles of thick, unburned brush. I was amazed. Over half of the 2,000 feet of inch-an-one-half hose was laid in light, dry fuel (the most explosive kind)—with fire below. I could smell smoke and see a glow. It was a classic set-up for disaster. To make matters touchier, a passing storm cell had turned the winds gusty and erratic, and lightning danced astride a ridge to the north. Our position was precarious—on high, exposed ground, sandwiched between fire below and lightning from above.

Scherf got the Division Supe on the radio to offer his assessment, and Dan altered our mission immediately. We would perform the eminently logical manuever of attacking the fire from below. Dan sent our bus. Such quick, decisive simplicity was a marvel. On big, inevitably bureaucratic, project fires, crew-level tactics are often bullied and abused by the overall strategy. Dan was good, but Scherf's competent assertiveness was also a factor. Many crew bosses—feeling low on the totem pole—would be reluctant to suggest shift plan changes to the Division Supe. This particular scenario was obvious, as there was unequivocal, unnecessary hazard, but it was still refreshing to see the system respond so adroitly. It should always be so.

Our bus bounced down a narrow, twisting road to the base of the slope, where we found a cache of hose and a full drop tank. Day shift had started a hoselay up the mountainside, and while the crew took a break, Scherf and I followed the inch-and-one-half toward the fire. Someone had apparently met trouble, because, after 300 feet we arrived at a dead end with the last joint of hose burned off, and a blackened nozzle lying nearby. It was eloquent testimony to either miscalculation or carelessness.

There were three major pockets of fire on the slope, surrounded by multiple spot fires, and in the darkness it was impossible to quickly determine if they were isolated by burned-over ground, or if we were on the verge of a blow-up.

A few minutes later, while our crew was humping more hose up the mountain, Dan arrived and decided we might need help. He dispatched our bus to pick up Ohio-1. Bob, our driver since the first night, later told us that after Ohio had settled into the bus, Dan hopped aboard and announced:

"Minnesota has its hands full, and I'm sending you to help. Be advised they're one of the better crews, and you'll have to hustle. Whatever you do, don't get in their way." If Dan was trying to keep us pumped up, he knew what buttons to push.

But the big flames were stimulus enough for that night, and soon we had a half-dozen nozzles working the pockets. It was invigorating to be right up against serious fire and engaging it directly. Our chronic lack of sleep was exacting a toll—it was increasingly difficult to rise and shine after a break, but when Ohio pulled up they could hear us hooting and hollering up in the burn, an energetic banter inspired by action. It was a battle to hold onto a nozzle, with everyone craving "a turn." There was a vivifying sense that we very well might be preventing a significant blow-up—that we were in exactly the right spot at precisely the right time. And we were killing an awful lot of fire.

By dawn the slope was cold and black, with no trace of flame visible from the road. As our bus headed down to camp in the morning twilight, Dan drove by in his Bronco. He stretched an arm out the window with a finger extended—number one?

"Either that," said Scherf, "or he's flipping us off." We roared, the laughter curbing the odd discomfort of being so obviously appreciated. As an Eastern crew on a Western fire, we would have been more at ease with being ignored.

It was significantly cooler that morning, and all were still sound asleep at 10:30 AM (incredible!) when some dingbat in a welding truck pulled to within fifty feet of the tents and fired up the engine that powered his welder. It sounded like a damn Mark-III. The entire crew jolted to a sitting position at once, and it would've been hilarious if not for the profanity on our lips and the murder in our hearts. The welder had his back to us, oblivious of his faux pas, and a few of us were crawling out of our bags, eyes smoldering like zombies from hell, when Bob rushed over to the welder and informed him he was about to die. Mortified, he instantly shut down the engine and was appropriately contrite, but another chance for prolonged sleep was shot in the ass.

When we had mustered at the Duluth National Guard Armory, the world was abuzz with the Iraqi invasion of Kuwait and the deployment of American troops to Saudi Arabia. There had been much wry joking about our "real" destination—"so you think you're going to a fire, huh?" But that afternoon in Oregon, the joke swerved into reality. Our crewmate, Brian, who had recently completed a hitch of active military service and was now in the Reserves, called home and discovered that he was to get in touch with his Air Force duty officer ASAP. It seemed he might be heading from a fire to a desert, and he wasn't entirely cheerful for the rest of the tour. He had been planning on full-time college, not Mideast war and figured he had done his time. But Uncle Sam is even more demanding than Uncle Smokey.

That evening it was back up to Division E, and for six hours we gridded the area we had hosed down the night before. But other than a few small hot spots well within the black, our sector was cold. There had been intermittent rain showers the past two afternoons, and despite the big blow-up, the Snowshoe Fire was winding down rapidly.

Just after midnight, Dan had Scherf assemble us on the road, and he instructed us to "hide and hunker" until dawn. There was no sense to keep stumbling around in the woods. It was a license to sleep, and we all tried, but I was first to give it up. It was—ironically—too damn cold. I quietly climbed upslope, and in a safe, black area, assembled some sticks and used a fusee to kindle a campfire.

In a few minutes I was joined by two others, and over the next half hour the entire crew straggled up one by one. (Except for Henry, who actually managed to sleep for a while.) As the circle grew, we graduated from sticks to small logs, and passed the rest of the night exchanging jokes, lies, and stories. The mountainside rang with laughter, and there was warmth beyond the heat of the campfire. It simply felt good to be there—part of a crew, fighters of fire in a remote corner of North America.

Another cool morning finally allowed most of us to sleep past noon. Bob stood guard against service trucks and any other threats to our bliss. It was luxury to feel rested.

I saw Razz that afternoon. He was back from the hospital, where a doctor had assured him he had a coronary disorder—a diagnosis later discredited by his doctor back in Minnesota. The Forest Service was shipping him home, and he would catch a commercial flight with a couple of the other wounded. He was disappointed—he would be missing hours and losing money. But there were further complications. Several weeks later the Forest Service tried to bill him for his hospital stay *and* the flight home—both items they'd mandated. Razz was shocked and outraged. It required long, arduous forays into the labyrinth of the bureaucracy (firefighting is a lark by comparison) to finally convince the Feds he wasn't liable for those expenses. (Even convicts get medical treatment.) Unfortunately, such is not an isolated case; the Forest Service once refused to pay my medical expenses for an injury incurred on the fireground and duly reported via the applicable forms signed by my Crew Boss. It's no wonder so many casuals feel they're considered expendable, and that the letters FSS—stamped on all our fire gear—are near universally taken to stand for "Forest Service Sucks!"

That evening it was back out to E for more gridding and cold trailing. A Probe-Eye (an infrared detector used to locate those final, elusive hot spots) was supposed to arrive near midnight, but never made it to our sector. No one got excited—the division was cold. We spent the last few hours hunkered down and/or patrolling to stay warm. The sky threatened more rain.

And it fell next morning—pouring and pounding hard enough to wake us. It didn't matter; we had the day off. After eight straight nights we were going to roll over into day shift the following dawn. We passed the afternoon snoozing, reading, playing cards, and grimacing at the leaden skies. No smoke was visible on the mountain, and it appeared the Snowshoe Fire, and hence our payroll, was just about dead.

It was weird to be headed for the fire in the morning, and even stranger to be doing it in the rain. A steady drizzle commenced after breakfast and lingered for hours. But we were assigned a 400-acre area to grid in another division, and we did find dozens of hot spots—chiefly smoldering duff in the midst of unburned woodland. We punched head and arm holes in garbage bags and slipped them over our torsos as rain gear. Looking like hoboes and derelicts (not far off the mark) we fanned out along a steep ridge and humped from spot to spot, digging out the heat and ringing the smolders with shallow trenches. A few of us started singing, not out of joy, but as a defense against the deep blues generated by slogging around in cold rain and wet ash. It always helps to *act* happy. The Strike Team Leader walked up behind us as we were thus engaged, and seemed approvingly amused.

Not so with a certain Army Lt. Colonel. Early in the fire, and much to our dismay, elements of the Ninth Infantry Division that had been quickly trained in the basics of fire grunting were dispatched to the Snowshoe. We considered it an overreaction, and it certainly cut into our possible hours; but it was the Army—back in the last century—that initiated organized fire suppression in the Western forests, and it seems they're never far away. But surely, with the 101st Airborne already in Saudi Arabia, and a huge military buildup underway, the Nineth Infantry had more germane things to do.

One of their Lieutenant Colonels thought so. We heard he had acidly remarked to a Strike Team Leader that he didn't "see how the Snowshoe is a national emergency when my troops are walking around in the rain." Good point. In all fairness to Overhead, however, it's often difficult to predict what resources you're going to eventually need on a large fire, and I guess it's better to have too much than not enough. I think part of the strategy behind mobilizing the military (besides giving them something useful to do) is that it frees up professional firefighters for the next Big One.

In any case, by late afternoon the sun returned, we had gone through our repertoire of shared songs, and the Strike Team Leader was happy with our work. It wasn't a bad shift, considering, and turned out to be our last on the Snowshoe. Next day we were bussed to BIFCE to catch a plane back to Duluth.

Our ride to Boise was uneventful, but my friend Sean (of the Yellowstone tour), who was now a Crew Boss, reported that his bus was accosted by a female flasher. A blue Camaro with two young women aboard drew alongside at highway speed, honking. Firefighters glanced out and were astounded to see bare breasts pressed against the glass of the Camaro's passenger side window. Pandemonium broke out, and the Camaro sped off. A few minutes later, someone called out, "Here they come again!" Everyone surged to the left side of the bus, and the Camaro pulled up for an encore. Cameras clicked. So at least a few fire photo albums are illustrated with something more fetching than money bubbles.

Just over a month later, I was on autumn fire duty in Minnesota, the Snowshoe and the Malheur only a memory, when my supervisor walked out to the shop where I was working. I happened to be coughing when he handed me a fax that was hot off the machine. As I covered my mouth in another burst of hacking, he quickly backed away and shot me a sardonic grin. The heading of the official Northern Fire Center fax read: Tuberculosis Infected Crewmember.

It went on to note that a firefighter from Tennessee who had worked on the Snowshoe had turned up with an active case of TB. It was recommended that all personnel who had come in contact with his crew should have a TB test immediately. I didn't think we had, but I couldn't be certain, and I didn't want to worry about TB every time I got a cold. I decided to be tested, and the fax further advised that I approach my county health department and inform them I may have been "exposed to an active case of TB, therefore, the test should be free."

Fine. I called the local Health Department, and the first thing they asked was, "Why isn't the Forest Service paying for it?" Very good question. But after all: FSS.

I saw the red tape starting to coil for a strike, so I figured the hell with it, and just made an appointment at the clinic with my own doctor. My tests were negative, but I later heard that one of our crew members developed a positive. For him it had indeed been "Malheur."

The Bonus Fire

That dry autumn of 1990 blessed us with an extended fire season in northeastern Minnesota, but by early November I figured it was over. On the ninth Todd and I swung into the forestry station parking lot simultaneously, grimacing at each other. An inch of snow had fallen overnight, and it was obviously our last day on the payroll for 1990. All but one of the regular DNR employees were on vacation—scattered across the countryside hunting deer—and Mike Magnuson (Mag), the remaining forester, decided to take advantage of the empty office and summoned us in to shampoo the carpeting. Fire season was going to terminate with a whimper.

As we dragged the rented steam cleaner around the station, Todd and I cracked wry jokes about "lint suppression" and "floor covering maintenance incident command." It was best to bow out gracefully, and we reminded ourselves that the past two weeks or so had been gravy. In fact, we had endured a ferocious storm in mid-October that left five inches of snow on the ground for a week. The Area Forester assured me then it was time to hang up the Nomex, and I agreed. But the weather turned, and I had worked a half-dozen fires since then. Still, this shampoo project was surely the coda. By mid-November I'm usually skiing, and it's not rare to see subzero mornings. It was deer season, not fire season; winter was imminent, probably overdue.

During the day, as we industriously sucked a year's worth of dirt out of the rug, the temperature rose into the high forties and most of the snow melted. It seemed unremarkable. The overnight low was predicted to be in the teens, with a chance of flurries, but just to be safe, Mag issued each of us a pager for the weekend. "I don't want to get caught short-handed," he said.

"What?" I replied. "You got more carpeting somewhere?"

We laughed. Short-handed? Three people was probably two too many for whatever fire we might expect.

At about six o'clock that evening I was getting dressed for a party at a neighbor's house when my pager went off. I heard Mag ask Todd to call him at home. Lucky dog! I was sure of the scenario: someone had a legal brush pile buring, but a passerby got nervous and dialed 911. Todd was going to snag an easy two hours' pay to mosey over and check it out. He was probably already gloating about how he was going to rub it in the next time he saw me.

About forty minutes later I was at the party—one beer down the road and heavy into munchies—when my pager beeped again. This time Mag asked me to call him. I did so immediately and he said, "Todd's at a fire south of Hibbing and he's reporting a half-mile wide head."

"You're kidding!"

He wasn't. "It sounds pretty wild. Todd hasn't even been able to determine how big it is yet."

I asked my host to save some beer and munchies, but it was only courtesy; I knew I wouldn't be returning. I rushed home for my Nomex, then headed for the station. It's a twenty-mile ride, and I reminded myself to drive according to road conditions, not according to fire conditions. The temptation was to fly down the highway at top end—feeling needed, important, above the law, and beyond mere common sense. No minutes ever stretch out longer than the tortured, slug-like minutes on the way to a fire. And nothing would be as mortifying (or stupid) as not arriving at all because you're in the ditch—or the hospital (or the morgue). I shoved a Nanci Griffith cassette into the tape deck to help me relax, and managed to hover closer to sixty miles per hour than seventy-five.

About two miles from the station I crossed a high bridge that offered an unobstructed view to the south. In the direction of County Highway 5, where I normally saw an isolated yard light or two amidst the blackness of forest and swamp, the sky was suffused with an expansive orange glow—as if the lights of some metropolis were brightening the clouds. I was astonished. I pounded the passenger seat to relieve the sudden increase in tension. Given what Mike had revealed about the fire's location, that ominous glow was at least five or six miles away. This was a tremendous fire—in November, at night, after snowfall. What the hell was going on?

Just beyond the bridge, a local business flies a huge, Perkins-sized American flag twenty-four hours a day, bathed in floodlights after dark. I glanced at it as I passed and noted that the wind was whipping it almost straight out. I guessed the velocity at fifteen-twenty-five miles per hour—a hefty blast for nighttime, and a real boon for fire spread.

The few minutes at the station were a hustling blur. Mag had alerted smokechasers who lived in town, and Jerry and Craig were waiting in the yard. I tossed them my garage key, and as they readied an engine—checking fuel, headlamps, handhelds—I radioed Todd for a size-up. He had been humping it through the brush, and his slightly breathless voice added to the air of urgency. He'd seen a lot of fire in his career, and he was deeply impressed by this one. He still had no real handle on its size, and it was possible there would be structures endangered. We arranged a rendezvous, and then Jerry and I got on the phones to track down more firefighters. We didn't suppose it would be easy during deer season. Significant portions of the local population move out to hunting shacks for the duration.

Mag arrived to handle the base station, commandeering radio and telephone with genuine gusto; he had also seen the glow from the bridge. Jerry, Craig, and I hurried out to Engine #1, our bodies abuzz with good hormonal chemicals. As I steered out of the station and turned south, I intoned a checklist:

"We've got functional headlamps?"

"Affirmative."

"Extra radio batteries?"

"Yo."

"Full canteens?"

"Three."

And so on. It wasn't that I doubted any of this—I knew we were ready—it was just a way to keep focused while waiting out another interminable (ten-minute) drive.

About a mile out of town, we sighted the glow. It was growing. There was spontaneous chortling and swearing in the cab—partly nervous, partly gleeful. This was my companions' first glimpse of the fire. I punched Jerry's knee. "Can you believe this? The Big One! In November."

"Awesome," Jerry replied, grinning.

"A real money bubble," added Craig.

"Affirm. This is truly a bonus." And hence the name of the blaze. For fire bums, big November paychecks are as rare and welcome as lottery winnings.

We tied in with Todd on a powerline right-of-way off County Highway 5. We spotted the flashing "cherries" on his engine's light bar. He'd turned off the highway and bounced along beneath the power poles over frozen ground for about a quarter-mile. We pulled alongside his truck as he was returning from a scouting foray on foot. Behind him a couple hundred yards, and across a narrow stream, we could finally see flames. In the foreground the fire was eating rapidly through alder brush and into a stand of aspen; beyond, distant power poles were silhouetted by a massive glow that was even more distant. My first impression was that the fire may have already run for a mile. The wind was brisk and steady, and as we watched, a spruce or fir torched out with a snapping whoosh of sparks and a twenty-foot tongue of flame. This was the biggest, hottest fire we'd seen all year, and it had yet to hit the windswept expanse of the right of way, a wide river of tall, brown grass. In daylight, I would have ordered an air tanker immediately (though none were on duty this late in the year).

Todd and I held a quick conference and decided that he and Craig would proceed on foot from that point, working north toward Townline Road to roughly map the blaze. There were homes on Townline, but as we spoke, the Chief of the Cherry Township Volunteer Fire Department joined us on the right of way and said he had just driven by the residences and they didn't appear to be in immediate danger. He would station himself on Townline to monitor the situation.

Jerry and I drove back out to County 5, and Mag requested we hook south and estimate how far the fire had run. The highway is straight as a shovel handle down there, and I eased south until it appeared we were directly abreast of the end of the fire. We had gone seven tenths of a mile. Mag pulled an aerial photo and saw there was nothing further south but spruce bog. We could ignore that for now.

As I swung around to return north, Todd came on the radio. The fire had slammed into the right of way and gained considerable momentum. It was racing toward Townline Road much faster than we had expected. Indeed, Jerry and I could see the sudden surge in brightness over the treetops, and I tromped the gas pedal, surrendering to the urge to drive according to fire conditions. It was still hard to accept that we had a fire of this intensity in November.

We turned east on Townline Road, and, though the entire blaze was now south of us, we saw no flames—only orange sky. We sped past two homesteads on the north side of the highway; the asphalt would be an effective buffer for them. The headfire was slashing toward Townline from the southwest, and the further east we drove, the nearer we approached the head. We had gone a mile and a half and were just beginning to search for an access of some sort, when we encountered a driveway. Two hundred yards in was a mobile home and some outbuildings, screened from the blazing powerline right of way by a stand of aspen, jackpine, and fir. I pulled in, the Cherry Fire Chief right behind. A man, woman, and child were standing at the corner of the trailer, staring south. The woods were ominously backlit by a red-orange cloud that seemed to fill half the sky—a wall of hot light just beyond the trees. It was brightening as they watched. I stopped beside them and rolled down the window, and the roar of the flames was distinct and pervasive, as if a huge waterfall was near and somehow tumbling closer.

"Should we evacuate?" the man asked.

"No, but be ready."

The Fire Chief strode up, and I requested that he page out his fire department to protect the homestead. He had just done it. I radioed Mag with our location. I asked the owner if we could use his yard as a staging area— "Sure, whatever"—and told Mag he could dispatch reinforcements to that address. He had a JD-850 bulldozer on the way, and he was trying to track down our J-7 Bombardier operator. A J-5 and another DNR engine were enroute.

A two-track road snaked out of the yard toward the fire. "Where does that go?" I asked.

"Right up to the powerline."

"Excellent. Is it good enough for this engine, in four-wheel?"

"Yeah, should be, but I'll lead you in. There's more than one trail and it could be messy."

The homeowner ran to an ATV parked next to a shed, and with a beckoning wave and a spray of dirt, he sped off down the road. I crammed the floor shift into four-wheel-low and followed him into the woods.

The first twenty-five yards were clear and spacious, but quickly constricted to little more than a wide ATV trail. It was winding and bumpy, and I fought the wheel in some spots, dodging rocks or easing between tree trunks. Brush scraped the sides of the truck, slapping at the mirrors, and with forest canopy overhead it was like driving through a dark tunnel. The fire was to our right, but we twisted through the woods for an eighth of a mile or so before we saw flames.

My neck tingled. This was a situation that screamed "Watch out!" There was fuel between us and the fire, and we were approaching the head down an essentially one-way road in country we had never seen in daylight.

At a wide spot in the trail I laid on the horn, and the homeowner spun around and stopped. No need for him to go further. I got out of the truck and he pointed ahead.

"This trail runs into the right of way about fifty yards up there."

Good. If we could kill the headfire here, we would establish an effective anchor point for starting a dozer line. I thanked the man, and he headed home. The Fire Chief reported via radio that he had a pumper, a tanker, and a brush rig arriving at the scene, and I asked that he just protect the homestead for now.

Looking south, Jerry and I could see a line of fire burgeoning across the powerline right of way, five-to-fifteen-foot flames whipped by gusts and aimed right for us. Sparks were blowing in ahead of the fire, spiraling to earth all around, but none had the stamina to ignite. I had Jerry back our engine into the woods on the opposite side of the trail, and I deployed our hoseline while he started the pump. Jerry's eyes were wide, and his quick, jerky movements betrayed anxiety. And why not? This was his rookie season and he had never seen a blaze like this, much less been in *front* of one—at night, when all fires are more fearsome.

If we had been out on the right of way, of course, there would be no chance of stopping a head like that. We would simply be overrun and burned. But between us and the right of way was a strip of aspen and alder about one chain wide, and I knew the flames would lay down as soon as they hit the trees. They'd still advance along the ground, but the intensity would fall off dramatically, and we had enough waterpower to knock them down. Jerry hefted a pump can to protect the engine and our rear, and I dragged the hoseline partway into the woods and waited for the fire.

It was an eerie minute. After the past hour of rushing—from party to home, home to the station, station to the fire—the tactical frenzy of initial attack had boiled down to this: waiting quietly for a fire to surge into our faces. I realized how fortunate we had been to find such a convenient, albeit hazardous, access. I mused on Jerry's nervousness, and how it was likely he would never forget this moment. I suddenly felt the need to qualify our stand.

"Hey, Jerry! Be advised that this is *not* standard operating procedure. But it's going to work because we got lucky."

He grinned and nodded absently, transfixed by the stampeding fire. A military motif was obvious. I had been watching a video series about the Civil War during the past week, and here was the classic order of battle—standing before an enemy charge. I had a brief glimpse of the terror that nineteenth century soldiers must have felt as they braced for inevitable fury. The fire wasn't yelling, but it was pushing sound before it like a wave that broke against the trees—a crackling roar as steady and intimidating as a hurricane blast. The flames were still a hundred feet away, but I could feel the heat on my face, the cold November air being warmed to August temperatures and rising beyond. On one level, Jerry and I were simply more fuel.

From somewhere behind the front of fire I heard a conifer torch out. It was a loud ripping, like a giant sheet being torn in two; a tree shriek. The forest was bright as sunset—weirdly suffused with yellowish light. For a moment I was afraid, not of being fried, but of having made a wrong decision. At this point I was the Incident Commander (IC). What if we couldn't stop the head? What if we were forced to flee, abandoning our engine to be burned over? This reasoned stand would suddenly be an unforgiving, humiliating blunder. I could hear it: "Why were you in *front* of the fire? Idiot! Incompetent! Carpet cleaner!" Of course the local Overhead wouldn't hurl insults like that, but their quiet censure would be even more painful.

Earlier in the season my crew and I had worked a two-acre grass/brush fire on top of a hill. It was no big deal, but apparently we missed an ember that had rolled downslope and smoldered in unburned fuel. We had been gone from the scene for two or three hours when the detection plane called in a smoke at that same location. He was still a few miles off but speculated over the air: "It might be a rekindle."

There are few filthier words in the firefighting lexicon. I cursed as I turned our engine in that direction.

Several minutes later the plane was orbiting the smoke. "Yeah," reported the observer, "it's *definitely* a rekindle." Such language on the airwaves! Then:

"Aero-1 to Leschak."

"Go ahead."

"Do you need directions to this fire?"

We exploded into pained laughter and fervent expletives. That son-of-a-bitch! There's no way he could've more expertly twisted the knife in our guts. I replied as sweetly and calmly as I could:

"That's a negative, Aero-1. You may continue on your route, and thanks for your help." My companions groaned, suffering genuine pain.

By the time we arrived and extinguished the fire a second time, it had expanded to five acres.

When we returned to the station Mag met me at the stairs. He sported a lopsided grin.

"You mean," he said, "you came back? I figured you'd have the good grace to just fall on a sharp pulaski."

As bystanders laughed I replied, "Yeah, I guess I should've; it might've been easier."

As this night fire rolled closer, however—showing itself—my confidence returned, and when I noticed a few snowflakes twirling past, I snorted. Snowflakes! In front of a howling headfire.

The first flames speared the edge of the woods and almost instantly shrunk from five-or-ten feet to two-or-three. I let them creep into the trees a few yards and then barged forward with the nozzle, spraying a high-pressure stream in a wide arc. In a moment the area directly in front of our engine was secure, and I angled left, hollering for Jerry to pull more hose off the reel. I doused another wide swath of flames and then pushed through the brush to the right, snuffing fire as I went—making blackness out of light.

For a few minutes Jerry and I struggled back and forth through the woods on a 200-foot front, snaking hoseline around trees and over deadfalls, cursing the tangled coppices of alder. We could see more big flames, but they were far to the west, and not yet across the right-of-way.

In the meantime, Tom and Torrel had arrived with a J-5 Bombardier from a neighboring forestry district, and I left Jerry mopping up our wet line and tied in with them. They had parked the J-5 trailer in a small sand-pit back toward the house, and I hustled there on foot. Torrel was feverishly rooting around in the tool box of a pick-up truck, hunting for a set of jumper cables. Unaccountably, the J-5 had a dead battery, and wouldn't be in service for several minutes. I chuckled. How many times in an emergency situation had I seen equipment that was working flawlessly the day (or hour) before, abruptly go belly-up? Murphy's Law is always in force on the fireground. At a night fire about a month earlier, the Area Forester—the local chief executive who *never* gets in on initial attack—happened to be one of the first people to the blaze. He grabbed a pump can and headed into the bush. Every last one of our pump cans had been checked out at least a dozen times during the season, but the boss pumped once and the trombone seized up. The can was useless, and turned out to be the only defective one in the bunch. There's no justice in the world.

I trotted back toward Jerry and met Todd. He had worked his way north and seen a significant portion of the fire. We discussed the anchor points I had in mind and decided that Todd would take command of the west half of the fire, and I would handle the east, along with overall command at the staging area. We could hear the JD-850 dozer approaching—a clanking/roaring/crunching that's always scary in the dark. Todd would lead it on a wide pass of line-building to the west. I'd ordered a second dozer from Mag and would start it east when it arrived. Theoretically, the dozers would circumnavigate the fire and eventually meet somewhere on the south side. We assumed it would take hours.

The 850 pulled up to the sandpit and the operator had no radio—another unaccountable glitch—so Todd hopped aboard with his hand-held, and the gigantic machine tore directly into the forest across from the pit, leaving a ten-foot wide line in its wake. Pole-sized aspens were uprooted, or simply cracked off and splintered beneath the treads. The homestead was no longer threatened and Todd's goal was simply to contain the fire—keeping it out of the timber "islands," and away from the highway.

I hurried back to Jerry, and we reeled in our hose and drove up to the powerline. A remnant of headfire was pushing east along the edge of the right of way, and I drove as close to the flames as I dared, and we redeployed our hoseline and snuffed it. The powerline was a 115,000-volt system with huge, double-pole and crossbeam structures, and the pair closest to the end of our trail was on fire. Flames licked up the creosoted poles for fifteen to twenty feet, and we advanced our nozzle and extinguished them. Looking west down the flat right of way, we could see at least another half-dozen poles on fire, but there was nothing we could do for them at the moment. This end of the trail was going to be our second dozer anchor point, and we soaked it down with the rest of our water.

Tom came on the air to say the J-5 was running, and he was headed our way. I directed him to proceed around the east flank of the fire, scouting, hitting hot spots, and wet-tracking where he could. Jerry and I started retracing our route back to the homestead; and now thick smoke had settled in, imbuing the forest with the ghostly aura of a horror movie graveyard. I crept along slowly in four-wheel-low, trying not to miss the turns the homeowner had taken on his ATV when he lead us in.

After a few minutes I spotted lights off to the right and assumed they were at the house and yard. I turned down a wider section of road that suddenly dipped downhill into a swamp. The truck plunged through a thin layer of ice and we were instantly bogged down in axle-deep, half-frozen mud. Damn! Ahead we could now clearly see the lights were not the homestead, but merely the running lights of the J-5. Tom, of course, had no difficulty traversing the swampy ground in the Bombardier.

I could've radioed him to turn around and yank us out of the mud, but I figured it was best if he continued down the east side of the fire. There was really nothing more for an engine to do at the moment anyway, so I told Jerry to switch on the cherries and stay with the truck while I backtracked on foot, found the correct trail, and hurried to the staging area.

The Fire Department was still standing by, and I released their pumper and brush rig, but requested that the tanker remain as a water source. We also needed people to follow the 850 and secure the dozer line, so I outfitted four of the volunteer firefighters with headlamps from a DNR engine parked in the yard, and they hiked off into the woods with instructions to put out any hot spots within ten feet of the line. No one had noticed any spotting going on, so that seemed a sufficient buffer for now.

I had expected the second dozer by then, so I got on the radio to Mag and learned the other machine he had ordered had thrown a tread while being loaded onto a lowboy. He was scrambling to find a replacement. But the J-7 was now enroute, as well as two more DNR engine crews—one from thirty-five miles away. It was quite a feat to be mobilizing resources like this during deer season. Mag was also preparing a supply truck; what else did we need? I ordered food, water, radio batteries, extra gasoline, more headlamps, a chain saw, and, oh, yes, how about a tin of Copenhagen snuff—as a stress-reliever? That was a joke, but when the supply truck arrived, Loren handed me radio batteries and a fresh tin of Copenhagen. It's a vice on which I try to keep a tight rein, have even gone cold turkey for months at a time, but somehow nicotine and fire have become inseparably linked in my mind, and I sometimes allow myself to backslide into addiction on the fireground. As a firefighter once told me on a big incident out West: "Hey man, you're out here breathing toxic smoke all day, a snag might fall and crush you at any moment, you could be caught in a blow-up and overrun with fire, the bus we ride in could easily roll off a narrow mountain road, an air tanker could drop a load of slurry on your head, and the federal government is trying to poison you with MREs—and you're going to worry about the health risk of a pinch of snuff?" Well, I do, but not in the midst of fire.

The logistics of a big fire are complex, and once I was back at the staging area I quickly exhausted two radio batteries trying for a rough orderliness. The radio traffic was relentless as I carried on conversations with six parties—Todd and the 850, the J-5, the crew on the dozer line, Craig (who was still scouting), Mag at the station, and three or four incoming units. There was also the police. Though paved, Townline is a shoulderless, two-lane backroad, not designed for heavy traffic. Nevertheless, it's bustling three times each day—at the shift change of a local taconite plant. But as 11:00 PM approached, we had a lowboy and a fifth-wheel trailer (for the J-7) parked on the highway, with at least one more lowboy due in. It was a definite traffic hazard, and soon a couple of Sheriff's Department patrol cars had a five-mile stretch of Townline completely shut down.

Such a steady flow of radio traffic is a stimulus to an altered state of consciousness. For an IC, charged with authority and, therefore, at the hub of this sizzling network, the flood of information is almost a substance; it is, in fact, an alternate reality. The radio messages etched a vivid image in my mind. I could see it all—the fire, the people, the equipment—as a living map or board game spread out before me. As I talked on the radio, I viewed the scene from *above,* as if soaring over the fire on the radio waves themselves. I had a distinct vision of my "players" and how they were all moving in relation to each other. That's not to say my mind picture was accurate in every detail, or even in its main characteristics. But the *relationships* of the units were critical, and those variables seemed to be coming through clearly. Each person was feeding me only his small view of the operation, and it was my task to integrate all the data into some kind of whole—that's the principle duty (and horror) of an IC. It's where the thrill is, and I did have the sense of controlling a dangerous, mind-boggling game of chess.

But I was physically isolated from the fire, pacing a shadowy staging area clutching a radio like a magic wand. Still, two days later, when I saw aerial photos of the burn, I was amazed at how closely my mental image resembled the actual state of affairs. I had either been truly plugged in, or had merely made a series of lucky guesses. It may not pay to dwell on which.

Robb arrived with the J-7 at about 10:00 PM, and I asked him to ferry me back in to Engine #1, and rescue it from the swamp. I might have had a tough time finding my way back, if not for the rotating red lights I had had Jerry leave on. We hooked a chain to the front of the J-7, and I hopped into the cab of Engine #1. Robb pulled it out with ease, but due to poor visibility, and the general distraction of command (thinking ahead of what I was actually doing), I backed into the J-7. I was only going about five miles per hour, and merely dented the bumper and tailgate, but it was embarrassing. It's why the IC (or at least *this* IC) should avoid mechanical tasks while mentally involved with strategy, tactics, and logistics.

"Sorry," I said, to Jerry and Robb (and myself), and then began to brief Robb on the fire situation and what I'd like the J-7 to be doing. I was using my finger to draw a map in the frost coating on the side of the Bombardier (I had a notebook, but I had lost my pencil early in the fray), when there was a grinding crash and the big machine bucked under my hand. For some reason Jerry had slipped behind the wheel of Engine #1 and backed it into the J-7. This time a tail light on the truck was smashed. Robb, who is normally mild-mannered (and as a regular DNR employee, usually in charge) blew up.

"What're you doing! Settle down! Just settle down!" Strong words for him. I guess we were either too tired or too wired. Ramming an engine into a J-7 twice in the space of three minutes is probably a stress-related glitch. Jerry was mortified, but it's one of those incidents that everyone laughs about the next week, and it'll no doubt pass into the corpus of local smoke-chaser legend, or actually, "anti-legend"—the good-natured self-deprecation that cements a crew.

We all took a few moments to mellow out, shaken by it all, and then I asked Robb to track the fire perimeter east, backing up the J-5 until our other dozer arrived.

By the time Jerry and I returned to the staging area, the second dozer was finally pulling in—a D-4 wide-pad that would perform well in the boggy terrain on the east and south sides of the fire. I outfitted the operator with a radio and headset (the one intended for the 850, but left behind in the chaos of initial attack), and had him follow me down the trail toward the power-line.

After Robb had extracted Engine #1 from the swamp, I took a good look at the trail spur that had led to trouble. One of the later-arriving DNR engines was parked across from the fateful turn, I noted its position in relation to the mudhole. My idea was wise, but one should never employ a mobile entity as a landmark. While I was back at staging, the engine was moved to the opposite side of the road—probably to make way for another vehicle—and as a result I took the wrong turn again and drove into precisely the same mudhole! Oh, shit, shit, shit!

Fortunately the D-4 was right behind, and he yanked me out in short order. I didn't ram him. And fortunately there were no other witnesses. (I had left Jerry at staging so he could get some lunch.)

In a few minutes I had the D-4 on track, scraping a line around the east flank of the fire. From the vantage point of the right of way (such as it was) I could see only one glowing patch in the sky—far off to the southeast. I checked in with Todd, Tom, and Robb, and determined we had no further fire spread toward the highway, and little running fire left anywhere but far down in the bog. All burning power poles had either been extinguished, or gone out by themselves. Now it was down to a dozer show—push a line all the way around it, and patrol with Bombardiers and grunts. At this point we had fifteen DNR personnel on the scene, and I released the rest of the fire department. Their tanker topped off what units we had at staging and departed.

It was well after midnight and the sky had cleared to late autumn brilliance. Orion was prominent in the east, and the temperature had plunged to fifteen degrees. I drained the pump casing on Engine #1 to keep it from freezing solid.

Over the next couple hours the ground forces trickled out of the woods. The west dozer line had entered terrain so low and wet that the surface fire was self-extinguishing at the line, and there was virtually no mop-up. The wind was finally easing up, and there was nothing to do but collect in the trucks to eat lunch and monitor the radio. I released the engine crew that had come the furthest. As soon as the two dozer lines met, we'd call this fire controlled, collect our toys, and head home.

But at around 3:00 AM Robb came on the radio with sad news. He had linked up with the 850 and reported that the dozer had hit a soft spot and was now "buried." I groaned. The 850 is the biggest dozer John Deere makes—comparable to a D-8 Cat—a very mean, incredibly heavy machine. Now what? I knew this information was going to make Mag terribly unhappy. His was the hardest job—sitting cooped up at the station for eight long hours so far, poisoned with coffee and fluorescent light. Since the excitement of initial attack and the hectic logistical scramble had petered out, he had no doubt been excruciatingly bored for at least the last four hours. But he had to remain on duty as long as crews were in the field. I hadn't spoken to him for at least a half-hour.

"Leschak to Hibbing."

"Go ahead, Pete." I could hear the expectation in his voice, the readiness to feel relieved when I said: "All units returning to base."

Instead, I keyed the microphone and intoned, "Yeah, Mag, be advised"—choosing words carefully now—"that the 850 is *mired.*" It seemed a kinder, gentler term, and appropriate for 3:00 AM.

"Ten-four, Pete. Understand the 850 is *mired.*" He wasn't fooled. Despite my discretion he'd heard "buried."

During the subsequent hour, I was able to report that in futile attempts to free the giant dozer, the J-7 had destroyed its winch (it actually shattered into pieces), and the D-4—which had worked around to complete the line—had snapped a stout tow chain. The 850 hadn't budged.

The dozers were under contract, and the owner of the 850 was snoozing in his pick-up at the staging area. I nudged him awake and offered a briefing. He had an idea. I radioed Tom to run the J-5 back to staging, and we loaded it with extra chains and a power saw. The contractor rode out to where his 850 was "mired," and pulled off what Todd later referred to as "a McGyver." He felled a seven-inch aspen and bucked the trunk so it was about two feet longer than the width of the dozer. The crew shoved the aspen under the tracks, and the contractor lashed it to the treads with chain. The 850 was then able to "walk" a few feet up onto the log. He then re-cinched the chains for another bite, and the dozer crawled up another yard or so. After three or four bites, the 850 finally gained enough purchase to pull itself out of the hole.

By 5:00 AM all the heavy equipment lumbered back to staging, and a half-hour later I was able to tell Mike what he longed to hear: "All units returning to base." I got home to bed just after sunrise. I didn't check to see if the neighbors had saved any beer or munchies.

By noon four of us were heading back to the fire. While Craig and I hunted for hot spots on foot, Robb and Kevin swung around the far perimeter with the J-7. Our detection aircraft scouted from overhead. Photos later revealed that the dozer line encompassed 430 acres, with about 350 acres actually burned. It was mostly grass and brush, with minimal timber loss, but it was a big fire by latter day northern Minnesota standards, and we expected substantial mop-up—especially in the peat areas. However, the ground moisture was high, and we found only a dozen lingering smokes, mainly in pine duff on the timber islands. We snuffed them all that afternoon. Ironically, a portion of the burn extended onto land we had tried to fire the previous June to create sharptail grouse habitat. We had passed an entire day running around with drip torches—even had a helicopter slinging alumagel—and it hadn't burned worth a damn. I guess we needed snow. That, and a campfire. Our arson investigator figured the Bonus Fire was ignited by an unknown deer hunter's warming fire. Whoever it was got lucky. The suppression costs totaled over $7,000, and the hunter would've been liable.

Just before sunset, as Craig and I trudged out of the woods—exhausted from battling fire for nineteen of the last twenty-four hours, I picked up an emergency page on my radio. It was for the ambulance of a nearby town.

Dispatcher: "Midway calling Cook Ambulance. Report to (address). There is a thirty-year old male eating a light bulb. Bleeding from the mouth. Please acknowledge this page."

It was gruesome, but I had to grin. We had had a hard day's night, but at least we didn't have to deal with *that*. And the carpeting at the station was clean for another year.

*"If you can't run with the big dogs, then stay on the
porch."* — Anonymous folk saying

Six-One-Echo

1.

The following year I left Minnesota on the summer solstice. Appropriately, it was raining. We had relished a snappy spring fire season, but now the forest was lush, the grass high and succulent—it was no place for a firefighter.

I was headed for Grangeville, Idaho, and the Nez Perce National Forest, where I had landed a job on a Forest Service helicopter crew. I had been assured an excellent potential for action and spectacular paychecks (by grunt standards). My friend Scott Hocking, the assistant helicopter foreman, predicted that by the end of summer I'd "be sick of fire." That seemed an unlikely proposition, but I was willing to test it.

Willing, but not eager. As I cruised down Highway 169, I was nagged by misgivings. I had applied for the job in late April—on a whim—not expecting much. Other than being transported via helicopters at Yellowstone, my only experience of air operations was from the ground. As the first week in June slipped by with no word from Idaho, I realized I was relieved. A glorious summer was shaping up in the northwoods. We were gardening, fishing, swimming, and had a wilderness canoe trip planned to begin on June 14. I wasn't really keen on leaving home for two to four months.

Then Scott phoned on the thirteenth and offered the job. They wanted me in Idaho on the seventeenth. Typical. Funding problems had caused a delay in hiring, and Scott was apologetic, but he had to have an answer ASAP. I told him I would call back in three hours with my decision. And then I bounced off the walls for an hour, raging at fate, the Forest Service, and the financial need that made the offer thinkable. I agonized and cursed,

167

but Pam merely shook her head. "Why all the fuss?" she said. "You *know* you're going." Yes.

Yes, but: would my car endure the trip—a decade-old rust bucket with almost 140,000 miles? Would I be able to do the job? I had much to learn in a short time, and I knew I was expected not merely to handle it, but to excel; Scott was a perfectionist. Was I ready to face the danger? Helicopter crews spend a lot of time in the payroll mode known as "H-pay," *hazard* differential. I admit it, I was scared. And could I be comfortable about leaving Pam alone to tend the homestead for months? No. But: "You *know* you're going." In the end it was the money and the challenge of new experience; it was impossible to say which carried the greater weight.

I offered Scott a compromise: let me start work on the twenty-fourth rather than the seventeenth. (I wanted to make that canoe trip—as a farewell to Pam and the northern Minnesota summer.) He readily accepted, later revealing that he never thought I would take the job on such short notice and already had a replacement in mind.

The highway west still evokes adventure, and, despite the numbing sameness of the North Dakota interstate, I felt a tingle of nervous anticipation. At forty years of age, I was leaping into something different, forsaking the security of home and hearth, and, in more prolix moments—"casting my fate to the winds." The car itself was a temptation of fate, and I didn't trust the old wreck. I was traveling light, packed so that if necessary I could carry it all on my back along the shoulder of the road, thumb in the air.

But most of the delicious anxiety centered on the assignment. Helicopter crew members are considered if not exactly "the elite," then at least honest-to-god professionals. There's scant room for error, and the welfare of others is a routine responsibility. Whether fully deserved or not, there's an aura of gallantry and romance surrounding helitack, and in a few weeks I would marvel at veteran firefighters regarding me with open respect and admiration. It would be unsettling, embarrassing. But that was the future.

As I crossed the North Dakota-Montana line (still in the rain), I actually had to battle a sudden, suffocating wave of regret—homesickness, road angst, guilt, simple fear. I pounded a fist on the dash, crammed a new cassette into the tape deck (the only trustworthy component of the vehicle), and said aloud: "It'll be all right." I worried about worrying, but each mile under the wheels was another notch of committment, and somewhere near Bighorn, Montana, the sun finally emerged, painting a bright rainbow over the foothills. That helped a lot, and by nightfall I was more than halfway to the Nez Perce and decided I was physically past the point of no return; the mind followed.

My first week in Grangeville was a hectic welter of government paperwork, apartment hunting, and intense training. It culminated in my first brush with hazard and injury. On Friday afternoon I innocently entered a local clinic for my mandatory physical, prepared for the standard inconvenience of an office call, but not primed for trauma.

It began normally—a three-magazine wait in the lobby, routine vision and hearing checks, urinalysis, weighing, and then another wait for the physician. It may be hindsight, but the doctor's manner was odd from the beginning—like the old gent was trying too hard. After a handshake and greeting he stared at my face. "Your nose was broken, wasn't it." No, not to my knowledge. He was skeptical. He drew a ruler from his breast pocket and held it up to my nose, squinting with one eye then the other. "Hmm. Okay I guess you're right." He placed a stethoscope on my chest and listened for a moment. He announced, "You had rheumatism as a child." No, no I didn't. He shifted the scope to the left. "Oh, Okay. I guess not."

I thought at first this was all a joke—bizarre, but perhaps his way of having a little fun on TGIF afternoon, releasing some steam after a stressful week in the medical trenches. He pressed a small lump I've had on my back for years, a benign fatty deposit. His voice was edged with alarm. "What's this!" Before I could reply he added, "Well, I suppose it's *not* melanoma." He then offered a short lecture on skin cancer, and the importance of checking for strange blemishes. "Are you married?" he asked, tapping my back. Yes. "Well, once in a while you and your wife should check all over each other's bodies." He chuckled. "Of course, some people like to get their friends together and make a party out of it." I chuckled along, albeit nervously.

He peered into my right ear and noticed a wax build-up. "Want me to clean it out?" Sure, why not? This was on the Forest Service tab. In a moment he was back with a steel probe. I'd expected a washing, not surgery. "Okay." he said, "your job is *not to move*—at all. This'll be painful, and I could easily puncture your eardrum." Before I could react the steel was scraping deep inside my ear. I grasped bare knees and froze. The pain was excruciating, and I broke a sweat. I dared not pull away. To my astonishment the good doctor then launched into a monologue about terrorism: "You know, the ear is very sensitive." (I knew! I knew!) "If any member of my family was ever kidnapped or otherwise harmed, this is how I would torture the culprits." I couldn't believe my ears, or what he was doing to them.

After about two long minutes of agony, my right ear was waxless, and I was drenched in sweat—sitting there in nothing but my briefs, and even they were damp. The doctor stared at me and said with a straight face, "I see you have a perspiration problem." I must've gazed at him in wonder, for he enthusiastically began a dead serious five-minute lecture about remedies for excessive perspiration. "Your feet sweat a lot, don't they." I tried to say I didn't think my level of sweat was abnormal, but he overrode my protest, extolling the anti-perspirant benefits of regularly soaking the feet in a tub of iced tea.

As I recall this astounding exam I have to ask: why didn't I flee? I suppose I was too stunned; also, I just needed to get that damn physical out of the way, and I figured each outrageous comment or act would surely be the last. But at least I wasn't the only one to suffer through this mad doctor's ministrations. When I returned to work and told one of my colleagues—a veteran of many seasons in Grangeville (or "Strangeville" as he called it)—about the ear episode, he laughed and said, "Hey, did he tell you about the iced tea?"

I resolved that I should definitely not get hurt while I was in town. I shuddered to imagine what it'd be like to have the man stitch a laceration or set a fracture. ("I see you have a pain threshold problem.")

My ODS (official duty station) was the Grangeville Air Center, or GAC (pronounced "Gack"), a Forest Service complex adjacent to the local airfield. What impressed me immediately was that the staff at GAC is a professional firefighting organization. Its raison d'être doesn't include timber, recreation, wildfire, or any other field in which the Forest Service might dabble. GAC exists for fire, wildland fire in all its manifestations, whether prescribed or unprescribed, accidental or incendiary, natural or man-caused. Other missions are accomplished, but only as side shows; and if not for fire there would be no GAC.

There are three branches at the Air Center: smokejumpers, air tanker operations, and helicopter operations. Thirty smokejumpers, their jump gear and fire tools, and a De Havilland Twin Otter jump plane are based out of "The Loft," a nickname for jumper headquarters derived from the two-and-one-half story tower where parachutes are hung as part of the packing process. Smokejumpers are at the pinnacle of the wildland firefighting hierarchy—the elite shock troops—comparable to airborne units in the military. The average jumper has eleven years of fire experience and probably matriculated from a Hot Shot or helitack crew. The walls of the chute packing room at GAC are decorated with annual group portraits going back to the mid-1950s, and I noticed that in almost every photo there were one or two jumpers on crutches or in casts.

I expected arrogance from these people and was pleasantly surprised to find very little, at least among the Nez Perce jumpers. (I would soon have a different experience with another unit.) I think part of it was that the GAC jumpers had recently seen one of their comrades die. Barely a month before I arrived, Bill Martin, a squad leader with some 226 jumps to his credit, was killed in Missoula while making a practice jump with a rectangular Ram-Air chute. (The official Forest Service parachute is an older-style round canopy.) The ensuing investigation was inconclusive; for some reason the Ram-Air was simply not deployed, and the reserve chute was activated too late. Bill Martin struck the ground at high velocity right before the eyes of some of his friends. If it could happen to him, it could happen to anyone; very serious business, and a definite hobble on swagger.

Still, there's justifiable pride among the jumpers, and on my first day it was made clear that I wasn't quite in the same league. When I introduced myself to Robin, the only female jumper at GAC (nationwide in 1991 there were sixteen women in the 387-person smokejumper corps) she said, "So, you're the new 'heli-slug'?" I think I may have won points by laughing and replying, "Well, back in Minnesota we prefer 'heli-slime.'" I realized that success or failure at GAC would hinge partly on knowing my place and it may as well be acknowledged gracefully.

The air tanker show consists of mixing and holding tanks for large volumes of fire retardant solution, and a ramp area for Air Tanker 119, a four-engined DC-4 that was built in 1945 and delivered to the U.S. Army in 1946. Now privately owned and contracted out, it's logged well over 25,000 flight hours, and in its role as a forest fire bomber, many of those hours have not been easy. Air tankers often ply unfriendly skies.

And as part of the helicopter operations, I'd soon be doing the same. Our branch consisted of Bob Quirino, the helicopter foreman for the Nez Perce; Scott, the assistant foreman (and fellow Minnesotan); and me, the grunt and rookie. Our helicopter, or more commonly, "ship," was a Bell 206 Longranger III (L-3, for short), contracted for the fire season and piloted by Jim Reed, a fifteen-year veteran of rotary wing aircraft. (In fact, when Jim and I compared notes, I realized I had seen him flying at the Silver Complex back in 1987, where he had been piloting a Vertol that made several bucket drops in our division.) The L-3, whose registration number was N7061E, or 61E ("Six-One-Echo") for everyday usage, was almost brand new, with only about 700 flight hours on the Hobbes meter. On stand-by it went for $1,592 per day, with a flight rate of $313 per hour. It's a tribute to the versatility of helicopters that even at those prices, 61E was often considered a bargain. It arrived with its own one-ton fuel truck, loaded with 500 gallons of Jet-A, and driven by Tim Adams, a twenty-two-year old who had finished a hitch in the Army only a month before. He had worked on helicopters for Uncle Sam, and was still miffed that he hadn't been shipped to Saudi Arabia for Desert Storm.

Our chief mission was to mount "initial attack" operations on fires—get people to the scene and then do all we were able to supply, support and suppress. By the end, 61E would be involved in about eighty initial attacks, or "IAs."

The boss of all three branches at GAC was a shambling bear of a man named Jon Foland, an ex-smokejumper also known as "Mr. Mud," because of his aggressive use of air tankers. The joke was he had the command "load and return" tattooed on his forearm. I was soon to witness Jon's air attack style "up close and personal," but his general philosophy of fire operations was made clear by a story I was told that first week. The account had been fondly polished, raised to the status of legend.

Since GAC is attached to a commercial airstrip, there are occasional traffic problems. One afternoon during the 1990 season, a corporate Lear jet landed at Grangeville and taxied toward the slightly ramshackle structure that passes for a "terminal." For some reason the pilot found it convenient to park the small jet directly in front of Air Tanker 119, which was on stand-by status for fire. (The Leer pilot may have thought it was merely the airport museum piece.) Jon rumbled out of the office like a gathering thunderhead and reached the Leer just as the dandified jet jockey, complete with fancy flight uniform, was descending the stairway. Jon, in rumpled T-shirt and blue jeans, was courteous, explained the mission of 119, and requested that the jet be parked elsewhere. The pilot demurred (who was this Idaho hick, telling an honest-to-god jet captain what to do?), saying that he'd only be a few minutes. Jon, the story goes, didn't raise his voice. He simply pointed to the large forklift that's used to load jump planes and handle bulk slurry, and politely offered to move the Lear jet himself. The pilot reconsidered, and the jet was quickly moved—without forks impaling the fuselage.

✳ ✳ ✳

2.

Alaska was the hot spot in May and June, with three or four big fires out of control, and by July 1st over 200 smoke-jumpers were there, making nearly 100 jumps per day. Several of the GAC people had been shipped north, and for a while Scott and Jim fantasized about our helicopter module being sent as well. The previous year 61E had been dispatched to "off forest" incidents regularly, and when you're "on the road" the payroll hours approach exponential growth. But when Ollie, Mr. Mud's boss at Forest Headquarters and the *biggest* chief when it comes to Nez Perce fire, was asked if 61E would be sent out of town in 1991 he replied, "Not no, but *hell* no!" Everyone agreed that Ollie's word was gospel. It's nice to be wanted.

I'd soon learn our value to the Nez, and the reasons for Ollie's possessiveness, but first I had to graduate from the Forest Service's official helicopter safety and operations course. Normally it's a week-long affair, but due to my late arrival I was sent to an abbreviated but intense (and effective) alternative session run by Paul Evenson, the head USFS helicopter honcho for all of Region I, and another native of Minnesota. In fact, of the nine people in the three-day class, six were current or former Minnesotans, generating a lot of enthusiastic banter about the redhot Twins, and how they were bound to choke. (They didn't.)

The course was conducted at the Dixie Work Center, home of Dixie Helitack and a grass airstrip tucked into the mountains at 5,126 feet elevation. It's about forty air miles southeast of Grangeville, on the edge of the Gospel Hump Wilderness, and nine miles north of the Salmon River. A clear, rocky stream called Crooked Creek waters the narrow valley, shaded by lodgepole and ponderosa pine. It was unremarkable to see mule deer in the "yard," or grazing out on the strip.

The Work Center is four miles south of the picturesque hamlet of Dixie, an isolated cluster of cabins and shacks sporting a dirt-road main-street (only street) and a bumpy gravel airstrip with a history of mishaps. One of the natives told me that when he gives directions to Dixie, he tells people, "Go to the end of the road and take a right; then go to the end of the road." The corral of Dixie Outfitters anchors the south end of the street, where horses and mules lazily munch hay in the shadow of a leaning, gray-boarded barn. If I had seen a photographer there some morning shooting for a Marlboro commercial, I wouldn't have been surprised. Across from the stable is a new guest lodge, a magnificent scribed-log structure with a wide, Western-style veranda; it's so perfect for the setting that it might've risen naturally from the ground like a stand of ponderosa. The main drag is rounded out by a general store/post office with a couple of gas pumps, a rickety four-room motel with gas lights for back-up, and the locally famous Lodgepole Pine Inn—the Lodgepole, for short—a saloon and restaurant that might be the world's only helitack bar.

On any given night during fire season it's a good bet the majority of pa-trons (or maybe all) are Forest Service helicopter people. Actually, I had heard of the Lodgepole back in Minnesota, from Scott and others who de-scribed it in the glowing terms one might expect from a preacher extolling the virtues of the pearly gates. And it is a genuine oasis for firefighters— cold beer, friendly proprietors, good non-government food, and an excellent juke box. Jim and Judy, the owners (and bartender and cook, respectively), treated regular customers like family, and before long breakfast was being scheduled for our convenience, and supper saved and kept warm on our longer days. When Scott turned thirty in August, they baked him a cake. We joked that a helipad should be constructed on the roof of the joint, and Jim and Judy were convinced the idea had merit.

The helicopter school was no-nonsense and somewhat frightening. Hard information, critical to the well-being of both crew and aircraft, was embellished by harrowing, true-life tales of mayhem and disaster. Only two days before, an L-3 working a fire in California nose-dived into the ground when its main rotors struck a large ponderosa pine. The pilot, an acquain-tance of Jim Reed, was killed. A USFS bulletin said he "was denied living space." An investigation was underway.

Federal documents bear a well-deserved reputation for obtuseness and euphemism (the above is a classic example), but as a synopsis of what I had to know as a helicopter crew person, my official job description form was concise, even colorful. For a "Lead Forestry Technician, GS-462-5" my "Major Duties" were: "Loads helicopter cargo considering methods, weight distribution, necessity for securing by tying down, total weight etc. . . . completes manifests of people and equipment being transported to fires . . .

Inventories and inspects helicopter assessories, tools, and equipment . . . Moves dirt, chops brush, and fells trees to build fireline using hand and/or power tools, lays hose, sets backfires. . . ."

Additionally, under a heading of "Complexity": "Performs a variety of fire suppression, leader, and helicopter duties . . . frequently performed under stress of emergency conditions." Under "Physical Demands and Work Environment": ". . . requires strenuous physical exertion for extended periods, which include walking, climbing, shoveling, chopping, throwing, lifting, jumping, and carrying over 50 pounds . . . work is performed at airstrips, helispots, unimproved helispots, and in the forest environment in steep terrain where surfaces may vary from paved to extremely uneven and rocky. The presence of various aircraft being loaded, unloaded, taking off, and landing creates special hazards . . ." For this I was paid $8.13 per hour.

And so we learned how to stay healthy around helicopters, and how to operate the exotic assessories that were our everyday tools: the belly hook where we attached longline (fifty-foot lengths of steel cable mated with power cord and used to "sling" external loads), a water-dropping collapsible bucket called a Bambi (after its brand name), blivets (flexible water containers—either potable or for fire suppression), and cargo nets. We studied the "remote hook," an electrically activated cargo hook attached to the end of a longline that can be operated by the pilot.

We went through the crash-rescue kit—a bare-bones field set-up with a pry bar, hacksaw, hatchet-like penetrating/ripping tool, and seat belt cutter, backed up with a fire extinguisher. We noted the location of critical features inside the ship like the ELT (emergency locator transmitter), a homing device designed to be automatically activated by the impact of a crash (assuming the impact doesn't destroy it).

We practiced hand signals, so that over the oppressive din of engine and rotors we could offer pilots sixteen separate instructions like, "hold hover" or "clear to take off." Emphasis was placed on the flying characteristics and load-carrying capacities of helicopters, particularly the L-3, and how even routine operations can be dangerous in mountainous terrain. For example, if your mission is to haul a payload from a point at 3,000 feet to a location at 9,000 feet, you must understand that the lifting power of a ship decreases significantly with elevation, and the load calculation must be based on conditions at 9,000 feet and not at the point of departure. Air temperature also affects performance, with higher temperatures making for lower density air and hence less lift and payload capability. Fortunately, temperature tends to drop as you gain elevation—a "lapse rate" of two degrees centigrade per 1,000 feet is the value accepted for purposes of calculation—so helicopters can still function relatively well at higher elevations.

The effect of air temperature was dramatically demonstrated to me a few weeks later as we were flying over the notorious Salmon River Breaks. The stream cuts through a deep canyon/ravine, and down at water level it's hellishly hot in the summer—routinely in excess of 100 degrees Farenheit. Over the rim of the canyon it can easily be ten to fifteen degrees cooler, and, as our ship cleared the rim and flew into the column of superheated air rising from the river bottom, we experienced the "elevator effect." The sudden decrease in air density triggered a loss of lift, and we dropped straight down for a few moments, stomachs left behind—light and floating. No place to be with a hangover.

Wind velocity is also a factor in helicopter performance, and air currents in the mountains, channeled over, down, and around ridges, peaks, and saddles, can be wickedly fickle, or in technical parlance—"squirrelly." The fuel capacity and consumption rate of a ship is also an important consideration, since it's a significant and constantly variable weight factor. Fuel is heavy. How much Jet-A to pump into 61E wasn't so much a function of "how far are we going?" (though obviously not trivial), but rather "how much weight can we add to the ship?" One of the most important items carried by pilots and helicopter foremen is a small calculator.

These and other details of air operations in the fire environment were hammered home in a friendly (we're all in this together) but dead-serious (just don't screw up!) quasi-military, "be ready for the worst" atmosphere. One of the cautionary proverbs at the front of our textbook encapsulated the desired attitude: "You must delete false pride, calculated risk, 'real world,' and 'good enough for government work' from your professional vocabulary." An ideal, to be sure, but it seemed to me that "calculated risk" was the very essence of fireground helicopter work.

This was proven to me on the final day of class—our "lab" session, where we actually practiced techniques around the ship, including "hover hook-ups." There are four basic ways for a helicopter crew to plug into H-pay: a) landing at "unimproved helispots" (that is, out in the middle of nowhere), b) hazardous flying conditions (like through a thunderstorm, or flying low and slow), c) actual fire supression activity, and d) hover hook-ups.

The latter are defined as any time a crew member secures an external load beneath a hovering helicopter. In practice, this is usually with a longline and remote hook attached, so the ship is anywhere from fifty to 150 feet overhead. However, in our training session we had a ten-foot lead line (a plastic-coated steel cable) hooked to a loaded cargo net, so Jim had to settle the helicopter down within arm reach, the landing skids less than six feet off the ground.

When it was my turn, I stood out in the middle of the airstrip, right arm fully extended, my hand nervously grasping the pear-shaped ring that's shoved into the self-locking belly hook on the very bottom of the helicopter fuselage. With another trainee (backed by the instructor) directing Jim via radio and hand signals, he lowered 61E on my head, sloping down and in with obvious skill. The ship swelled above me, like a great white whale descending from the sky, the tall grass flattened by rotor wash, and an artificial gale whipping my pant legs. As the skids bracketed my shoulders, I remembered to touch one with the pear ring—to bleed off any static electrical charge that may have built up on the skin of the ship. (Under certain conditions there can be enough juice to deliver a shock, and Jim was delighted to tell us about the times he had seen hookers knocked flat by a heavy charge.) Then, as the ship rocked gently overhead, I slipped the ring into the belly hook, tugged lightly to make sure it was secure ("don't yank the ship out of the air!"), and strode away from beneath the helicopter, watching it all the way; you don't turn your back on a hovering ship. When I was clear, Jim lifted off, the cargo net spinning freely on its swiveled hook.

It was a simple operation—"could teach a chimp to do it," we joked. Nevertheless, it was also a rite of passage, the finale and confirmation of our course. But they don't give you the H-pay for nothing, and later Jim explained that if he ran into trouble during a hover-hookup he'd always try to swing the helicopter to his right, and we should always dive away to our right, thus moving in opposite directions. If he "augered in,"—that is, crashed—it would offer us a better chance of survival, assuming there was enough warning for us to react at all. Hi ho.

At that point, though not exactly related, we were solemnly told how a few years before, during a helitorch operation, a helicopter crewman had been observing a take-off when he noticed that one of the cables of the torch was draped over a skid. Rather than direct the pilot to ease the helicopter back down (or leave that to the guy who was marshalling the ship with hand signals), he rushed in to flip the cable clear as the skid was rising. His jerk on the cable destabilized the helicopter, and as the pilot fought to regain control, the tail rotor swung around and the crewman was decapitated—before a horrified audience of his peers.

There's an obvious symbiotic relationship between pilot and crewmembers (especially between pilot and foreman), but also a great gulf. Jim, for instance, harbored a virulent, longstanding animosity toward some foremen with whom he had worked previously, who "thought they knew more about flying helicopters than I did." And it's true that some helitack people develop what our text referred to as "false pride." On the other hand, the arrogance and conceit of many professional pilots is legendary. One of the standard gags: Q. "What do pilots use for birth control?" A. "Their personalities."

In reality, given the jeopardy and craziness of fireground air operations, anyone who's earned genuine cause for pride can be forgiven a display occasionally, as long as it doesn't compromise safety or morale; particularly a good pilot. They bear ultimate responsibility for aircraft and crew, and their collective grace under pressure is also legendary. A story filtered down from Alaska in early July. It seems that a helicopter owner in the lower forty-eight phoned his pilots, Bob and Jack, to see how things were going.

"Well," drawled Bob, "the helicopter won't start."

"What! Why not?"

"Well, Jack and I have a difference of opinion on that."

"How so?"

"Well, Jack says it won't start because it's upside down. I say it won't start because it's in ten feet of water."

I suspect this was an apocryphal tale, but if someone did invent it, or more likely, jazz up a real occurrence, it was only because it rang true.

Pilots must be good, manipulating controls as if hardwired to their nervous systems, but above all they must be cool—and take every opportunity to project the chill. For example, Jim, like many pilots, has two modes of speech: his normal, workaday, regular-guy tone, and his fighter-jockey cockpit radio voice, the righteous, unflappable monotone of aces about to die—often garnished with a down-home, don't-really-give-a-shit drawl. It can be soothing when events are waxing wild and crazy. Still, there's potential danger in the aura of "cool." As our text also admonished: "You must not let your actions instill the attitude of competition between pilots. [It] may hinder their performance, and compromise safety." I could see how it might happen, but Jim, nearing age fifty, denied any inclination to "hot dog" or "cowboy it."

"There are," he said, quoting a timeworn airfield maxim, "old pilots and bold pilots; but no old, bold pilots. I plan on collecting my Social Security." Sounded real fine to me; my life would be in his hands more regularly than I liked to acknowledge.

✳ ✳ ✳

3.

Two days after I was officially carded as an HECM—Helicopter Crew Member—the Nez Perce was struck with the first lightning "bust" of the season. I was returning to GAC after lunch, and from the highway I could see 61E on the helipad. At that moment its rotors began to turn. I tromped the gas pedal.

Grangeville isn't in the Forest but down in the rolling hayfields of the foothills, and it's not unusual to enjoy blue sky and sunshine at GAC while watching thunderstorms pounding the wooded mountains only a few miles away. That's what happened on July thirteenth, as isolated dry thunderstorms raided the Nez, igniting fires in the Red River Ranger District. Smokejumpers were dispatched immediately, and 61E was ordered to Mullins, a cow pasture leased by the Forest Service as an emergency helibase.

Scott and I kept an array of tools and equipment laid out on the ground next to the ship, and, as Jim warmed it up, we loaded the Bambi bucket, a couple of cargo nets, and our personal gear. The rest of our inventory was stashed in the support truck, a four-wheel drive pick-up with a topper that Bob would send along later.

The best part of helicopter flight is lift off. A fixed-wing aircraft must take a long run at take-off, revving down the strip at full bore, seeming sometimes to labor—against all odds—into the air. A helicopter lends the illusion of an anti-gravity device, surging like a tethered balloon that's been abruptly released and wafting nearly straight up toward the clouds; then, nose slightly down, it can power away at a right angle to the ascent, the closest thing we know to the reported feats of flying saucers.

This heady transition from earth to sky is the fast hot heart of flight, the pure elation of god-like privilege. Couple that with the fact that we were bound for fire in the mountains (run boys, run!), and you may understand why I yelped as we rose from the grass and shot away from GAC like a barracuda of the air.

We wore flight helmets linked to an intercom system so we could chat among ourselves while monitoring outside radio traffic. Scott reminded me that part of my duties was to scan the sky for flight hazards—in this case, other aircraft near the field. He also suggested that I try to follow our progress on my Forest map and develop a feel for navigation.

Above the dappled patchwork grid of farms and roads, it was fairly easy to keep track of position, but as we ascended the flanks of the mountains and crested the first ridgeline over an ocean of conifers stretching to the far blue horizons, I was almost instantly confused. The convoluted drainages looked the same; each knob, butte, and hump, the most obvious principal landmarks, were lost to me in an alien landscape of immense range and contour. The map across my knees became a puzzle. It was finely detailed and colorful, precisely coordinated in township, range, latitude, and longitude, and conveniently crosshatched down to section level, but in my straining eyes it bore little relation to the spectacular terrain below. Part of the problem was that I had scant appreciation for the character of our motion. I wasn't used to covering ground at 120 miles per hour. I asked Scott, "Is that Blacktail Butte?" No, it was Quartz Ridge. Blacktail Butte was four or five miles *behind*. Oh.

In front was a torn rampart of cumulo-nimbus clouds, a line of thunderstorms rolling away to the east. We saw an occasional downstrike split the blue-black strata, but the only apparent rain was wispy arcs of virga, lashed to curving by high wind. Little if any moisture was reaching the ground. Turbulent air coiled in the wake of the storm, and 61E was jostled and bullied, but it wasn't as bumpy as I expected, and I found that gratifying. Still, the season was young.

In less than twenty minutes, Jim banked us steeply down into a draw, and a long swath of flat grassland opened up below: a meandering stream, a road, a couple of small ranches sprinkled with hay bales and horses, and a faded orange wind sock stuck on a pole, denoting the emergency airstrip at "Mullins International."

The intercom buzzed and Jim enunciated what sounded like the final item on a checklist: "And watch out for the powerline at the end of the meadow." Ten-four; a definite flight hazard.

As our skids settled into the grass—still green, but destined for tinder—a Forest Service pick-up pulled off the road and up to the gate in the barbed wire that isolated Mullins from the local livestock. Three firefighters hopped out—the first wave. We knew by now we had at least three or four fires with which to deal, a clump of lightning starts about thirty miles to the east in the River of No Return Wilderness.

While Scott and Jim produced a load calculation—considering air temperature, elevations, fuel on board—I manifested the firefighters and their gear, recording names and weights. These were experienced people; their personal weights were inscribed on their hardhats, and their packs were tagged according to poundage. One of the tools in our support truck was a small hand scale for weighing unfamiliar items, but by the end of that day the weights of all common fire gear and tools were at the tip of my pencil. I was to complete a manifest for every single mission of 61E, no matter how trivial some would seem. If all went well, the data would be logged and forgotten. If, however, there was a crash, my manifests could conceivably become some of the most important documents in a court of law. It was wise to keep them legible and accurate.

Since these were wilderness fires, no chain saws were allowed without special permission, so the firefighters had grabbed an old-fashioned two-person crosscut—the kind of tool more commonly seen these days gracing the walls of backwoods taverns, or perhaps painted with quaint country scenes and sold at flea markets to decorate the mantles of yuppies from Boise. But in the Nez Perce it's still a fire tool, and for helicopter transport we bent the wide, but flexible blade into a horseshoe shape around the top of a pack and tied it securely with parachute cord. The teeth, long and razor-sharp, were sheathed in a split length of old canvas fire hose.

Scott had the load calculations—our allowable payload was 880 pounds. Since one of the firefighters was only 150 pounds with his gear, we were able to load all three, along with two thirty-pound "chaser" packs (containing food, water, and sleeping gear), the crosscut and three hand-tools (two pulaskis and a shovel), and all their personal gear, or PG (small day packs with canteens, rations, fire shelters—equivalent to the standard yellow web gear). And of course Scott was in the front seat to help navigate, find an appropriate helispot near the fire(s), and see that the ship was safely unloaded.

Safety was the prime component of my air operations existence, and even though these folks had been on helitack gigs before, I delivered a quick safety briefing, guided by a wallet card I had been issued for the purpose:

approach the ship in a slight crouch, in full view of the pilot and preferably accompanied by a crew person; have helmet secured by chinstrap, gloves on, collars buttoned up, sleeves down, earplugs in; no running; tools carried horizontally (to keep them out of the rotors), no smoking in or near the ship, no loose gear, no unnecessary movement while in flight; be aware of body position for crash landings, plus location of ELT, fire extinguisher, radio, and battery switch; DO NOT EXIT SHIP UNTIL GUIDED BY HELICOPTER PERSONNEL.

This last, seemingly picky and innocuous to the uninitiated, would be a critical consideration later that day. One helispot was so cramped and uneven that Jim had to keep the rotors powered up, suspended between flight and rest, just to remain stable. If someone were to jump down on a skid at the wrong place and moment, it could alter the center-of-gravity (always important with helicopters) enough to induce what's known as "dynamic rollover," where a ship actually flips on its side, and disintegrating rotors can dismember both crew and machine.

We loaded the handtools (taped together for safer handling) and a couple of packs into the small cargo bay on the port side rear of 61E, and the rest was piled on the floor or the two empty seats. I made sure the firefighters were properly seatbelted, that all doors were latched, and that nothing was hanging out of the ship. (61E had already been slightly damaged on another contract when someone left an unused seatbelt dangling and banging outside the door. It dented the fuselage and scared hell out of the pilot.) We tried to be quick with all this without being rushed. But the effect of screaming rotors, torqued to a nearly invisible blur just overhead is unsettling. The high-pitched, almost keening sound seems an automatic stimulus to anxiety and tension, especially in an emergency situation. It feels as if your heart responds directly to the whine, overriding the mind that knows it's only necessary noise.

There's also the omnipresent threat of the unprotected tail rotor, which even a short person could easily walk into and be literally chopped apart. It happens. There are stories of people mesmerized by the rotor, walking toward almost certain death as if captivated by a malevolent viper—possibly akin to the strange urge to jump that people often experience when on a cliff or tower. We were taught to establish an imaginary line at the rear of the L-3's cargo compartment, and *never* stray further aft when the ship was running. Scott told me how he had once seized an experienced firefighter who was stepping right for the tail rotor. I made it my practice to avoid the entire tail section, even when the ship was shut down. There was nothing for me to do back there.

Once the personnel and gear were stowed, I positioned myself about a hundred feet in front of the ship and scanned the sky for other aircraft, including birds. Traffic in the skies over Mullins—both organic and inorganic—usually isn't heavy, but it's smart to make these safety procedures habitual. Assumptions are always hazardous, and aircraft can appear virtually anywhere, anytime—and they often do suddenly. (A few weeks later I was in the front seat as we lifted out of Dixie, and we had no sooner cleared the field when a Cessna 172 sped in from the north on a landing approach, seemingly by materializing out of the treetops just to our left and below. It wasn't a near miss, but I could clearly see the pilot, and I was astonished by how instantaneously the plane appeared, and how breathtaking were our relative velocities. There'd been zero warning, and the Cessna had obviously *assumed* there was no activity at Dixie. Jim jumped on the radio to establish contact, and then energetically cursed over the intercom, a handy means to vent anger and emotion that was better left off the airwaves. I contributed an appropriate epithet of my own, and we both felt better—if not more comfortable. From our perspective the careless Cessna was equivalent to an anti-aircraft missile.)

So I always checked the sky before take-off, my hand-held radio glued to my ear. During a big bust, the airspace over the Nez could quickly become relatively crowded with helicopters, air tankers, observation craft, and jump planes. When I was satisfied all was clear, I showed Jim a thumbs-up, and 61E powered aloft. One of the firefighters gave a happy (or nervous) little wave as the L-3 banked away to the east.

The freshest challenge of helicopter operations was working and thinking in terms of a full three-dimensional arena. Not only were we concerned with the events and features of terra firma—helispot configurations, tree heights, fuel types, fire behavior, straight-line distances—but also more esoteric variables like: What was the wind doing 200 feet above Drumlummen Ridge? What was the altitude and course of Air Tanker 119? What was the outside air temperature at 8,000 feet? Would 150 feet of longline be enough to link our airborne world with the ground-hugging cargo that needed to fly? Would the turbulence near a thunder cell be too rough for comfort and/or safety, or would there be hail mixed with the rain ahead, ready to bombard the ship like a swarm of meteors? Actually, given all the critically time-dependent parameters like fuel consumption (thirty-five gallons per hour for the L-3, or about 245 *pounds* per hour), flight time (affected by wind direction and velocity, flight hazards), the daily progression of sunrise and sunset times (since operations one-half hour before or one-half hour after were forbidden), plus the workaday arrangements of various schedules, rendezvous, and ETAs, we dealt with a four-dimensional environment in a constant state of flux, where almost no datum was trivial as far as efficiency and survival were concerned.

While 61E was on that first IA of the afternoon, I heard Jumper 14 (the GAC Twin Otter) radio Grangeville and report that it was too windy for parachute work. That meant more assignments for us, and two additional Forest Service trucks soon arrived at Mullins with firefighters and gear. I delivered another safety briefing, outlined our payload limitations for the day, helped sort gear, and began to develop a real warmth for the job of HECM. It was clear these people—mostly young (late teens, early twenties), seasonal fire employees—were granting me automatic respect. It wasn't fawning by any means, but solid attention and regard. Since I was a GS-5 helicopter operations firefighter out of GAC, it naturally followed that I must be competent, professional. This was something new. As a smoke-chaser or AD I had often felt like the opposite assumption was being made. I was guilty until proven innocent; no matter how well-trained or experienced, a "casual" must invariably bear the burden of proof: Are you worthy or not? Show us. It matters little that casuals are regularly the backbone of suppression forces on major fires, or that some states (like Minnesota) would be essentially without an effective wildland firefighting organization if not for the seasonal corps of accomplished casuals.

It was sharply stimulating to be awarded this routine deference—like the first breath of air on a crisp autumn morning—and I had to make a conscious effort not to play the prima donna, or "heli donna," as Bob said, an all too common fault of helicopter people who allow the respect to inflate their heads, and hence become less deserving of same. Indeed, before I had even left Minnesota my fire colleagues had razzed me about "mutating" into a "rotorhead," and how I'd probably be "ruined." Mag said he would schedule a "deprogramming" session for me as soon as I returned. Fortunately, I was too keenly aware of my tender knowledge of helitack for my head to swell.

Six-One-Echo was far away amidst the mountains and I couldn't hear Scott's radio transmissions, so I had to keep track of events via Red River's half of the conversation. I surmised there were three fires in need of immediate attention—in nasty terrain, with dangerous helispots—and that the air was mean and bumpy.

When the ship returned I could see Scott and Jim were already stressed, faces grim and pinched. Flying (and landing) conditions in the wilderness were rugged. "It's ugly," said Scott. "We're getting beat up out there." The post-storm sky was roiling and vindictive, offended by air machines. But I quickly loaded two more firefighters and their gear, shoved a copy of the manifest into Scott's hand, and 61E launched for the second fire.

Soon after, Tim arrived with the fuel truck, and our support truck pulled in a few minutes later. Bob had enlisted a part-time helicopter crew person named Walt Bailey to deliver the pick-up and join us for the duration of the bust.

Walt was an oldtimer like me—age forty-one—and a seasonal Forest Service employee who normally maintained campgrounds, but was available for fire work and had been trained in helitack. He was delighted to be at Mullins; it was a chance for overtime and H-pay, and a break from routine. And he was certainly no "heli donna." "I like helitack," he told me, "but I don't like helicopters." He wasn't excited about flying, was content with ground work and driving the support truck.

The latter was a rolling warehouse, crammed with everything but an extra helicopter. Items ranged from cargo nets, longlines, and blivets, to fire tools (pulaskis, chain saw, portable pump), extra radio batteries, and camping gear, to rations, cubees, and manifest books. If need be, we could set up a makeshift helibase, complete with warning signs, circus flagging, a crash-rescue kit, and a wind sock. We even carried a wad of extra chinstraps to hand out to firefighters who showed up without them.

When 61E returned, it was low on fuel, and, per regulations, Jim shut down and Tim clamped a grounding wire to the ship so he could pump Jet-A into the fuel cells—but not to capacity—Scott wanted to carry as much payload as possible.

And for the rest of the day it was a hectic shuttle from Mullins to the firegrounds. I scribbled in the manifest book, balancing people and gear as 61E began to visit multiple sites on one run, manning a new fire and bringing additional supplies to another—cubees, bladder bags, a replacement for a defective radio. I did more arithmetic in a few hours than I'd done in the past year. Walt and I fell into a rythym of briefing, manifesting, loading, marshalling—while monitoring radio traffic, designing loads, and then instantly reshuffling a planned payload as the ship landed and Scott was requested to give one fire priority over another. Walt and I were stevedores and flight attendants, traffic controllers and coaches ("you go, you stay; do this, don't do that; yea team!"). I was surprised at how strenuous and inherently stressful it was, and how involved with the fires I felt, even though they were thirty miles away. It was a swiftly-paced, exhilarating operation, crackling with tension and radio chatter.

By dusk we'd shipped fifteen people to three fires, along with approximately 1000 pounds of gear and supplies. Scott and Jim were frazzled, weary-winged with the strain of tight, scabrous helispots and buffeting wind. At one point in the long afternoon Jim had hovered seven or eight feet off the ground while Tim checked the skids for rock damage. They were okay, but there had been some craggy touchdowns.

On the plus side, all three fires had been kept small and were under control. (Firefighters would spend the night, sleeping next to the black and checking for lingering hot spots in the morning, not leaving the fire until the last scintilla of heat was snuffed.) We'd made thirteen hours of overtime (it was a Saturday; God bless weekend lightning), and we were to have dinner at the Lodgepole and sleep in the Dixie Motel.

For those who may harbor resentment against helicopter crews, such accommodations are probably one reason. The folks we had transported were sleeping in the dirt and sucking warm water out of sooty canteens; we were soon sipping Michelob Dark and taking hot showers before bed. Actually, I was surprised. I had been fully prepared to camp in the grass at

Mullins, but as we leaned against the bar at the Lodgepole I felt not a twinge of guilt. I had long since paid my dues as a fire grunt. The beer was cold, and it was a tonic to listen to the desultory gasconade of tavern talk. If anyone begrudged us this, to hell with 'em.

We returned to Mullins just after dawn and shipped four people to a pair of new fires. We also delivered a couple of blivets to the previous day's fires.

A blivet is a collapsible plastic water container that holds about seventy gallons and is fitted with a hose connection. It's slung into a fire at the end of a longline, and can be used to fill bladder bags or directly feed garden hose. In the latter application, Jim would try to set the blivet upslope of the fire to provide some gravity pressure for the hose lay. Each blivet had a rope bag attached, and before Jim released the catch on the remote hook, a firefighter would pull the rope out of the bag—specially braided in the smokejumper style so it would play out quickly and evenly with no snags—and secure it to a tree or deadfall to prevent the unit from rolling downhill. It happened once, later in the season. A blivet wasn't adequately secured, and everyone concerned watched in bemused mortification as the bright orange sack teetered uncertainly, and then accelerated downslope, the shifting water inducing a kind of slinky, flywheel effect as the blivet bounded out of sight into the valley below. Fortunately no one was in the path. What an embarrassing way to exit—bashed by a blivet! Sounds like something out of Dr. Seuss.

But the best blivet story was told by Pat Wilson, the smokejumper foreman at GAC. On a fire in the Clearwater National Forest (just north of the Nez Perce) in 1990, two blivets were slung in to a smokejumper crew. Apparently one of their colleagues was around when the blivets were filled back at the helibase, and the smokejumper squad leader on the fire received a cryptic radio call. He was instructed to "check for a message" inside one of the blivets. Upon arrival, the "message" blivet was found to contain fifty-four cans of beer immersed in the cold water. The crew toiled over the fire until after midnight, painfully aware of the beer, and finally the squad leader said, "Okay, dammit, the bar is open. But whoever's drinking beer has to piss on a hot spot."

We sent no messages in our blivets, but by sundown we had moved over 6,000 pounds of people and gear during our two days at Mullins. Much to our satisfaction, we were then told to return to our digs of the night before, and Jim's radio confirmation to Grangeville became our unofficial motto: "Inbound to Dixie."

The next day provided a sobering dose of R^2, that is, "reality squared"—a vivid realization and reminder that we're the prey of fate and that it *can* happen to us; "us" being everyone, but most particularly firefighters and flight crews.

Jim, a mechanic as well as a pilot, performed a pre-flight check of the ship each day, and that morning he discovered something that bothered him.

"Seems like there's too much play in that swash plate," he told Scott. It was part of the main rotor assembly. "It's probably not serious . . ." His voice trailed off.

That kind of talk from an auto mechanic is a relief; from a helicopter mechanic, it's chilling. Jim hemmed and hawed for a few minutes more, and then convinced himself he should fly alone to Lewiston, home base of 61E, and have the swash plate checked in a fully-equipped shop. As pilot, it was his call, and he departed immediately. (I later discovered that Tim had advised him not to fly at all.)

Scott, Walt, and I passed the day at the Dixie Work Center, cleaning equipment, doing paperwork, and helping out with chores around the Center. By 1830 Jim returned and gave us the news. A close examination in the shop had revealed a bad bearing in the main rotor system—bad to the point of making metal shavings—which had caused the sloppiness in the swash plate. It was concluded that within perhaps three to four more flight hours (easily attained on a single busy day), the bearing would have failed, and the main rotor would have "separated from the ship." Disaster. Probably death. If not for Jim's meticulous pre-flight check (and not all pilots are so finicky) it could have happened that very afternoon. Scott summed up our feelings: "Holy shit."

It was especially disturbing to know that particular bearing was rated as a 1,500-hour part, and had lasted less than 800. Jim vowed to keep an even closer eye on the swash plate. Then, before dark, he and Scott flew out to pick up the four firefighters (and their gear) that we had transported the day before. The fifteen firefighters we had dispatched on the first day of the bust were all hiking out via a trail near the fires, aided in their logistics by one of the observers in a nearby fire tower.

Fire towers are still in routine use in Idaho, with solitary observers spending an entire season at some remote lookout, hunting assiduously for wisps of smoke. During lightning storms they're incommunicado, perched on insulated stools watching blue sparks dance around their high-profile aeries. I heard that one lookout was working on a novel and had written 700 pages so far. Another had the radio voice of a seductress—a liquid, sexy tone that always caught your attention. I was told she didn't have the looks to match, but was an excellent observer and not to be trifled with. Her tower was in the wilderness, and she was very protective of "her territory." Once, to a helicopter pilot obviously taken with her Marilyn Monroe/Mae West manner, she offered an invitation to drop in for a visit. When he was stupid enough to do so, she immediately issued him a citation for an illegal landing in the wilderness.

The very names of the towers made for colorful radio traffic: Oregon Butte, Coolwater, Corral Hill, Pilot Knob, War Eagle Mountain, Hell's Half. And though a detection flight out of GAC was regularly scheduled during dry periods, the lookouts obviously earned their keep, picking out the bulk of the smokes, and serving as indispensable radio relay centers in the transmission-unfriendly terrain.

But the lookouts spotted no new fires the next day, and, after conducting a training session for a couple dozen firefighters at Elk City, we returned to Grangeville. The first bust was over—my initiation as it were—and I felt like part of the team, a few shades less green.

One week later a minor bust sent us scampering back to Dixie. We flew over a fire before landing—it was barely a mile from the airstrip—and observed a classic lightning-strike blaze. A black circle ringed the base of a tall lodgepole snag, with low flames visible on the tree itself. Three or four small spot fires were scattered around the snag, smoldering in punky wood blown out by the force of the strike. It would be no big deal if we got a couple of firefighters there soon—a matter of dropping the snag and mopping up with dirt or the water from a bladder bag.

Chad and Brian, members of the Red River fire crew, were waiting at the strip, and I quickly loaded them on the ship. Scott and Jim located a decent helispot within a half mile of the fire, and, after Chad and Brian were established on the ground, Jim briefly hovered over the smoke, allowing Chad to take a compass bearing. Such small fires can be hard to find on foot.

Within twenty minutes we manned a second nearby fire, and, in the meantime, Oregon Butte had pinpointed a third. As I was manifesting the next helitack team, I kept a wary eye on the black cloud mass arching up over the ridges to the east. Six-One-Echo eased onto the concrete pad, and I loaded Andra and Sean. I saw Jim and Scott exchange a skeptical glance as they watched the sky. The new fire was east of Dixie, and the way looked ominous. I knew Jim was figuring the storm clouds formed an isolated cell, and he could find a path around it, but the L-3 appeared particularly tiny and vulnerable as it climbed over the ridge and faced a hemisphere of sky the color of midnight. I saw a distant stab of lightning and was not disappointed to be on the ground.

The ship was gone for only five or six minutes when I heard it returning. They had encountered volleys of lightning and a horizon-encompassing storm. I knew Scott absolutely hated to scrub a mission; however, he and Jim had developed a casual but effective tactic for deciding when it was time to punch out. If either of them said, "Well . . . what do you think?" and the other replied, "Well . . ." then that automatically added up to *negative*—get the hell out. And they did.

I unloaded the ship, and Jim decided we should take off immediately and make a break for GAC. He was certain there'd be hail at Dixie in a few minutes, perhaps severe enough to damage the helicopter, and we knew it was partly sunny and calm at Grangeville. Scott stared at the sky for a moment, watching the wind sock spinning circles in the gusts, and said, "Let's go!"

I was scared, tempted to spit, "Screw the helicopter!" The cloud mass was a dark, twisted tidal wave, closing in rapidly from three sides and curling overhead like an evil dome of hell. Fat raindrops, flung by wind, began to splatter my helmet, and Andra and Sean shouted "Good luck!" as they hurried away for shelter. I was startled by that—didn't even think to say, "Thanks"; it's rare and unnerving to hear that jaunty phrase when it's not just polite banter. They meant it; they had been happy and relieved when Jim turned around. "Good luck!" and a wave. Indeed, indeed.

I belted in and secured my flight helmet. "Ready?" asked Scott. "Affirmative," I lied.

We jumped out of Dixie like a rocket, streaking away to the northwest at full speed. It was as if we had risen from the lap of a malevolent giant trying to enfold us with its titanic, curving arms. Far ahead, like the hopeful glow at the end of an impossible tunnel, was a tiny patch of bright sky. An opaque wall of rain engulfed Dixie as I watched, and there were lightning bolts flailing the ridges to either side. The drainages filled with virga and billowing clouds, and pitch darkness descended from overhead. We were a whisker ahead of the storm front, "our rotors between our legs," shoved by wind, and flat-out-to-the-max.

Slowly the patch of brightness began to grow. For a few minutes I had a white-knuckled grip on my shoulder belt, bracing for the bumps and rocking, but the air ahead of the front was surprisingly smooth, and I gradually relaxed as it became evident we were going to win the race.

Scott started singing over the intercom, cold-heartedly butchering a harmless country-western tune. "Oh-oh," said Jim. "We're in trouble now. The only time he sings is when our asses are hung out to dry." I went on the air to good-naturedly insult Scott's voice, and we kidded back and forth, defusing the tension of the flight. The storm slowly fell behind, and the brightness ahead opened up onto an oasis of blue sky. In fifteen minutes we were landing at GAC—soft breezes and sunshine.

✳ ✳ ✳

4.

A major facet of our job was to support the smokejumpers—supplying them, slinging out their jump gear, picking them up (when possible), and occasionally doing a medevac.

One morning, as we were sitting down to breakfast at the Lodgepole, the phone rang. Judy beckoned Scott into the kitchen—it was Ollie. Scott hustled to the phone. Ollie wouldn't call us at Dixie to exchange pleasantries and inquire after our health. He had an emergency.

Overnight, on a fire in the Moose Creek area, two smokejumpers had been clobbered by a falling snag. One was seriously injured—lacerations, cracked ribs, a punctured lung. His companions did what they could, but he laid in agony for several hours, awaiting first light. A hospital helicopter out of Missoula picked him up as early as they dared, in semi-darkness at a godforsaken helispot that Scott and Jim would soon see and never forget. Gulping coffee, they hurried out to the strip and took off. Six-One-Echo's assignment was to pick up the second, less seriously injured jumper.

Shortly after sunrise Jim squeezed the L-3 down onto a narrow, angled bench on a wooded mountainside. The main rotors were two feet from the side slope, and as soon as the skids touched down the dirt beneath began to crumble and slide away. Jim had to keep the ship powered up as Scott gingerly loaded the victim into the back seat. It was a zero-tolerance operation, no room for error and even too tense for Scott's singing.

Two days after our retreat from the storm, we were back at the Dixie airstrip, detailed to pick up a squad of eight smokejumpers. They had worked a fire above the Salmon River Breaks, arguably some of the meanest topography in the West and were hiking down to a sandbar along the river. We had slung out their jump gear (parachutes and protective clothing) the afternoon before, and now six of them were ready to fly out at noon; the other two would remain until the end of the day, patrolling the fire through the conventional burning period to ensure it was dead.

Scott told me to take the mission, and Jim was in a frisky flying mood as we roared down the full length of the airstrip about twenty-five feet off the ground, nose pitched forward, watching a dozen startled gophers bolt away to the right and left—it was a thrilling, raptor's eye view, but only a prelude.

Just before the strip gave way to forest, Jim eased 61E into a rising/banking portamento of a turn, and, as pine tops flashed past the plexiglass beneath our boots, we surged into the canyon of Crooked Creek, heading down to the Salmon.

"Just hang a right out of Dixie!" Jim chortled. He leveled the ship about even with the canyon rims. "What do you think of this terrain?"

I had already caught my breath, neck hair tingling. All I could reply was, "Awesome."

The canyon was formed by undulating rock spines alternating with steep, wooded draws. The fir and pine, some stunted by the harsh environment of the slopes, looked like bonsai trees, unreal in this massively tortured landscape. The creek was a shining ribbon several hundred feet below, cascading over boulders and deadfalls. Jutting dramatically from the near-vertical ramparts were several craggy spires that looked like pedestals for mountain goats. Crooked Creek was aptly named, and from our altitude it seemed 61E was twisting and banking through a labyrinth gouged out by the folding crust of the planet itself. The weathered bedrock was not only below, but just outside our doors on either side. Over the canyon rims, the far ridges rose in grand serrations to melt into the bluish-gray boundary between earth and sky and finally merge with white puffs of cumulous cloud.

"This is fantastic," I said.

"Yeah?" Jim had a different perspective. "The first time I flew in country like this, my asshole puckered." He explained that if we had an engine failure or other serious malfunction, there was no place to ditch safely. "Look around. We wouldn't have a prayer. Dead meat."

Well, leave it to a pilot to lay that kind of slant on the scenery. But I saw his point—clearly. One advantage of helicopters is that even without power they can "auto-rotate," that is, the force of air passing through the rotors will keep them turning, creating enough lift to maintain control for an emergency landing. But in the canyon of Crooked Creek we would simply auto-rotate into sheer rock faces, or if fate was kind, into a creek bottom studded with jagged boulders and cockeyed snags. This unpleasant prospect lent a certain sharp edge to the beauty—like an honorable scar on a handsome face—an extra touch of grandeur.

Since day one I had been forced to consider the possibility of experiencing a helicopter crash and, though the odds were against it, reach an accommodation. As Barry Lopez has written: "You accept the possibility of death in such situations, prepare for it, and then forget about it." Beyond conscientiously performing my own pre-flight duties—correct loading, secure doors, brief passengers—there was little else I could do to ensure the integrity of the ship. Keeping us in the air and/or safely ditching was the pilot's job, and, at least in that sense, a crash was not my problem. Or so it was helpful to think. Jim's puckered asshole served only to polish the glory of Crooked Creek's canyon.

As we settled onto the sandbar, Jim had me lean out my door to keep an eye on the tail rotor—make sure it cleared some patches of sage brush. This was definitely an "unimproved" helispot, and I was plugged into H-pay. I scratched out a manifest, loaded the four lightest smokejumpers (because we would have less fuel on board for the second trip, and hence more payload capacity), and Jim was off. I stayed behind with the other two, enchanted by the monumental geology of the Salmon Breaks and by the fact that I had merely dropped into this imposing wilderness redoubt for a stay measured in minutes. Trés chic. Other folks rode rubber rafts or kayaks for days—harrowing days—to attain this spectacular spot, and I was buzzing in and out like an Arab potentate. And I was getting hazard differential to boot. What a country! Small wonder there were fire grunts coveting my job.

On the flight back to Dixie, Jim and I debated about the canyon and the Breaks. I maintained it was gorgeous territory. He snorted and said it was only desolate. Yes, but that's one reason it was beautiful; and so on. In

Jim's view I was still very much the tenderfoot, not really a bona fide flight crew member, and he even brought up the consequences of a crash again, and how the canyon would offer no mercy. Fine. I wasn't sure if he wanted to keep me humble, or if he was whistling in the dark for himself. Maybe both. I grunted my acknowledgement, and we left it at that. There was no point in getting rattled.

The rest of the afternoon was quiet, and at 1700 hours it was time to pick up the other two jumpers. Scott asked Walt if he wanted to go, and Walt decided that, though he wasn't excited, he should log a little flight time—and H-pay.

As he and Jim approached the sandbar, they saw a couple of backpacks, but no smokejumpers. However, a little further upstream there were now two tents and a beached raft. Jim cursed. This was a wilderness corridor, and if his rotor wash set tents to flapping it might generate complaints. He wanted to get in and get out as rapidly as possible—where were those damn jumpers?

As the skids hit the sand they spotted them. The two smokejumpers, grasping cans of beer and balancing heaping plates of hot food on their knees (and grinning like fools) were surrounded by seven young women.

Imagine the scenario and mutual fantasy: The women, in the midst of a long, backcountry river trip, put ashore for the evening. Shortly thereafter, a pair of brawny, soot-stained smokejumpers—regularly celebrated as heroes, "wilderness warriors," and fine physical specimens—come hiking down out of the Breaks like wandering gods. For their part, the jumpers, expecting only a sweaty wait for a routine ride, stumble upon a slice of paradise—a bevy of attractive women in their twenties who are delighted to see them, shamelessly fawning and flirting. It was a stinking beer commercial!

When 61E landed, one of the women whispered to Kevin, who had just been on his first fire of the season: "Ohhhh . . . you have to go? I'm sleeping single again tonight?"

As Walt was loading their backpacks, Kevin rushed up and shoved his radio into Jim's hands. "Here! Take this!" he shouted. "I'm staying. Tell them I quit!" He was only half joking. With reluctance that actually hurt, the jumpers climbed into the ship, and as Jim lifted off the bar, the women formed a chorus line and performed an impromptu farewell dance. Kevin snapped a picture with the small 35mm camera he carried. (They were indeed good-looking women, and the photo is destined to become an icon at GAC.) What tormented Kevin the most was that he had set the time for the pick-up himself, before they'd hiked to the river. If only he'd waited. . . . But then it was all an impossible fantasy. As Kevin rode away from the Dixie airstrip in a Forest Service truck, we heard him banging his head on the dash and intoning, "There is no god, there is no god. . . ."

Walt mentioned that he had enjoyed the flight after all.

* * *

5.

In late afternoon on the last day of July we were dispatched to a fire about forty miles south of Grangeville, just inside the Payette National Forest. It was thirty miles or so west of where I had fought the Whangdoodle back in 1989. We had been listening to the radio traffic for about twenty minutes, jumpy and itchy, anticipating a call, and when it finally came we blew out of GAC like startled ducks.

It had been a long, hot day of impatient expectation, seeking out barely justifiable odd jobs to pass the hours. It's the truly difficult aspect of the operation—waiting, and doing so gracefully. Anyone can nurture high morale and alertness out on a fire, but keeping sharp and chipper on slow days at the base is a challenge and separates the dilettantes from the pros, the glory hogs from the A team.

And the challenge isn't restricted to the tedium of the base. Pat Wilson, who sometimes filled in as an aerial observer, revealed how he once battled the monotony of a detection flight on a quiet day. His pilot, monumentally bored with flying the same route over and over, kept nodding off to sleep. Pat was forced to man the dual controls and scan for smokes at the same time. It got old. So late in the shift he jammed the yoke forward, pitching the small plane into a steep dive from 10,000 feet. Then he frantically shook the pilot awake while shouting, "We're going in! We're going in!" It was an exciting moment, said Pat, but fleeting; ten minutes later the pilot was snoring.

When we got the good word to head for the Payette, an air tanker was already enroute, along with a couple of helicopters out of McCall. The fire, in rugged terrain (what else?) near a place called Devil's Hole, was at two acres and building. Scott and Jim went ahead with the ship, and I wheeled out of town in the support truck; Tim followed with the fuel rig.

By the time I arrived at the "helibase," a rock-strewn wide spot adjacent to the highway south of Riggins, 61E had made its first sortie, dropping off a couple of firefighters and leaving Scott behind to manage the helispot near the fire. The two ships from McCall were Bell Jet Rangers—smaller versions of the L-3—and the Helibase Manager divvied up the duties thusly: since there were some ponds relatively near the fire, one Jet Ranger would do bucket work; the other would attach longline and start slinging in supplies; and 61E, with the largest payload capacity, would be moving people and their gear—as quickly as possible. We had about two hours of daylight.

Six firefighters were waiting for me, lounging in the back of a pick-up truck with their gear. They looked unkempt and unprepared, and I assumed the worst: these must be inexperienced summer recruits, or worse, timber cruisers hurriedly mobilized for an emergency. (The Payette had other fires going.) I decided I should give them a detailed safety briefing while Jim re-fueled, making allowances for any greenhorns.

As I launched into my spiel I noticed I didn't exactly have this audience in the palm of my hand. In fact, only two were even looking at me, one glowering, and the other, a female, had her upper lip slightly curled in dis-taste—as if I were something freshly ejected from a nostril. And then, as I finally focused on their tools and gear and noticed the logos, it dawned on me that these were McCall smokejumpers. We had heard it was too windy to jump the fire, so these raggedy-assed (I had to provide chin straps for two of them), but arrogant folks were our first helitack crew. By the end of the season I had worked with jumpers out of GAC, Missoula (the smokejumper Mecca), and McCall, and only the latter blatantly regarded me as sub-human, or so they managed to project. (A friend from Minnesota who worked helitack at Krassel, near McCall, later told me he felt the same way.)

I was too busy to take much offense, but that night, when I had time to consider the episode, I was grateful for it. I recalled how they made me feel—cheap, embarrassed, inferior—and realized it had been a threat to my self-confidence, and hence to my performance, thus potentially jeopardizing everything and everyone for which I was responsible. I resolved to never allow myself to perpetuate a fireground pecking order nor to act that way toward people I might be tempted to deem beneath my station as an HECM. Renouncing arrogance transcends common courtesy; it speaks to basic is-sues of teamwork and safety. It's ancient and trite, but true, and seems es-pecially apt for air operations: "Pride goeth before destruction, and an haughty spirit before a fall." (Proverbs 16:18)

Since the fire was only about five miles away, Jim's turnaround time was short, and, as he lifted off with the first load of McCall prima donnas, Tim and I scrambled to toss loose rocks from the landing space. When we had a decent area cleared I spiked down a bright yellow square of oil cloth that Jim could key off for touchdowns.

The next ninety minutes were a frenzy of manifesting, re-manifesting as orders were changed, loading, briefing, and marshalling—the latter being more critical than usual since we had three helicopters sharing relatively cramped quarters. Radio chatter was a nearly constant buzz as the Incident Commander organized the initial attack, the Helibase Manager coordinated the shipping, and the pilots kept out of each other's way.

Our next squad of firefighters really were mostly rookies, with some never having been on a helicopter, so, on top of the usual hustle, I had to make certain they knew the rules and then watch them like a hawk, per-sonally guiding them to the ship. Since our flight time was limited, I had to make several decisions (some aided by Overhead, some not) about balancing loads between people and gear. With usable water near the fire, hose and pumps were a priority, but of course we needed enough people to use them effectively. How much hose? How many people? The short answer: as much and as many as possible. In practice, I gave people top billing and then stuffed in extra gear whenever the payload capacity permitted.

As evening approached, it was still hot, and I was slimy with sweat; unless I used the chinstrap, my hardhat slid off greasy hair every time I bent my head. Even the Velcro strap on my radio pouch was saturated, and apparently lost its sticking power, for, as I strode away from the ship after the last load, bent over beneath the rotors, my $700 King radio tumbled out of the pouch, and I inadvertently drop-kicked it as it fell, sending it bouncing over the hard ground like a loose football. Cool, real cool. But it still worked (that's why it cost $700) and no one witnessed the slapstick; I was particularly gratified that no McCall smokejumpers were hanging around.

Shortly thereafter, 61E raced for Grangeville to beat the official sunset, and I headed north with the support truck. The fire had gone to three-and-a-half acres, and I was bemused by the difference in the scale of resources required for such a fire in the mountains, and what might be needed for a three-acre blaze in Minnesota. This Devil's Hole incident had demanded two air tanker sorties, three helicopters going full tilt for over two hours, and sixteen firefighters—all mediated by the atypical feature of nearby surface water. Back home I had been on three-acre fires that required merely a trio of smokechasers with pump cans. That's topography. (And pump cans are usually more fun.)

In retrospect, it's clear the Devil's Hole gig was more or less my final training session before things got wild in the Nez Perce.

On Sunday August 4, we were standing by at GAC, brutally killing time, when the next bust rocked the airwaves in mid-afternoon. Jumper 14 was off, and we were inbound to Dixie. Gayle Wilson, the owner of 61E, was sitting in for Jim, who was on a required day of R & R. (The Forest service mandates that pilots have two days off out of every fourteen.)

Gayle was a good pilot, but a little rusty, and clearly tense as he was dispatched directly into longline work—our full 150 feet—slinging cargo nets of extra food, water, and tools to three fires manned by smokejumpers in the unforgiving terrain west of Jersey Mountain. It's one thing to fly a helicopter; it's quite another to fly it with 500 pounds dangling 150 feet below. And it's something else again to do that while dealing with the innate treachery of mountain air currents. And we cut Gayle no slack. As soon as the supplies were delivered, I removed one fifty-foot length of longline and then helped Scott hook up the Bambi bucket. The fires were near enough to the Salmon for Gayle to do some good with water drops. The blazes were active, threatening blow-out, so he pushed it until dusk. When he finally set down in the valley at Dixie, he had to switch on the landing light.

In the meantime, a half-dozen firefighters from Elk City had arrived at the strip, and, since they would be camping, Scott felt that he and I should do the same for the next week or so. The Dixie Motel was available, but he didn't want to engender hard feelings by seeking its relative comforts. I don't believe we would have, but it was a wise gesture, and I certainly didn't mind sleeping on the ground. In fact, as I rolled out my foam pad and sleeping bag, the partly cloudy sky over Dixie cleared to a glittering starscape framed by high, wooded ridges. I heard an owl far back in the forest, and, as I snuggled into the bag I experienced the warm, satisfying sensation of being in the right spot at the right time, not wanting or needing anything else. Here, at least for the moment, was my niche.

At first light, Gayle ferried the ship to GAC, and Jim flew it back. By that time Scott and I had set up a pump and hose lay at a nearby water hole ("watch for rattlesnakes," we had been warned) and filled six blivets. Several fires needed additional water. We also "built" a half-dozen cargo-net loads of cubees, cases of MREs, bladder bags, and miscellaneous supplies. Then for the balance of the morning we did hover hook-ups.

Again I was impressed with Jim's skill. We had the remote hook tethered at the end of 150 feet of longline, and Jim would lean out the door of the ship, deftly maneuvering the hook to "float" in at eye-level. I was able to smoothly (more or less) snap the ring of a lead line into the hook as it sailed by. In almost one motion a blivet or cargo net would rise from the ground, and Jim was off for a fire. The remote hook, painted blaze orange and equipped with four handle guards (so we could almost always find one to grab) is designed for such work, and though the Forest Service officially recommends that hookers have the pilot lay the remote on the ground before approaching, it was a lot more interesting—and safer, in my opinion—to do it on the fly. The key, of course, was to never take your eye off the hook, despite the loud distraction of a helicopter hovering overhead.

The next day I flew with Jim on another smokejumper retrieval down Crooked Creek to the Salmon. The temperature was in the high 90s, and I was sweating just sitting in the cockpit. The jumpers, along with some Red River fire grunts that we had helicoptered in, were to hike about three miles and meet us on the dirt airstrip at Shepp Ranch. We swept out of the canyon and hovered over the strip, but it was deserted.

"Well, where are they *this* time?" asked Jim, referring to our last retrieval on the Salmon, which had since become known as "the fantasy pickup." He followed the strip down to the river and banked upstream. There, just off a wide gravel bar, ten firefighters—stripped to their underwear—were happily cavorting in the cold water. They weren't particularly enchanted to see us. A group of their colleagues had been retrieved via a pleasant jetboat cruise the day before, and, due to a misunderstanding, they thought they were going to enjoy the same privilege—a thrilling (and refreshing) river run back to town. Our arrival meant they had to suit up in full protective gear and get all hot and sweaty again. Jim and I were unsympathetic. "I should just land on that bar and shut this damn thing down," he growled. "You and I could use a swim." Nice thought, but there was no way he would actually do it. We had a reputation to protect.

We spent the next day, August 7, mounting a few minor IAs, "demobing" some of the earlier fires (removing people and gear), and running more smokejumper pickups. Earlier in the season it would have been hectic; now it was routine, even a bit slow. But on August 8, the fire season burst wide open.

Smokejumper reinforcements had been flown into GAC from McCall and Missoula, and there were jumpers scattered on a half-dozen small fires in the Red River district. In the morning we transferred our show to Mullins and began supplying and/or retrieving them. These were almost leisurely missions, but as the temperature rose and the wind freshened, new fires began to pop up. It's not unusual for new smokes to appear for several days after a lightning storm, smoldering in sheltered pockets until the humidity and wind are sufficient to finally coax them into flame.

By 2:00 PM it was a circus. We were mounting IAs as fast as we could turn around, Air Tanker 119 was aloft, another load of smokejumpers was leaving GAC, and an extra helicopter was on the way. The Nez Perce radio net, barely adequate with a routine fire load, was hopelessly jammed with traffic. Communications—the most critical aspect of the endeavor—had been problematic all season, and it was maddeningly common to be "stepped on" or to interrupt someone else's transmission. It was dangerous. At one point in the afternoon I loaded a two-person fire team onto the ship—Troy, a veteran, and Tom, a timber cruiser who was going to his first fire via his maiden helicopter ride. Enroute to the smoke the radio waves became so congested and chaotic (with a faulty repeater somewhere in the system squealing each time it was tripped) that Scott actually pounded on his helmet in frustration, briefly hammering away with both fists. (Jim had simply shut off his Forest Service radio.) In the back seat Troy and Tom, who weren't plugged into the radio, stared at Scott in alarm, nervously wondering why their helicopter foreman was apparently going berserk. Troy told me later that he guessed at the cause of Scott's outburst, but Tom had no idea, and, when Troy glanced over, he saw that his companion was white and rigid, both hands raised off his lap with fingers reverently crossed.

When they arrived over the fire, Scott and Jim could find no suitable helspot anywhere nearby, so Scott radioed Grangeville and requested smokejumpers. It was a sensible, unremarkable decision, but there's a tradition of friendly rivalry between helitack and jumpers, with the unwise and the unprofessional (fortunately in the minority) sometimes taking unwarranted risk to "ace out" the "competition." So back at GAC, as Pat Wilson hit the alert siren for his jumpers, he yelled, "Hocking ordered jumpers! Hocking ordered jumpers! A twelve-pack for Hocking!" One of the smokejumpers sent in from McCall was astonished. "You mean," he said to Pat, "that a rotorhead *asked* for jumpers?" Wilson was indignant. "*We* work together around here," he snapped. Two days later a twelve-pack of Hamm's showed up at Mullins.

Around mid-afternoon, Sue Phillips, the topnotch—though harried—dispatcher at Red River asked Scott to check out a reported smoke near Butter Creek, east of Red River Hot Springs. We were surprised. We had done two smokejumper retrievals in that immediate neighborhood only a few hours before. I had taken one and Scott the other, and there had been no hint of smoke. We figured this couldn't be much, probably a wispy trace that was just now beginning to flare. I loaded two firefighters and Jim lifted off. Less than a minute later they had barely cleared the ridge to the north when Scott ordered an air tanker. Sue asked him to repeat. She was obviously a shade nonplussed, a rare condition for her. No one was expecting this, and a moment later Scott reported a blow-up—torching, possible crown fire, and major potential for spread. In a few minutes we could see the smoke from Mullins—the top of a burgeoning column partially obscured by the ridge.

A system that had been in high gear was slammed into overdrive. Within minutes Jon Foland was in the air, manning the jump seat of a Cessna and prepared to take command as Air Attack Supervisor. In addition to 119, he already had air tankers departing McCall and Missoula. Jumper 14 was enroute with eight GAC people, and a DC-3 with a dozen more jumpers was ordered from McCall.

Scott dropped off the two firefighters he had on board, directing them to find a safety zone and wait for reinforcements and slurry drops before attempting to move in on the fire. By the time 61E returned we had fifteen firefighters at Mullins and more on the way.

"Get your gear together," Scott told me, "you're going to the fire." I would accompany the next ferry of firefighters and then remain at the helispot, marshalling and unloading as we transported people and tools. "This could be a big one," he said.

By then Jumper 14 was over what was already known as the Butter Fire, and we waited at Mullins until we heard that the eight GAC jumpers had exited the aircraft. We then had a window of opportunity before the air tankers began to arrive, and we packed the L-3 to the limit of the allowable payload—myself and four firefighters with requisite gear. Jim complained about our relative heaviness as we lifted off, injecting a note of dismay, but I realized by now it was only recreational bitching and that such negative comments were simply part of his normal style. If Jim *stopped* bitching, then it was time to worry. His flying skills made up for his personality quirks, and I ignored most of his chatter.

The fire was visible as soon as we cleared Mullins—at least eight to ten acres and swelling rapidly. A dense mass of brownish-white smoke roiled out of the forest, occasionally split by tongues of flame. It was—in local parlance—a "gobbler," voraciously eating upslope with room to roam. Directly above the fire I could see an orbiting speck that must be Foland. I pointed. "Have you got a fix on Air Attack, Jim?" He peered and nodded, then contacted Jon's pilot on "victor" (VHF, the aircraft band) to outline our approach.

There was a large meadow about a third of a mile southeast of the fire, a grassy expanse bisected by a sylvan creek, and about 300 yards long by 50 to 100 yards wide. Here was our helispot. As we settled in toward treetop level, it was clear that much of the meadow was spongy, uneven bottomland, and Jim was careful to hunt for solid footing. In soft ground the ship could easily sink, miring the skids, or even tip over if one skid suddenly sunk deeper than the other. We landed at the extreme northwest end of the meadow, near the treeline where the ground began to slope upward to the woods. The skids dented the ground, but didn't subside.

I scrambled out of the front seat, and the smell of smoke pervaded the air. It was a tonic. This was the closest I had actually been to a fire all summer. I hurriedly unloaded the firefighters and marshalled Jim out. Tendrils of smoke were drifting into the meadow as 61E banked away for Mullins.

We collected our gear and took bearings. The fire was north and west, and we could hear it snapping and surging through the forest. Smokejumper packs, stuffed with parachutes and jump gear were scattered around the meadow, along with several heavy-duty cardboard boxes of extra food and tools that had also been dropped. On the eastern edge of the opening a single parachute dangled from the branches of a large fir. No doubt it represented a mortified jumper—the meadow was a huge drop zone by Nez Perce standards, and should have been an easy target. Someone was in for severe razzing.

The jumpers, along with the two people Scott delivered earlier, had already left the meadow for the fire. The folks with me would wait until they had a full crew, then follow. In a few minutes we heard the first airtanker. Its muted droning gradually surged to a head-turning roar as it swept over the forest at low level, preceded by the screaming swoops of a twin-engine lead plane. Foland, consulting with the smokejumpers on the ground, directed the tanker sorties from high overhead, and, as each plane emptied its tank, we heard him give the inevitable order: "Load and return."

Jon—"Mr. Mud"—had a well-deserved reputation for initiating and sustaining extremely aggressive air assaults. I was told his personal record was 22,000 gallons of retardant dumped on a five-acre fire—that's like spilling a bottle of beer (twelve ounces) on each square foot. It was a legendary operation, and the joke was that the fire crew present dug handline not as a conventional barrier, but in order to channel off rivers of slurry. Jon freely acknowledged that, yes, he had probably wasted a few gallons of retardant here and there and thus raised the dollar cost of some fires, but in the long run how much time and money (and forest) had he saved? No way to tell, of course, but it was an unassailable argument. As expensive as air operations are, it's significantly cheaper and more efficient to stop a fire at five acres than have one bust out to 500 or 5000 acres (or more) because the air attack was overly timid and, thereby, eventually lost a million dollars in the cause of saving a few thousand. Jon would further support his point at the Butter Fire.

When the third air tanker cleared the scene, 61E returned with more firefighters, and Jim kept shuttling until we got word that the DC-3 out of McCall was on its way in. By then we had fourteen people staged in the meadow, and the crew boss and I figured that was going to be it. As soon as the McCall jumpers were down, the air tankers would be back, and after that daylight would be waning. Dick Hulla, the GAC smokejumper squad leader, who was temporary IC, emerged from the forest and directed the crew to one of the flanks.

My job was to continue as helispot manager, and I was alone in the meadow as the first McCall jumpers hopped out of the circling DC-3. They left the plane in pairs, drifting in from the northwest, and as the first one sailed into the drop zone—only yards from where I stood—I saw he had a teddy bear riding in his leg pouch. This man turned out to be their squad leader, and he quickly collapsed his chute, squirmed out of the harness and prepared to receive his people.

By the time the second pair of jumpers landed, Hulla had returned to the meadow. A jumper struck the ground almost at our feet, and when he leaped up and removed his helmet, I stared. His hair and beard were silvery gray, his face creased with wrinkles. He looked like he was at least sixty years old. Hulla noticed my expression and laughed. "He's not as old as he looks," he said. "Late forties, maybe fifty." Still impressive. The man nodded and broadly grinned; he'd also noted my stare.

Then we heard a frantic shout from above and behind, and turned to see that a member of the third pair was in trouble. She yelled again, cursing. It was obvious she wasn't going to make the meadow. We heard branches snapping as she hit the treetops about forty yards back into the woods and saw the chute drape over the crown of a lodgepole pine, stretch, then stop. Hung up. "I'm all right! I'm all right!" she cried as Hulla and the teddy-bear man headed into the trees to assess the situation. To deal with such problems each jumper carries 100 feet of nylon let-down rope in a leg pouch of their jumpsuits, but it's a very hazardous fix. Control has been lost. The chute might be only precariously snagged and give way at any moment, or a branch or top might snap under the strain, and in either case a jumper could fall ten stories and easily be crippled (like as not in remote country) or killed. I heard Hulla shouting some advice.

The fourth pair landed farther down the meadow toward the creek, perhaps influenced by seeing their colleague drop short. I heard an actual "squish" as one struck a mudhole. He leaped to his feet, loudly but good-naturedly griping about getting his boots wet. But everyone seemed glad of the built-in cushion of flat, spongy ground. More often than not they had to roll with the punches of rocky ridges, or slopes of wicked talus.

I was surprised to see that the sixth pair sported RamAir parachutes, red and white striped, spinning and swooping like raptors on a thermal. These were BLM (Bureau of Land Management) jumpers on loan to McCall, and everyone paused to watch their descent. The rectangular RamAir is more maneuverable than the standard round canopy, so this expansive meadow provided little challenge. It seemed to me they were even hot-dogging a bit—circling overhead as if leisurely picking out the optimum spot for touchdown. They glided in, almost wafting, until poised about a hundred feet above their chosen points, then vigorously pulled on the toggles and dropped straight down into the grass. Compared to the round chutes it was a pinpoint landing, and clearly softer.

By this time the woman in the tree (a rookie, I later learned) had been able to lower herself to the ground, and I was amused to see she was wearing a hot pink web belt—a fashion understatement if ever there was one. She was also loudly vilifying the directions she had received from the spotter (jumpmaster) before leaving the plane. Her jumping partner, obviously a veteran, told her to forget it. He said that during his first two years in the outfit he had always been so airsick by the time they reached the fire that he had never understood the spotter's instructions anyway—had just done his own thing, and still did.

When we accounted for everyone, we backed off a little as the DC-3 made some breathtakingly low passes the length of the meadow, dropping boxes of supplies via small cargo chutes. The teddy bear man directed the operation from the ground, and jumpers shouted their approval as the boxes swung down and safely landed in our half of the drop zone. I pitched in to help carry it all to the helispot, and, after Hulla led the McCall contingent away to the fire, I spent an hour picking up the rest of the GAC jump gear and lugging it to a single pile near the edge of the woods. By now there was a fair-sized cache of cubees, rations, fuel (for chain saws) and tools.

As the second wave of air tankers bombarded the fire, Robert, one of the people Scott had dropped off at the very beginning, hurried out of the woods to retrieve a saw pack. I had to chuckle. He had been on the fire for two and one half hours, working like a fiend; his shirt and helmet were streaked with retardant, his face was black with soot and smeared with snot, and he was drenched with dirty sweat, but he was also radiant—happy as a fly on shit and grinning like a fool.

"Having fun, Robert?"

"Oh, man! What a great fire! Great fire."

I slung the saw pack onto his shoulders, and he hustled off, eager to get back on the line. A genuine fire hog; the boy might go far—if there was any place to go. A fire can be "great," but, unfortunately, it's rarely a career track. But Robert had made me restless. I had nothing left to do, and it was maddening to be so near a fire and not join in the battle. No matter; I had to man the helispot until directed otherwise. There was so much critical radio traffic during air operations that I didn't dare intrude with a trivial request about my role for the rest of the day.

I munched an MRE for supper, and, as the wind died and sundown approached, a horde of mosquitoes materialized, and I was forced to keep swatting and moving. I was tempted to just grab a pulaski or shovel and head for the fire. If I was going to be expending energy I might as well be digging line. But after the air tankers left again there was a relative lull in the radio chatter, and I contacted Hulla to see if he had any word on my status.

He surprised me by coming back with, "Stay or leave? What's your preference?" Since when did my preference count for anything? Before Scott had dispatched me out of Mullins he had told me to be prepared to spend the night. Via the radio, I knew that 61E had been busy with new IAs since I had seen it last, and it would soon be too dark to fly. I honestly didn't want Jim to make a special low-light trip just for me. I told Hulla I was willing to stay and I would be happy to tie in with one of the crews and work the fire.

"Stand by," he replied.

About three minutes later he called and asked if there was much smoke in the meadow. Negative. Okay, then 61E was inbound to Butter. I was disappointed; I had been looking forward to getting out on the line.

In less than ten minutes I heard the rotors. Mist rose from the creek, and the sun was behind the ridge, hugging the horizon. It was dusk in the meadow, and 61E hove into view in a burst of colored flashing—running lights and landing beacon ablaze—like a swinging sciopticon beneath the high smoke of Butter. It was silly, I knew, but I felt suddenly privileged, almost royal, to realize that this powerful, beautiful airship was flying in just for me. There was even a twinge of guilt. It seemed decadent to climb aboard without at least hefting some cargo onto the L-3. But this was it— my taxi.

Before we reached Mullins, the sun set beyond the ridges in a vibrant splash of deep orange, tinting feathery cirrus clouds to gold, then pink. This, I thought—encompassing all I had seen and done that day—is very good. And we had tallied more overtime and H-pay to boot.

✼ ✼ ✼

6.

The next day it topped 100 degrees at treeless Mullins, and, despite the savage heat, we labored like mules, still in the thick of mounting IAs. The Nez Perce was strapped for veteran firefighters, and most timber and trail crews had been mobilized. It became part of my responsibility to form IA teams with the personnel available, and via brisk interviews and a certain grim catopsis born of long experience, I separated the sheep from the goats. I tried to pair our remaining vets with rookies, made sure that only qualified people (at least *officially* qualified) packed chain saws, that neophytes were carrying plenty of water and other critical items, and that we generally didn't ship someone to a location and situation that instantly plunged them in over their eyeballs. I reminded nervous greenhorns of basic procedures. For example, in the hustle and excitement of initial attack, some folks were forgetting to turn on their handheld radios after they left the ship, and it drove Scott nuts trying to figure out if people were okay and had found their fires, or whether their radios were even functional. Nothing's more frustrating than being out of touch with a fire crew. Good communications are a security blanket for all concerned. A lot of ugly things can happen out on a fire, and it's always comforting for people to be able to tell that they're not happening.

Two-Sierra-Bravo, a Bell Super 204 (Huey)—a larger medium-class helicopter (61E was considered to be a light ship)—had assumed our responsibilities at the Butter Fire, hauling in crews and making bucket drops on hot spots. Predictably, Mr. Mud had taken flak for dumping nine airtanker loads the previous afternoon, but at mid-morning the Butter blew out, and the IC was screaming for more tankers. The fire grew to twenty-five acres, and Foland ended up ordering a total of 43,000 gallons of slurry. By evening the situation was firmly in hand, and Mr. Mud had seen his modus operandi justified. "Load and return!" If anything, the first day's sorties had been conservative.

By late afternoon Jim had accumulated seven and one-half of his allowable eight hours of flight time, and we had transported over two dozen people to twelve new fires. GAC had long since run out of smokejumpers, and the jump plane out of Grangeville was staffed with squads from McCall and Missoula.

But the next day the bust abruptly tapered off. There were no new IAs, and we spent the tenth and eleventh days demobing firefighters and slinging out jump gear. The action gradually ground to a halt by the afternoon of the eleventh, and for the last few hours we had nothing to do but stand by, crawling under the trucks for what paltry shelter they offered from brain-broiling sun, reading and napping. Such slack, boring shifts (thank God I enjoy books) have sometimes bequeathed helicopter work a bad name, and what rotorhead hasn't heard the epithet: "shade-seeking, juice-sucking helislugs!" Well, we would have gladly done some work if there had been any to do ("they also serve who only stand and wait"), but around 3:00 PM it was demonstrated yet again that there's little justice in the world.

I emerged from beneath the support truck, bleary-eyed and rumpled, and reached into our cooler for a can of apple juice. I had just raised it to my lips when a school bus rumbled by on the road. It was carrying GAC smokejumpers, demobed from the Butter Fire, and they gleefully hooted and waved, obviously relishing the fact that they had caught a helislug red-handed, "juice sucking," with the rest of the crew under the trucks. Ah, well. I raised the can in a toast.

A few hours later we flew back to Grangeville. In eight days I had logged 102 hours on the clock. Scott and I had spent one day off in the last thirty-five, and they made us take another one. I admit I wasn't completely opposed to the idea.

Typical of fire operations, the following week was as phlegmatic as the previous one had been hectic. A crew was still mopping up the Butter, and we established a helibase (that is, parked the ship and our trucks) in a pasture known as Sable. Our mission was to support the Butter project until it was wrapped. At the crack of dawn each morning, before direct sunlight warmed the burn, Scott and Jim loaded up a Probe-Eye (an infrared camera) and its operator and cruised low and slow over the black. They pegged two hot spots the first day, and one the next. Firefighters tracked them down, and the Butter petered out to ennui. Each afternoon we slung out some of the accumulated gear, garbage, and supplies, but ninety percent of our time was passed in passing time. On the third and final day of our Sable internment, Jim was so afflicted with tedium that he killed a portion of the afternoon inside the ship, wistfully programming 61E's navigational computer (LORAN) with coordinates for Cancun, Honolulu, Disney World, and other exotic escapes. I reminded myself that anyone can thrive on adrenalin; it's how you survive boredom that is a benchmark of professionalism. I read a book, completed a crossword puzzle, and twice moved the support truck to maximize what shade it offered. And yes, chugged a lot of juice.

A week later I was helping some smokejumpers do a little spruce-up painting at GAC, when an incendiary fire broke out on the South Fork of the Clearwater River, about ten miles away. Gawking and fidgeting, we could see the smoke from where we stood—let's roll! The fire was along a road, so engines were dispatched from Forest Headquarters, and a few minutes later Air Tanker 119 fired up, its four 1,500-horsepower engines generating a windstorm across the ramp.

Scott was wired, pacing like a caged tiger. "Send us. Send us," he muttered; then, eyes heavenward: "Why, oh, why don't they order a helicopter?" Good question. The fire was only a few chains from the river and we should've been airborne instantly, but there seemed to be some confusion out there.

Ten smokejumpers piled into a van; it'd be quicker to drive than fly. Their mood was bouyant—it had been a long, slow day at GAC, the chief excitement being an "ice cream flip" around mid-afternoon. Once or twice a day several people would gather in the Loft with a designated ceremonial half-dollar. We formed a circle, and someone would flip: "Heads." Each person who subsequently flipped a head was then "out." Tails stayed "in," until by process of elimination one person was left holding the coin. This obviously unlucky individual then purchased ice cream (or juice, if it was a "juice flip") for the entire crew. (Another popular diversion was Twin Otter Roulette.) The numbers one through thirty-two were written on a garbage can lid, and people bought a number for one dollar. The next time the Otter landed and parked, one of the numbers matched with a pre-determined point on the wheel when the lid was aligned a certain way. This winning number took the pot—part of which had to be donated to the "welfare fund," from which employees could borrow in an emergency. I believe the attraction of this game centered on the novelty of employing a large, twin-engined aircraft as a gambling device.

Tanker 119 was about to make its first pass over the fire when 61E finally got the call. Scott and Jim hustled for the ship, and Tim and I hopped into our respective trucks. I was out of town before the L-3 lifted off, driving happily toward an ever larger column of smoke.

A few minutes later Scott and Jim were nearly killed. They were flying down the meandering, gorge-like valley of the South Fork, not far above the river, staying clear of 119 and searching for a good bucket-dipping spot. They rounded a bend into another straight stretch and Scott yelled, "Wire!"

Jim automatically yanked on the collective control, and the L-3 shot almost straight up. They missed the powerline by fifteen feet. Another second or two of level flight, or a marginally less alert foreman, and 61E would have been snagged, destabilized, and almost certainly destroyed. Harrowing, but there was no time to meditate on what might've been. They found a deep hole within sight of the fire, and Jim landed on a gravel bar. Scott hooked up the Bambi bucket on fifty feet of longline, and Jim was in action. I arrived about ten minutes later, driving slowly past the fire to get a feel for what was happening. It appeared to have started near the road and was ten to twelve acres and spreading fast. The jumpers had taken the left flank, building a quick and dirty control line uphill. Engine crews were pumping from the river, protecting a house and couple of outbuildings with a hoselay.

The valley of the South Fork is narrow and ultra steep, and the fire was ripping upslope and flanking briskly to the east—more structures were threatened. Tanker 119, powerful but lumbering, could only lay retardant along the crest of the ridge in hopes of slowing the blaze when it got there. No one doubted it would. As Pat Wilson said later, "I've never seen one stopped at mid-slope yet." But attempting to contain the east flank, Foland (now orbiting overhead) ordered two Thrushes—small, single-engine crop dusters that looked like P-51 Mustangs and held 200 gallons of slurry. I watched in heart-pounding amazement as their intrepid (some would say, insane) pilots dived downslope into the smoke, released their loads of retardant, then pulled up into steep, howling climbs only a couple hundred feet above the river. Each time a Thrush disappeared into thick smoke, I found that I was holding my breath until it re-emerged. It was a magnificent, frightening spectacle.

But before the Thrushes arrived, Tim and I performed a mundane, unglamorous chore that earned us more kudos than anything else we did all season.

After I found a secure spot for the support truck, I called Scott on the radio. He was stranded on the gravel bar, so it was up to me to locate a suitable helispot. Jim would need a place to land in order to refuel, and we would soon be called upon to transport firefighters and supplies as well. Not only that, but Four-Sierra-Bravo was also on the way and would require the same. ETA: twenty minutes. I looked around in dismay. This compressed valley didn't sport much open ground. Tim and I hurriedly checked out a couple of tiny meadows near the base of the fire, but one was simply too rough and steep, and the other was near a powerline and offered no access for the fuel truck. Then Tim pointed across the river and upstream: "That spot might not be too bad."

There was a flat swath of pasture on the river bank, about half the size of a football field. It was hemmed in by forest, but open on the river side. We could see an old shack at one end, and some fence line—private land. I trotted over to a trailer house on our side of the river. A man was outside, watching the fire, and I asked him if he knew who owned the pasture.

"I do," he replied; then gesturing at the raging fire, "and that land too!"

I offered my opinion that a lot of the mature timber wasn't being seriously damaged (at the lower end of the fire it was mostly burning grass and brush), and then explained our needs and politely requested use of his field.

"Sure! But you'll need a key to the gate." He retrieved it from inside the trailer. We thanked him profusely, promising to inflict no damage to his property, and then jumped into the fuel truck. Fortunately there was a bridge not too far up the road, and in a few minutes we had located and opened the gate and were admiring the helicopter-friendly qualities of the man's pasture. It was smooth and flat, with a perfect orientation to the fire. We could see both flanks and the head, and it was all *above* us and downwind. (We had a ringside view of the amazing Thrushes.)

The single imperfection was a large piece of driftwood in the middle of an excellent landing zone. Tim walked over, picked it up, then shot straight up into the air. He yelped like a startled dog and bolted away. "Snake!" he yelled. "Snake!" Such is life along the river banks.

But when we cautiously returned to the driftwood the snake was gone. "What kind was it?" I asked.

"Who cares!" We tossed the chunk of wood out of the way.

I contacted Scott and briefed him on our new home. It was a routine mission accomplished, but he made us feel as if we had stumbled upon the treasure of El Dorado. Later, Tim and I were ceaselessly praised by Scott and Jim. I guess people just felt terribly uncomfortable until they knew we had a place for the helicopter to set down safely. They also realized that along that stretch of the South Fork such real estate was at a premium. And everyone was gratified that we hadn't pissed off a taxpayer (whose other property was on fire).

Despite our aggressive air and ground attack, the fire crested the ridge and spread beyond, eventually burning about 125 acres. Even before sundown, crews were converging from all directions, and we pushed the limit of available flight time. The valley was already in deep shadow when a bus pulled into the pasture carrying a twenty-person crew from the Idaho prison system. Six-One-Echo was just settling in from across the river, and Jim got on the radio: "Start loading those people."

They were a tense, aroused bunch. Atypically, they had a clear view of most of the fire, which was still rocking and rolling. One of the proverbs of the fireground is: "If looking at a fire makes you crazy, then don't look at it." Exactly. The fury of a cranking blaze has a fomenting effect similar to the whine of rotor blades. This crew had both, and, it turned out, many had never been on a helicopter.

My main assignment in this instance (other than actually loading the ship) was to get them briefed and organized without augmenting the inherent stress and excitement. Projecting calm efficiency wasn't easy to do while shouting over the noise of the helicopter and racing the fading daylight; also, I had discovered early on that pointing out crash procedures isn't particularly soothing. I did my best, briefing and manifesting simultaneously, but it was soon evident that in at least one case I had failed.

On the first load out, one of the firefighters was so afraid or excited or both that he was literally shaking—so agitated that if I hadn't been there to buckle his seat belt I doubt he could have accomplished it himself. As soon as the ship was off, I wondered: should I have sent that man at all? But imagine the crushing shame if I'd ordered him to leave the helicopter. Would that have been more harmful? Besides, I reasoned, when he arrived at the fire (in about five minutes) he'd soon be working so hard that any fear would quickly be transmuted into garden-variety weariness and pain. In any event, what was done was done, and I pushed it out of my mind; I couldn't afford distractions.

We managed to transport all but five members of the crew before 61E was forced to speed toward GAC and the sunset. Bob Quirino had shown up to help coordinate the helicopter operations, and we trucked the remaining firefighters to the base of the east flank and sent them up the hill, scratching line as they went. I drove back to Grangeville in darkness, dodging deer on the switchbacks. I flicked on the dashboard radio and heard the Doors singing, "C'mon baby, light my fire."

* * *

7.

By the end of August it was time to go home. We had heard of fires back in Minnesota, and that, coupled with the fact I needed to find a new apartment in Grangeville (a returning teacher had dibs on my place for the school year), convinced me to head east. But my last solo mission on 61E was one of the highlights of the season.

Six smokejumpers had parachuted into a fire a few miles from Buffalo Hump and the old Concord Mine, and Scott sent Jim and me to retrieve their jump gear. There was no helispot near the fire, so Jim set down on an old grass airstrip adjacent to the abandoned mine. With the helicopter "idling," I hopped out and pulled our remote hook and 150 feet of longline from the cargo bay. I attached it to the belly hook, snapped it all together, and then carefully strung the line out along the ground in front of the ship, making certain it would rise without snagging a rock, root, or other potential hazard. I pressed on the keeper of the remote hook with my right hand and signalled Jim with my left. He tripped the switch; the release was working. I clasped two rolled-up cargo nets into the remote hook, tugged on the swivels to make sure all was secure, then flashed a thumbs-up, scrutinizing the sky and the longline as 61E lifted away.

When Jim got to the fire he lowered the two nets to the ground, and the smokejumpers quickly spread both out and filled them with gear. Then Jim made two trips back to Concord and dropped them off. He landed, expertly laying the longline in front of the ship as he descended. I packed all the jump gear and miscellaneous items (about 400 pounds) into the ship, taking care to create a stable, balanced load, and re-rolled the cargo nets into tight ovals, hitching them with swivel hooks. Then I took apart the three sections of longline, deriving great satisfaction in being able to smoothly re-coil the stiff, feisty line using a nifty overhand-underhand technique Scott had shown me. It was a simple task, but of such are great and complex events constructed, and "he who is faithful in little is faithful also in much." You can stow the longline sloppily, or you can do it quickly, neatly, professionally. In either case it'll ride, but the crux of the matter is attitude: think like a pro, and you are one—no matter what your salary.

When I climbed back into the front seat, I was streaming with sweat and feeling euphoric. As I buckled my harness, Jim gave me a cockeyed look and chided, "You didn't have to do it that fast; no big hurry."

I laughed. I knew that if I had indeed taken my time, he would have chewed my butt for being too slow. I had learned back in June that when Jim or Scott said "take your time" they really meant: "do it quickly, just don't screw it up." In helicopter fire work there are often only two operational modes: dead stop or full bore. By acknowledging that I had done the job "that fast," Jim had just given me a rare, albeit backhanded, compliment.

But that's not why I felt so good; my quiet exhaltation as the L-3 powered up and rapidly rose higher than the mountains was only partly rooted in what I had done. While waiting for Jim to return from the fire I gloried in the solitude of the flower-speckled meadow, standing in knee-high grass just above the timberline. Behind me was Concord Hill, a bare, gnarled peak with eons etched on its face. In front was the Buffalo Hump, pushing 9,000 feet and a breathtaking caricature of its namesake silhouetted against the rich indigo of alpine sky. The old airstrip sloped down and away to the edge of the world. This was one of the highest areas in the Nez Perce, and I had a distinct sense of being perched on the crown of a vast region of mountainous forest. The silence was hypnotic, that brand of perfect stillness that seems to force hearing inward—to the hiss of one's breath and the drumming of one's heart. I suddenly felt so vibrant, so manifestly alive, that I laughed aloud and merrily waved both arms at Concord Hill and the sky beyond. When I heard the distant hum of rotors a few minutes later, I was sorry the silence was pierced. I must return to this spot someday, I thought, and spend a night under the stars. And then I laughed again as the L-3 settled into the saddle between the peaks and ridgelines that crowded the strip, for the whine of the rotor blades reflected back in from all directions, and now the sound was as potent as the silence, and the helicopter spun out its name: Six-One-Echo echo echo echo echo. . . And I knew then I would be back the next summer; I was hooked.

I returned to Grangeville on June 7, 1992, the weather dry and GAC primed for action. A Spokane newspaper reported that the Forest Service was expecting "the worst fire season in thirty years" in the Pacific Northwest, surpassing the Siege of 1987 and the trials of 1988. High country snow had melted early, and local rivers were already shrunk to mid-August levels. Throughout the regional fire service was an air of impending apocalypse. I was in the right place at the right time.

Our first bust arrived on June 10. We rushed out to Mullins and Dixie to mount initial attacks on four or five small fires, and it seemed as if the dire predictions would pan out as advertised. But two days later, fire operations were killed off by three inches of snow, and it proved to be an omen.

After a fairly active June, July was wetter than normal, and one particularly heavy downpour in Grangeville actually flooded portions of the tarmac. In a display of bitter irony several smokejumpers donned full jump gear and tried to paddle a rubber raft out to the Twin Otter.

During the second week of August—usually a rockin' and rollin' fire time—the chief task at GAC was scraping paint, and people were talking about surviving the coming winter on "Minute Rice and noodles." There was no overtime and H-pay in painting the garage.

Then things changed.

On August 19 I slammed into trouble. I thought it appropriate that, four days before, I had been swilling tap beer at the Triangle Tavern in Grangeville, listening to smokejumper Walt Currie rhapsodize over his salad days in the parachute corps—back in that lustrous era "when the winds were swifter, the trees taller, the slopes steeper." Sharing our table was a rookie jumper, raptly focused on the forty-eight-year-old fire dog with three decades of experience. The greenhorn's visage reminded me of a youngster glued to the flickering image of Mr. Rogers.

Currie spoke fondly of his mentor, a super-macho ex-Marine jumper (now retired) who had been a merciless taskmaster. Once, on a big fire that had "gone project," this demon worked Walt and his comrades for thirty-eight hours, and, when they finally reported to the fire camp, he ordered them to "go put on some clean Nomex." When they were all changed into crisp duds, he marched them to the check-in station and announced that he had "just arrived with a fresh crew." They were sent back to the line.

We roared appreciatively at the account of such audacity, pounding our mugs on the table, but it's fortunate most crew bosses aren't so bold and intemperate—more firefighters would die.

Nevertheless, it was boldness, of course, that launched us into trouble on the nineteenth. We knew we had embarked on a hazardous mission.

Like some heavenly malediction, a massive lightning bust struck the Nez on the eighteenth, igniting about 140 fires in a few hours. Our painting project was forgotten. It was evident that we had an emergency when the Indian Hill lookout, an expert observer with seventeen seasons in the tower, simply gave up pinpointing fires and tallying downstrikes. It was dusk when John radioed in and said of the myriad winking blazes: "It looks like a small city out here."

Next morning, 61E was dispatched to the Slate Creek airfield, a grass strip on the banks of the Salmon River south of Grangeville. It was near a spot where I had gone on a "ground pounder" with a squad of smokejumpers two months before. (A "ground pounder" is a fire that's driven/walked to, rather than jumped.) A truck with hot brakes had started a fire along Highway 95, and it scorched about four acres of grass and brush. Our chief fire control problem had been smoldering heaps of cattle dung that stubbornly resisted extinguishment, and the operation had been dubbed "The Cow Chip Complex." But that was in June, a typically benign month—firewise—in central Idaho. We were now living in late August, and the amber hills above Slate Creek spoke eloquently to the potential of the season.

Our main function was to run IAs out of Slate Creek, manning and scouting as many small fires as possible before they grew beyond what two to six firefighters could reasonably handle. Several teams of smokejumpers had also dropped into the area, and another priority for us was to retrieve them as they squelched their fires, so they could be quickly cycled back through Grangeville and deployed on other blazes.

Around noon on the nineteenth, we received word that jumpers on a fire near Scott Saddle would be ready for pick-up at 1800. They were wrapping up a routine "two-manner," and there was a good helispot nearby. We recorded the legal description and logged it on our "itinerary" for the day.

Retrieving smokejumpers had provided a pair of memorable moments over the course of the summer—one ugly, one sublime. The first had been during an earlier bust confined largely to the Moose Creek area in the Selway-Bitterroot Wilderness. Several jumpers from both Grangeville and Missoula had parachuted in to a half-dozen fires, and we set up shop at the Moose Creek airstrip, slinging out their jump gear, and flying those folks who could hike to a decent helispot. On one such mission Scott and Jim had settled into a marginal, uneven helispot where 61E wasn't as stable as Scott preferred. He felt the jumpers, who were from Missoula, should take extra care in boarding the ship, and that it was his duty to remind them—especially since these were people with whom he hadn't worked before. Often, due to the intense noise level in the neighborhood of the helicopter, we would grasp a shoulder and draw people close when we spoke to them, barking directly into their ear to ensure the message was received. Scott approached the jumper in charge, and as he put his hand on the man's shoulder, the guy angrily swatted Scott's arm aside. It was the arrogance of the elite: no common helislug was going to tell him what to do. He'd probably been on a helitack crew himself as some point, and figured he knew it all. Maybe so. But it was reminiscent of my safety briefing experience with some McCall smokejumpers the year before, and to openly display such an attitude was bush league—and hazardous. Scott's own anger flared, and in a spurt of ire he informed the jumper that he could either listen to instructions, or he could slog ten miles through the wilderness with full gear—his choice. The man grudgingly listened.

This kind of "cooler than thou" attitude isn't rare, and we were able to capitalize on it for the second memorable retrieval. Back in June, Jay and I (he was my fellow 61E crew member in 1992) had been sent to a training session in Oregon, and, while purchasing snacks at a local grocery store, we encountered a rack of novelty items that included gag license plates. We simultaneously lunged for the same plate. It read: "Get In, Sit Down, Shut Up, and Hold On!" We laughed, mutually recognizing our new helicopter safety briefing card.

Jay had this sign stuffed in his belt one day, as he and Jim flew out to begin shuttling eight Grangeville smokejumpers off a cold fire. Randy Nelson, their squad leader, was fond of giving us shit—mostly good-natured. He was also an ex-helitacker, a very proud jumper, and a hardcore firefighter who was quick to express contempt for anyone he considered below par, especially if the person happened to be a "helislug."

Acutely aware of this, Jay modulated his radio voice into an officious, demanding rasp and said: "Smokejumper Nelson. Muster your troops for a safety briefing!"

Jim, ignorant of the planned hijinks, offered Jay a quick glance that inquired "Are you nuts?"

On the ground, Nelson was wild. A fellow jumper urged calm as Randy instantly reddened, spewing bitter epithets about "goddamned helidonnas" and promising violence as an educational tool. One of the jumpers noted later that Nelson "was foaming at the mouth."

As 61E eased into the helispot, Jay could see Randy was livid, and he played it to the hilt. Strutting from the ship like a duke, attired in immaculate Nomex, he drew himself up before the jumpers and addressed them in a formal tone of command: "According to United States Forest Service regulations, I am compelled to deliver this safety briefing. . . ." Nelson was making zero effort to conceal his loathing when Jay reached behind his back, whipped out our "briefing card," and held it up. After a moment of surprised silence, the eight jumpers burst into raucous hooting—one actually sank to the ground in his mirth—and Randy turned an even deeper shade of red. He realized he had been set up, had sucked for it completely. But the prank had been so skillfully executed, he could only join in the laughter. It soon became a standard bar story, and to his credit, Randy looked sheepish every time the episode came up.

In late afternoon at Slate Creek I heard the Scott Saddle jumpers call Dispatch. I assumed they were finalizing their pick-up plans. Instead, they reported of the fire: "We lost it."

Indeed, the wind had abruptly strengthened shortly after noon, waxing gusty and erratic. Further east, the energetic Porcupine Fire was generating a swollen column of smoke, and the radio net was jammed with traffic.

We had been humping all day—chiefly IAs—Scott and 61E were on another mission when Dispatch requested that we bring firefighters and a bucket to the reinvigorated fire at Scott Saddle. It was in steep country (where else?) and had the signs of a major blowout. Scott returned to Slate Creek airstrip when his latest IA was accomplished, and as Tim refueled 61E, Scott told me this next venture was mine. He was fried and needed a break. I felt a surge in my gut. I had never run a helicopter IA mission by myself, and it sounded like Scott Saddle was evolving into a major challenge. I nervously manifested two firefighters and the Bambi bucket, and loaded them as soon as the fueling was done. Buffeted by gusts, 61E rose and banked away from the Salmon, heading up into the mountains.

Jim, I think, was nervous too—not because of the mission, but because I was in the front seat instead of Scott. Having me there on "milk runs" was one thing, but we were steering for an uncontrolled situation, and I had not yet earned his full confidence. That was made clear several weeks earlier when he and I had gone to pick up a couple of firefighters at a helispot in the middle of a clearcut. Unfortunately, the fire grunts—who had a chain saw—didn't make the ten-minute effort it would have required to clear a Cadillac landing pad. It wasn't terrible as it was, and increasingly foul weather encouraged us to get in and out as rapidly as possible, but there were some scattered logs and stumps to dodge, and a few protruding stubs that appeared to be about two feet high.

As we descended, I cracked open my door to watch the skids and tail rotor. Jim slowly settled in between a couple of logs, straddling a low-cut stump.

"Looking good," I said. The stubs were behind the cabin and safely below the tail boom.

"How's the tail rotor?" Jim asked.

"Clear." Our skids, after all, had just touched the ground and the rotor hadn't struck anything—we couldn't get any lower. But Jim wasn't prepared to take me at face value.

"No it's not!" he chided. He lifted the ship a few inches off the ground and moved it about one foot foward. We set down a second time.

Well, whatever makes you happy, I thought; but I was angry. The tail rotor *had* been clear, and when I got out of the helicopter I held my hands about three feet apart, indicating to Jim the span of safety. If he had really believed the tail rotor wasn't clear he never would have set the ship down in the first place. However, I got the message: I was still a rookie. I told myself that was okay; dangerous overconfidence wouldn't be my problem as long as I worked with Jim.

It was about twenty-three miles to Scott Saddle, only a twelve-minute ride, and I was glad I didn't have a lot of time to worry. I mentally reviewed the procedure of hooking up the Bambi bucket, and tried to follow our route on the map. This was unfamiliar territory, and that laid on an additional strata of stress. Through a jumble of radio chatter, we heard that helicopter 699, a Bell Super 204 was on the scene, and that Air Tanker 119 was due in shortly. Air Attack was circling the fire, which had already expanded to over ten acres.

About halfway there, someone jabbed my shoulder, and I started, getting another surge of combat chemicals. It was Derek, one of the Red River firefighters I had loaded into the backseat. I looked around, and he pointed out the starboard window, yelling over the flight noise: "Another fire!" I saw the plume of white smoke rising above the forest canopy and assumed it was the fire to which Jumper 14 was dispatched—we had heard them on the radio. In any case, we had bigger fish to fry, and I nodded at Derek and waved my hand as if to say, "Yeah, I see it, but never mind." I attempted to determine a rough legal for the fire in case I was wrong about Jumper 14, but in a few moments I spotted the Twin Otter at three o'clock and a thousand feet above. It was heading for the smoke.

"Jumper 14," I said over the intercom, and pointed out the bubble.

Jim glanced quickly. "Yeah." Ahead, the huge gray-brown smoke column at our destination was twisting to the clouds. Yes, Jim was nervous; I was scared.

Earlier in the day I had related a story to one of the firefighters staged at the airstrip. During the hot Minnesota fire season of 1988, I had worked off and on with a DNR oldtimer—nearing retirement—who had had a bellyfull of fire. One morning we got a fire call as soon as we came on the clock, and, as I hurried to an engine, I called out to the grizzled veteran: "Hey, Loren! You coming with us?"

He pulled a butt from his lips and pointed at his feet. "Hell no! The only ashes that touch these boots fall off the end of my cigarette."

He later assured me that "fighting fire is like shitting your pants—you grow out of it."

Well, I hadn't grown out of it yet, and on the way to Scott Saddle I wasn't entirely certain I might not pee my pants. Derek's unexpected poke had rattled me. We constantly urged our helitack crews to keep alert in the backseat, watching for flight hazards (other aircraft, birds, wires) rather than just gawking at the scenery, but that was the first time a passenger had hailed me, and my first thought had been: damn! what trouble do we have now?

That was soon clear. We approached the blaze from the west, wind at our tail, smoke rolling away. The pine forest was gorged with fire, as if the arms of flame were jostling for space, or tearing out of the earth itself to seek the freedom of open air. It looked like a mob of bonfires—All spreading—the woods couldn't burn quickly enough. We saw a couple of engines at the end of a logging road, and some yellow shirts scattered along the south and west flanks. The Salmon River was just below, and on the opposite bank—in the Payette National Forest—another fire was running upslope through two drainages. I hadn't even heard about that one.

Jim contacted the pilot of 699, who was already making bucket drops, and they agreed on a flight pattern to keep out of each other's orbit. There was a good landing area off the southern flank of the fire—a bare knob about five chains from a line of flames that was slowly backing downslope. It would put Derek and his companion below the fire, in clear view of people already working it, and provide enough room for me to comfortably hook up the Bambi bucket and one section of longline.

We landed, and I slipped out of the front seat, hurrying to send Derek on his way, and glad of the tension-releasing activity. It was a dazzling moment. As our two firefighters grabbed their packs and pulaskis and hustled off, Air Tanker 119 thundered through the smoke and banked west. A red mist of slurry lingered in his wake. Helicopter 699 made a water drop off to our right, and the 300 gallons nailed a jackpot that spewed a jet of steam. The fire's roar was drowned by the whine of our turbine and rotors, but my brain was charged with the heady scent of smoke, and, from a hundred yards distant, I noticed the heat of the blaze on my cheek.

I was excited, hands shaky with adrenaline, and I mumbled to myself— "take it easy, take it easy, don't screw up"—as I rolled the 140-gallon bucket out of its bag. I shook it open and stretched out the cables, attached the longline to the belly of the ship and taped the electrical connection, strung the longline to the control head of the bucket and snapped the hook into place, plugged in the electrical cords and taped them, then grasped the control cable release. I signalled Jim and he tripped the switch on his stick. The cable pulled smoothly out of the head; the connections were sound. I backed off and stuck a thumb in the air, holding my breath as Jim slowly lifted straight up and the bucket became airborne. It looked good—cables free and straight—and Jim dropped toward the river and out of sight behind the backside of the knob.

I was rooted to the spot, clutching my radio, anxiously waiting for 61E to reappear. I couldn't be absolutely certain the Bambi system was working until Jim made the first pass. After a long two minutes, the L-3 slid around the other side of the knob, rising upslope with a full bucket. Jim hovered over a hot spot about 300 yards away, and I heaved a sigh of relief when I saw the cascade of water plunge down into flames. My job was finished for the moment.

Six-One-Echo and 699 were working a line of fire backing through brush down toward the river, first one ship dropping, then the other, keeping the same rotation to the water and back. Perhaps if enough firefighters arrived soon, they could establish an anchor point for further operations, and/or keep the fire from eating right to the river bank. It was apparent the helicopters couldn't do much with the main body of fire.

I turned to face it, gazing upward at a hellish marvel. The terrain was rocky and steep, with trees and brush forming a green mosaic amid the stone. As the forest was consumed around them, the illusion was that the very rocks were afire. At one spot was a wide, jagged cleft in a sheer rock face, and long tentacles of flame were shooting out of it, snapping ferociously, fed by some unseen fuel. It was a volcanic-like scene, and now I could hear it howl. It was obviously going to grow.

The lookout at Chair Point was about twelve miles west, and in a few minutes I heard her call Air Attack.

"There's some weather moving in," she said, and reported twenty-five mile per hour winds. I looked west and saw a bank of dark cloud on the horizon. It was time to get the hell out. The bucket drops had been snuffing fire, but it wasn't enough, and I could see that squirrelly air currents were vigorously bouncing the helicopters around. With even stronger winds (and perhaps lightning and precipitation) bearing down, the operation was going to become too dangerous in a big hurry.

But Air Attack acknowledged Chair Point without comment, continuing to direct the ground assault and making no mention of suspending bucket drops. I paced the helispot like a caged cat. "C'mon!" I shouted to the air. "It's time to go!" I vividly recalled a rough-weather flight from a month before, when we had been shoved around the sky by the cold breath of a charging front, and the collective control stick had actually been knocked out of Jim's hand. And this weather sounded even worse. We needed to scamper, and I was chagrined that Air Attack was not directing us to do so. This fire was a loser until the weather changed. I was just about to radio Air Attack with a suggestion/request for our escape when I heard him release 699. Good! But then he told Dispatch he was "hanging on to 61E for a while longer." What! I didn't know then that the pilot of 699 had contacted Air Attack on "victor," the AM aircraft band, and stated in quite explicit terms that he had had enough and was pulling out.

As ominous clouds piled up in the west, I watched Jim make another drop and bank toward the river. This was nuts, and I tried to call Air Attack but couldn't punch through the buzz of traffic. In frustration I yelled at the sky again: "Time to go! Time to Go!" Even Tanker 119 wasn't coming back. A light helicopter had no business there any longer.

Six-One-Echo made another drop, and I was intensely relieved to see the nose of the ship swing away from the river and head for me. Jim was done. With the radio impossibly jammed, I wasn't sure if Air Attack had released him or not. No matter; I just wanted to skedaddle.

Jim's driving was usually butter-smooth, but this time he lurched in with the dangling bucket, hammered by updrafts, downdrafts, and the generally fickle gusts. The Bambi swung like a pendulum for several seconds, but the instant the skids touched ground, I scuttled under the ship to disconnect the longline, then hurried to re-package the bucket. I'd been taught to work methodically, ensuring that the bucket was properly stowed, with cables straight and neatly taped into two bunches, and the longline tightly coiled with hook and pear ring latched and power cord connected. The idea was that the neater these appliances were maintained and stored, the more reliably they would deploy and function when needed most.

I was trying to work more rapidly than normal, but I didn't realize at first that it wasn't rapid enough. I heard Jim yell.

That was surprising. Understand that he had to be shouting with some conviction: I was wearing my flight helmet, which is equivalent to having earplugs; the usual rotor/engine noise was present; and Jim was inside the helicopter.

I looked up and saw him waving his arms and literally bouncing up and down in the seat. Now what? I rushed over and he jabbed a finger downslope to his right and shouted something loud and obscene about me hurrying. A glance was all I needed. Flames were rolling up the north side of our knob, and the helispot was going to be burned over very soon—a matter of minutes, or less. That arm of the fire had exploded out of nowhere.

I ran back to the bucket, and for a split second I considered abandoning it and just hopping into the ship. But I wasn't conditioned for such a loss. Instead—perhaps unwisely—I snatched it up as it lay, cables twisted, control head dangling, and half-ran half-stumbled to the rear of the helicopter and shoved it into the cargo bay; water was still slopping out of the folds. Then I seized one end of the longline, yanked open the back door, and dragging the line hand-over-hand across the ground, piled it willy-nilly on the seats and floor.

Even during those frantic moments of sudden fear, I cringed as I abused our equipment, and actually worried about scratching or denting 61E. So thoroughly had I been brainwashed in regard to care of the machine and pride of appearance, that even as fire threatened to engulf our helispot, I considered the protocol of fuselage/plexiglass protection and how expensive the damn doors were. Small wonder I wouldn't just leave the Bambi bucket.

I slammed the back door (another cringe) and all but vaulted into the front seat. I had barely buckled in when Jim lifted off and we swung steeply to the left and shot downslope and away. I had never been so joyful to be flying. The flames claimed our spot.

Jim keyed his mike. "We're having fun now," he said. "And look at that, I'm only pulling eighty percent!"

I smiled. He was referring to the reading on the torque gauge—a device that measures how much stress the helicopter is under. During tricky take-off conditions—with heavy loads, bad wind, or a steep ascent—Jim would often call out the torque gauge reading. It was a way for him to defuse his nervousness and reassure himself (and the crew) that we had a margin of safety.

"Only eighty percent," he repeated. I knew he'd been scared. I sure was.

With my right hand still trembling a little, I reached over and patted his knee.

"That's real nice, Jim."

"Fire prevention specialists cannot accomplish the fire prevention job alone." — National Wildfire Coordinating Group, Handbook 4

Inside the Bear

I was displayed in full costume before a kindergarten class, being worshipped by wide-eyed children. My wage was $8.36 per hour, and frankly, that was my primary motivation. However, I was also there because in 1942 the Japanese Imperial Navy lobbed a few cannon shells onto the southern California coast. Damage was slight, but it's the thought that counts, and the thought was to ignite massive forest fires across the American West. The Japanese also dispatched balloons carrying incendiary charges wafting into United States airspace.

It wasn't as goofy as it sounds. The available manpower for firefighting was being sucked into the armed forces, and awesome quantities of heavy equipment such as bulldozers—critical to forest fire suppression—were being shipped to combat zones. A conflagration or two could be set off (like the fires in Yellowstone in 1988) and significantly detract from the American war effort.

This enemy threat, coupled with the usual causes of forest fires, prompted the supervisor of the Angeles National Forest in California to contact Washington and convince the Federal government to push a fire prevention awareness program. With the help of a Los Angeles advertising agency, a public service organization called the War Advertising Council sponsored a nation-wide media campaign. Slogans like "careless matches aid the Axis" gained wide currency, and in 1944 Walt Disney's Bambi—whose major adventure was escaping the hungry flames of a forest fire—appeared on a colorful poster that proved to be one of the most popular of the war years.

But I wasn't preaching to the kindergartners from inside a fawn suit. I was dressed in a full-body, $2,000 bear costume. I was Smokey, and until I wiggled into that deluxe outfit I didn't fully realize the startling power of that bear.

217

Part of Smokey's influence rests on a core of reality. In 1945 the government advertisers experimented with a new symbol—a teddy-like bear dressed in dungarees and a ranger's hat. According to the National Wildfire Coordinating Group, Smokey was "a natural peacetime symbol that combined the emotional appeal of an animal with the ruggedness of a firefighter." Smokey quickly captured millions of hearts, and the incidence of forest fires decreased. Then, in May 1950, the lovable image came dramatically to life. There was a man-caused, 17,000-acre fire near Capitan, New Mexico. After being overrun by flames and nearly killed, a crew of firefighters discovered a black bear cub clinging to a charred snag. Its paws were burned, but miraculously, the little bear had survived the "blow-up." The firefighters carried him out, and veterinarians from the New Mexico Game & Fish Department treated his wounds. Immediately christened Smokey, the cub was drafted into government service and transferred to the National Zoo in Washington. He quickly became a star, and served until 1975, when he was retired and replaced with a younger bear. The original Smokey died in November 1976, and was buried at a state park dedicated to his memory in Capitan.

So everyone knows Smokey is real. Unlike Santa Claus, the Easter Bunny, or Bambi, Smokey was (and is) flesh and blood in our midst—an avatar of sorts. One may travel to Washington to visit him. It's this basic truth, I think, that accounts for the respect and love that washed over me while I was inside the suit. That, and the Smokey Bear Act of 1952, which stipulates that the Smokey image may be employed only for the promotion of fire prevention, and if the U.S. Forest Service grants a license for the use of the image (consistent with Smokey's standards and status), the resulting royalties must be spent to further strengthen the program. Therefore, we'll probably never see Smokey modeling Levi's 501 jeans, or extolling the fire safety aspects of smokeless tobacco products. Smokey is pure, true to his mission of public service, and unsullied by even a whiff of corruption. This fact is implicitly realized by the citizenry, and Smokey is offered a level of devotion that elevates him to a civic deity.

If the costume wasn't so hot and uncomfortable, I'd be tempted to *live* in it, constantly enjoying the benefits of universal admiration. On the drive to the school, I waved to passersby from the front seat of a Minnesota Department of Natural Resources pickup, and people smiled, yelled, and waved back, as if greeting a bosom buddy they hadn't seen for years—honest enthusiasm was evident. (Except for the people who were simply too startled to react to a long, furry arm protruding from a vehicle window.) At the school we (I had a state forester with me) had to report to the principal's office. I took a seat in an anteroom after politely declining the apples and doughnuts so graciously—and shyly—offered by the office staff. As I waited there, the principal strode in from the hallway. Here was a dignified, somewhat imposing administrator in a three-piece suit. He looked to be in his mid-forties, and there was a businesslike, no-nonsense demeanor to his step. When he saw me sitting there, his face went dark for a moment, with eyebrows slightly pinched, as if preparing a disapproving scowl. But instead a smile suddenly creased his face, and, without breaking stride, he raised a hand and said, "Hi, Smokey!" There was no irony in his voice. As he closed his office door, I heard him say "That's great!"

Meanwhile, our plan was this: the state forester would enter the classroom alone and deliver a short talk about fire prevention in the forest. Then he would hand his portable radio to one of the youngsters and ask him or her to call Smokey. I was also equipped with a radio, firmly grasped in a hairy paw and pasted against my "ear." We had turned the volume down so we wouldn't cause a ruckus in the school.

In a few minutes a small, timid voice came over the air: "This is . . . this is Amanda calling Smokey."

I keyed the mike and lowered my voice to a friendly ursine rumble. "This is Smokey; go ahead Amanda."

The classroom was only about thirty feet away, and I heard the kids squeal with delight.

Then: "This is Amanda, Smokey; we want you."

"Ten-four, Amanda; I'll be right there." I felt warm and righteous.

As I entered the classroom, there was a general gasp—the suit makes me nearly seven feet tall—but I waved, giving a cheery "Hello kids!" The little faces settled down to simple enchantment.

The state forester asked if anyone had any questions for Smokey, and a precocious boy was on his feet immediately. He asked me how it had felt to go through the fire in New Mexico. I was impressed with his knowledge, but his teacher looked baffled, and after I had said something suitable about the pain and danger, she asked, "What fire?" I then explained about "my" adventures back in 1950. The boy looked satisfied and a little smug.

However, that was the only real question. Several children had statements to make. They obviously had heard a great deal about fire safety and were proud to tell it to Smokey. They mentioned "stop, drop, and roll," dialing 911, and having an escape plan—making no distinction between residential fires and wildfires. One girl solemnly stated that if your house catches on fire you should, "throw the babies out the window so the firemen can catch them."

The forester tried to get us back on track by reminding them about campfire safety for the coming Memorial Day weekend, and the teacher pointed out that although Smokey was a friendly bear, they should stay away from any bears they might see in the woods.

Finally the forester said, "Smokey has to go now," and I was just lifting my arm to wave good-bye when a little girl in the front row ran up and threw her arms around my leg. "I love you, Smokey," she said. In a moment two more kids rushed up to grab my other leg, and then the whole class surged forward, mobbing me with affection—squealing, yelling, and pawing at my fur. I tried awkwardly to pat heads and squeeze arms, but I was overwhelmed. The forester was backing out the door, bemused, and at a loss. Two boys were trying to jump up and hug my neck, and I suddenly recalled the powerful scene in the movie "Jesus Christ Superstar," where Jesus is thronged and eventually buried by a frenzied crowd of lepers, cripples, and blind people trying to touch him and partake of his healing gifts. Smokey had delighted and enthralled these children, and now they wanted to love the huge teddy bear.

For just an instant I was alarmed to be inside that stifling costume. My vision was poor and the kids had me off-balance—what if I stumbled and fell on top of them? But then the teacher was there to gently prod and peel them away, and I eased out the door into the hall, laughing. I knew what it felt like to be a superstar.

The official U.S. Forest Service rules for the use of the Smokey suit state that, "Authorized individuals shall behave with dignity when wearing the costume." A good policy, of course, but easier said than done when you're being overrun by a swarm of ecstatic children. Nevertheless, a puissant impression was made, and I suspect that if one of those kids ever starts a grass of brush fire, they shall be racked with guilt for betraying the bear.

Smokey lives, Smokey sees; and ultimately, you can thank the Japanese navy.

"I have met a few fellows that claimed they enjoyed
fighting fire, but I have always thought there was something
wrong with their heads." — H. A. Calkins, U.S. Forest Service, 1925

Fire Bum

I smelled smoke from the highway. It was the sweet odor of free-burning wood—birch or aspen, possibly maple; definitely not pine.

Nearby residents said they noticed it four or five days before, from out of the west, but weren't concerned at first. Woodsmoke is common in this rural area. However, it was early July, and no one lived back there, so it wasn't likely a woodstove. They called the local fire department, who called the Forestry office, who called me.

It was a pleasant surprise. Northeast Minnesota's spring fire season had been over for weeks. We were deluged with rain in June, and the woods had burgeoned into green luxuriance—moist, flowery, and damn near fire-proof. I was laid off and didn't expect to be on the local payroll until fields and forest turned crispy in late September. So when Tim, the District Forester, phoned to see if I was available (Ha! Does a fish swim? Do ticks suck?), I joyously donned my Nomex and hurried to the station.

The "incident" was mine. The foresters were busy with forestry—timber sales, pulpwood scaling—and were out of the firefighting mode. "Find the fire and deal with it," Tim told me.

"I love it when you talk like that," I replied.

As if he didn't know. I turned forty in the spring of 1991, and passed the landmark day at the station, waiting for a fire. But the detection plane went down at 1800 without spotting a thing. We put the engines in the garage, and a few minutes later I headed for my car. I was almost there when Tim shouted out the door of the office.

"Hey! Hold on! We got one."

Someone had phoned 911 and they'd paged the DNR.

I rounded up the other two smokechasers who hadn't made it to their cars, and we hustled to the garage and fired up an engine. Lights flashing, we rushed off down the road.

The fire had burned through tall grass adjacent to a suburban home, and torn into a stand of Norway pines. As my crew dragged a hoseline toward the blaze, I got on the radio to Tim.

"Leschak, Hibbing; we've got running fire in grass with some fifteen-foot Norways torching out."

Normally Tim, a well-seasoned incident commander, would've had something tactical to say—a pertinent question perhaps, or at least an official acknowledgement. But all that came back over the radio was: "Happy Birthday."

However, I didn't believe I would be facing torching pines on that day in June.

The people who had reported the fire directed me to an old logging road—a skidder trail, really—that snaked far back into the woods. It barely showed up on the aerial photo Tim had given me. I turned off the pavement and drove for about 200 yards. The way ahead looked spongy. My truck had four-wheel drive, but from bitter experience I knew that could mean I would only get stuck farther out than I would with two-wheel drive.

The previous April, for instance, we were dispatched to a fire whipping through tall grass toward a pine plantation. As we arrived, the owner motioned us into his driveway and across his backyard. I dodged a garden and a shed, and a twenty-acre field opened before us. The whole fire was visible. Its right flank had run into an aspen stand and was just creeping. The left flank was progressing, but would probably slow dramatically when it hit an old set of wheel ruts. The head fire was charging briskly for the young pines.

I motioned Steve to slam the floor shift into four-wheel-low, and I tromped the gas pedal. If we could roll to the head and deploy our hoseline, we could pinch off the fire before it started devouring trees. With the head fire knocked down, we could then leisurely secure the slower-moving flanks.

It was sound strategy, and as we careened through brown grass, jostled around the cab by ruts, bumps, and hummocks, our confidence was high. Phil was intoning a tense mantra of "All right! All right!"—high on the rush of initial attack. The idea was to "flank the flank" until we found a spot where we could barge through a break or low flames, and drive into the black. Then we would approach the head fire from the rear, in the relative safety zone of burned-over ground.

I saw our opportunity open at a place where the flanking fire had been reduced to smoldering by short grass. The field had been solid so far, and the ground ahead looked firm, but shortly after I decided to steer for that smolder, the truck started to bog down. I floored it, trying to power through, but in a few seconds we were stopped, buried to the axles in sudden, unaccountable mud. I rocked it once, jamming from drive to reverse with motor howling, but it was useless, we were mired.

While Steve defended the truck with our hoseline, Phil and I grabbed pump cans and chased the fire on foot, cursing as the first pines flashed into blackened sticks. Fortunately, I had called for the J-7 Bombardier as back-up, and a few minutes later the operator was able to squelch the head fire before major damage was done to the plantation. Later, he also towed our engine out of the muck. It was embarrassing.

The episode is summed up by the saying on a placard Tim keeps in his desk. Attributed to an old German artillery manual, it reads: "All skill is vain if an angel pisses in the flintlock of your musket."

Not wishing to tempt the angels again, I decided to park my truck and hike to the mystery smoke. I strapped a King radio across my chest, hefted a pump can onto my shoulders, and pulled a mcleod out of the tool box. I got Tim on the radio to inform him I was on foot, then strode down the trail, whistling. It was a sunny summer morning, rich with blue sky and bird-song, and the friendly forest was closing in around me. I was on the payroll again, and somewhere ahead was a fire that belonged to me.

During the regular fire season, a detection aircraft would have circled the blaze long ago, reporting in detail on its location, size, fuel types, and rate of spread. Useful data, to be sure, but death to suspense. In laid-back July, I was a solitary hunter, completely trusted to do as I had been trained. There's immense gratification in being awarded control of an incident—no matter how small.

And I had assumed this fire was small. But as the aroma of smoke per-sisted and intensified, I reminded myself I had no idea of the severity of the blaze. The twisting trail was hemmed in by hazel brush and a dense mixed forest of aspen and fir, so the view ahead could be measured in yards. It was possible I would come upon the fire suddenly, unaware of its true nature until I was on top of it. I might be surprised; I had been before.

On the same day that we had bottomed out at the pine plantation, Aero 1, the detection plane, had reported a fire described as "small, attended, and about to go out; nothing much." The observer sounded bored. Aero was al-lowed to continue its route, and we were dispatched to check it out. We groaned. Probably no action, but we would likely encounter an irate citizen resentful of our intrusion and leery of being cited for an illegal fire.

As we approached the indicated location, however, we saw a column of black smoke rising out of the trees. We were still a mile away and it ap-peared to be an awful lot of smoke for "nothing much." I was surprised; Aero 1 was usually a reliable scout. What we were seeing would become known as the Doghouse Fire.

The column grew steadily, and we soon realized that it was near a homestead. We wheeled into the yard and were confronted by a wall of fire in the woods beyond—flames shooting fifteen feet into the air and licking up tree trunks. An exhausted man, sweat-stained and sooty, was futilely beating at spreading surface fire with a smoldering broom. Over an acre of brush and trees was involved. The fire must have blown up just as Aero was banking away to head north.

My first impulse was to order a helicopter, but a quick size-up showed the "wall" of flame was a pile of debris (brush, trash, asphalt shingles) burning fiercely in the woods, and that the rest of the fire wasn't moving too rapidly for three of us to handle. After we had extinguished the fire edge with pump cans, and laid a protective hoseline to the pile, I ordered another Forestry engine and a local fire department tanker to aid in mop-up.

The homeowner had slumped gratefully onto his porch steps as we arrived, and, when the situation was in hand, he offered us soft drinks and introduced himself: "Hi. I'm the idiot who started this fire."

It seems he had been burning off a patch of tall grass around the doghouse, and in the dry conditions it got away, snapping through the brush until it ignited the debris pile and fanned out from there. He waved toward the point of origin. The doghouse had been consumed, and a forlorn golden retriever was pawing through a smoldering heap of dog food. He was stabbing with his snout, trying to eat the blackened pellets. "I guess he likes it cooked," the man said. Maybe, but it was an expensive entree. The bill for suppression costs totalled about $300.

All these fires were in the "rural-urban interface" where residences and other structures mix with woods. The interface presents a treacherous, demanding arena where almost anything can happen. The distinction between municipal and wildland firefighters and firefighting tactics is easily blurred, and, if likened to a playing field, it's a realm of curve balls, fumbles, steals, and trick plays.

What opens as a relatively innocuous grass fire (perhaps even a deliberate, legal hayfield burn) may spread to a garage or barn (or biffy), or, if especially greedy, to a home. On the other hand, a structure fire may extend into the woods, and on its merry way to the neighbor's house involve a propane tank, a vehicle, a pile of old tires, or perhaps a case of dynamite being used to blow stumps. You name it—it's lurking in the weeds.

I once heard of a forestry crew in a brush rig that swung off the pavement into a field of tall grass, rushing to intercept the flank of a running fire threatening a rural homestead. It's a common tactic—that's what all-wheel drive and maneuverability are for—but lost somewhere in the sea of waving grass was a discarded engine block that they abruptly pinpointed the hard way.

On one of my first adventures in the rural-urban interface, I was strenuously working the flank of a grass/brush fire with a pump can, my vision intermittently obstructed by heavy smoke, when I tripped over the rusting strands of a fallen barbed wire fence. I ripped open a brand new boot, and could just as well have torn my shin, groin, or face. I hate barbed wire; a downed fence line—corroded, tangled, perhaps partially absorbed by a living tree—can be flawlessly camouflaged. And there's a mess of it out there.

Though the risks and traps of the interface are legion, and could undoubtedly be tallied by the volume, one of the chief challenges (as usual) is people. There's no variable so complex as human behavior. After responding to wildfires in populated territory, either the suburbs or semi-wild townships with farms and/or seasonal homes, it can be a genuine relief to confront a remote, honest-to-God forest fire where people aren't a factor. Even a raging blaze with torching conifers can seem a relatively uncomplicated, almost refreshing affair, without the unpredictability and additional stress of victims, perpetrators, bystanders, or volunteers.

My engine was once dispatched to a fire at the edge of town. We spotted the smoke as soon as we left the station, and it looked serious. I ordered the J-7 and another engine. A helicopter was already enroute. In less than five minutes we turned off the four-lane into a wooded area dotted with homes and small farms. (I know I'm involved with the interface when I take a four-lane highway to a wildfire.)

We discovered later that a local resident had left trash smoldering in a barrel sitting out in dry grass. (A fireground maxim: "You don't generally get called to a fire because someone did something smart.") The grass ignited, and a brisk northerly wind pushed the fire across a ten-acre field where it barged into a mixed forest of aspen, birch, and balsam, also lighting off an abandoned car, several tires, a stack of old railroad ties, three or four discarded petroleum drums, and the cedar posts of the inevitable barbed-wire fence. In the next clearing was the neighbor's house, garage, and woodpile. It was they who dialed 911, certain they were about to be overrun by flames.

I swung my engine into the driveway and stopped in front of their garage. The fire had emerged from the woods and was creeping across the lawn. We could see an old man in front of the woodpile, vigorously beating at flames with a shovel. I rattled off the order of our initial attack: Kevin would grab the hose line, knock down the fire at the edge of the yard and work into the woods; Corinne would start the pump, then don a piss can and begin hitting the west flank back toward the field; I'd take another can and head southeast, scouting the extension and potential of the headfire.

We jumped out of the truck and scrambled around it like ants. I was squirming into the straps of a pump can and jabbering on the radio: the J-7, soon to arrive, should unload in the field, charge for the east flank and work around to the head; our second engine crew would fall in behind the J-7 to mop up. In the distance I could hear rotors; and then I heard Corinne say, "No thank you."

An elderly woman had hurried out of the house and was urging Corinne to come in for coffee! Corinne was smiling as she brushed past the woman, "I'm kind of busy right now, ma'am." The woman's face tightened.

She was clearly miffed that we were spurning her hospitality in favor of fighting the fire that was eating into her yard. As she focused her attention on me, I ducked in back of the engine and trotted off toward the relative nonchalance of the head fire.

It appeared we were lucky. The fire had run up to a narrow creek, and though there were several hot spots along the bank, this natural barrier seemed to be holding. I radioed the helicopter, and the helitack foreman confirmed that from his vantage the creek looked like a stopper. Then the ship set down in the field so a Bambi bucket could be attached. There was still flanking fire in the alder brush to the east, but I could hear the J-7 beginning to work the perimeter of the burn from the north, so I doused fire in the alders until I was out of water, then returned to the engine to replenish and take stock of our situation.

Kevin had secured the yard, and was mopping up with class-A foam in a windrow of logging slash at the edge of the woods. The second engine crew had come to him to refill their pump cans. The helicopter was now making water drops along the west flank.

I grabbed a full can from our engine and was about to head west to see how Corinne was doing, when the old woman materialized in front of me. She had a pitcher of orange juice and a bowl. She filled the bowl and held it up. "Have some juice!" It was more a command than an offer.

"Thanks, ma'am, but maybe later. We're still pretty busy here." She glared at me as if I were a five-year-old who'd refused to take his vitamins. This firefighting stuff was obviously just a lame excuse invented by a recalcitrant boy who ought to know better. I weakly grinned—guilty as hell—and hustled away.

In the meantime her husband—the old guy with the shovel—had battled his way into trouble. He had joined Corinne on the west flank, still swatting away, and, when the helicopter started making bucket drops, he refused to get out of the way. Corinne cajoled, trying to convince him of the hazard, and pointing out that the hundred-gallon dumps of the Bambi were snuffing more fire than his #2 shovel. He ignored her. The pilot tried hard to work around the old man, but visibility from a helicopter over a fire isn't always the best, and on one of the final sorties the stubborn gent was knocked flat by a load of water. Sputtering and gasping, he cursed the pilot: "He hit me on purpose!" No, but the old man was out of the game. He turned pale and struggled to breathe, then mentioned he had a heart condition. Kevin, also an EMT, rushed over to monitor his vital signs. He came within a whisker of ordering an ambulance, but after a short rest the guy perked up and resumed his vilification of the pilot.

After the fire was under control, when we were packing up our gear and actually had the time and inclination for a little coffee or orange juice, the woman was nowhere to be found. I figured that offering beverages to her "guests" in the middle of the initial attack had simply been her method of dealing with the stress. Or perhaps we were being punished for our bad manners.

We drove to the neighbor's house to check out the point of origin. It didn't require genius to see where the fire started. The burn fanned out from the barrel in a classic spread pattern so obvious that, if we had drawn it on a blackboard, wildland arson students would've accused us of over-simplifying. The ashes in the drum were fresh.

When I knocked, the owner shuffled to the door with an air of "Fire? What fire?" No, he hadn't used that barrel for a long time. He had no explanation for why the fire had originated on his property and spread to the neighbor's. Okay. I was polite, almost jocular—well, shit happens, right?

When I returned to the truck I radioed for an official investigator, and we headed back to the station—other fires were in progress. By the time the investigator reached the scene, the barrel, of course, had disappeared. It was a good argument for carrying a camera in the engine, but a better reason would have been to capture the old man decked by a bucket drop. Perverse, but true.

However, I'm being unfair—and hypocritical. Actually, I deeply appreciate the carelessness of the general public in regard to wildfire. If not for their rotted-out burning barrels, tossed cigarette butts, unattended brush piles, over-ambitious field burning, unquenched campfires, and a host of other questionable practices and outright screw-ups, my fire season pay-checks would be significantly smaller. Out West, lightning strikes are a reliable source of ignition for many hundreds of fires each year, but in northern Minnesota if we seasonal fire grunts depended on Mother Nature, we'd be orphans. One way or another, the majority of our fires are caused by humans.

One afternoon, about a month after "The Orange Juice Fire," Corinne and I were dispatched to a blaze at a homestead out in farm country. We could see a black column of smoke from six miles away, the ugly brand of discharge associated with some manifestation of petrochemicals.

A local volunteer fire department beat us to the scene and executed a quick and dirty knockdown of a fire that encompassed only about 500 square feet, but had involved a typical rural trash pile of tires, sheet metal, a toilet bowl, heaps of smoldering yard wastes, a pile of old shingles, decaying lumber, and miscellaneous auto parts. It was a mop-up nightmare, and after the customary token effort, the fire department left it to us. Most volunteer fire outfits can mount an effective initial attack on a wildfire, but aren't usually interested in the practiced subtleties of an efficient mop-up. So be it. It's more mission and more hours for us, and their primary responsibility is not wildfire.

Corinne and I waded into the task, prying up hot slabs of sheet metal to ferret out the embers underneath, tearing apart the half-melted mass of shingles with a pulaski (and trying to stay out of *that* smoke), and dragging partially burned lumber into the black.

The eighty-year-old woman who'd started the fire came out of the house to chat and apologize. She and her sister, also elderly, lived alone and were both diabetic. That morning (after a frosty night) the woman dumped their woodstove ashes on the gravel of the driveway adjacent to the trash pile. Apparently some coals had bounced into the grass, and as the day warmed and the wind rose, the latent heat was kept alive until it burst into flame at around 4:30 PM. Both sisters had rushed out to battle the fire, flinging buckets of water as fast as they could run to fill them.

"You know," the woman told us, "we almost put the fire out too, but," and she hooked a thumb toward the house and sneered, "but *she* got tired!"

I gently chided her for not phoning 911 sooner, but I had to marvel at the feistyness of a pair of diabetic octogenarian sisters refusing to call in a fire until they'd at least tried to attack it themselves. These were no pampered city folks, and it was unfortunate she hadn't more carefully aimed her ash pail. The woman returned to the house, and Corinne and I shook our heads and grinned. "We'll check on them before we leave," I said.

But a few minutes later the woman appeared at the door of the house and cried, "Come here and help me!" Oh, boy. It wasn't hard to guess what she needed, and, when Corinne and I hurried into the kitchen, we found the other sister slumped in a chair at the table, violently shaking. Diabetic shock. As I radioed 911 for an ambulance, Corinne managed to get some orange juice down the woman's throat, and by the time the EMTs arrived about ten minutes later, she was looking much improved.

Tim was in the neighborhood with his engine and, hearing our radio traffic, decided to stop by and offer assistance. The small house was cluttered with two lifetimes worth of stuff, and while the medics strapped the woman into a stretcher, Corinne, Tim, Lonnie, and I moved furniture to clear a path to the front door. As we wheeled her out, with two EMTs primping to protect her from the chilly wind and prepare her for the ambulance ride, she waved a hand in irritation and growled, "Oh, quit all this fussing! I'm not dying yet." Indeed. And if she hadn't gotten tired they probably would've beaten that fire and aced us out of the action.

Firefighting is often a mess of uncertainty and surprise. The recipe takes the complex chemical reaction of combustion and mixes in the vagaries of weather, the countless variations of fuel types and consistency, a treacherous array of topographical possibilities—all spiced with the unpredictability of human effort. The latter, of course, is the wildest card of all. In July 1989 I got a phone call at 3:00 AM. Would I join a fire crew headed for southern California? Sure. I packed and drove to the staging area in Duluth. A few hours later we boarded a chartered 727. It landed in Boise, Idaho. This development was greeted with general merriment. In this modern, ultra-channeled, over-organized society, one has to love a process so alienated from routine.

And that's the chief reason I was delighted to be hiking through the forest, slapping at deer flies and plucking wood ticks off my pants: this was not a civilized activity. Tracking down a wildfire—that is, stalking a dangerous beast, is a throwback to our frontier heritage. It's man against nature in a microcosm of the raw, elemental struggle that forged the American character. For better and for worse, the frontier toil and conflict is what made us. I carried a mcleod instead of a musket, but in spirit I was a scout, a mountain man, a Daniel Boone off to face the unknown. I was being paid to act out a youthful fantasy—hearkening back to the 1950s when my playmates and I wore coonskin caps. Our heroes were clearly defined. Though forty, I felt fresh; as young as all America 200 years ago. I was spitting on the fact that the frontier is gone—dead-ass done. Most of my cohorts are ensconced in secure, twentieth century routine—nine-to-five and putting on weight. That's not terrible. A regular income produces undeniable advantages: health insurance, a savings account, a pension plan. I often miss those amenities, and it's probably extremely stupid not to have them. A single mishap and. . . . But, I tell myself, I can always go back to a conventional job if things get tight enough. I worked a swing shift for ten years; I could do it again. Of course it nearly drove me mad, and sometimes I believe I'd rather die, but . . . .

A half-mile in, the spongy trail turned to gravel as I crested a rise and broke into an old clearcut. The aspen regeneration was amazingly thick—saplings packed like stalks of grass. The cut was over eighty acres, and the sky opened up. To the west, screened by popple tops, I could see the smoke. There was more than I expected, and it was pure white. Something homogenous was burning cleanly. Another quarter-mile and a couple turns of the trail, and I was there.

I chuckled. It was a huge mound of wood chips—the size of a two-stall garage. It was half-burned and super hot. The prevailing westerly breeze over the past few days had pushed the fire east through the pile, leaving a "crater" of hot ashes on the windward side. The remaining stack of chips was twelve feet high and burning from the inside out.

I studied the ground. From the burn pattern it was obvious the fire had run from the edge of the trail into the mound. My guess: kids on ATVs using matches to create a little excitement. The fire had also swept past the chips and spread into the woods, igniting some slash that had burned hot enough to kill several saplings. About a half-acre was scorched. I assumed the rainfall we had received three days before had put out the running fire, but the pile of chips was generating enough heat to withstand all but a heavy, prolonged downpour. My five-gallon pump can was useless; I may as well have brought a squirt gun.

I radioed Tim and outlined the scene. "Is there any usable water around there?" he asked. "Stand-by." I made a sweep around the fire, as far as a half-mile out, searching for a pond or creek. Our portable floating pump can offer an effective stream through 2,000 feet of hose. Water is usually the first option in northeastern Minnesota; it's almost always near enough. But not at the Chip Fire. I found two puddles choked with cattails.

I was sorry. A pair of us could have easily passed an enjoyable (and profitable) two days hauling in hose, extinguishing the fire, and hauling out hose. Portaging and nozzle work is always satisfying.

I reported to Tim, and by mutual consent we decided to put a control line around the fire and let it burn. It was probably best to get rid of the chips anyway, or they'd catch fire again at a later, more inconvenient date—like the middle of fire season, surrounded by tinder dry woods and cured slash. Tim would see about getting a bulldozer. No sense digging a handline if we had access. (We learned later that the mound was the residue of a local government project employing wood chips as roadbed material in a swampy area. Several hundred cords had been shredded into fill.)

I sat down and took a long pull off my canteen. I mused on how my fire buddies would chortle when I told them of the Chip Fire—properly embellished, of course. No doubt it would evolve into an inside joke of some sort. Scott and Phil were already in Idaho for the summer, following the fire season west. With any luck I too would soon head out that way for a three-week tour on some burning mountain. A week before I had been on stand-by ("fifty to seventy percent chance" of dispatch) for an incident in Arizona, but the weather had improved out there. Or deteriorated, depending on your point of view. My gear was packed and would remain so for the rest of the summer. All I needed was that $2,000 phone call.

The rest of our crew was scattered across the local economy in a potpourri of jobs that only paid in money. Stephen Pyne, author and ex-smokechaser, aptly calls seasonal firefighters a "migrant folk society." And so it is—a strange band of fire mercenaries, or fire bums, as Scott says, hooked on adrenalin, ready to go anywhere, and perversely glad to hear of drought. None would do it for free, and our time sheets are closely kept, but in the end it's not the money. How could it be? There's not enough. It's done for ephemeral, romantic reasons—like whiffs of sweet distant smoke on the morning breeze.

And of course there's always the angel piss.

"I went out to the hazel wood,/ Because a fire was in my head . . ." — W. B. Yeats

Epilogue

It's deep winter—February second to be exact. This morning it was –14 degrees Fahrenheit (not terribly frigid for this part of the world), with five inches of fresh snow layered over the foot already on the ground. I ventured out and skied until my feet got cold. I also did some writing, but it came hard. I haven't sold a story since early December. I've got forty-four manuscripts and queries circulating, and nobody's biting. We've been flat-ass broke for several days—living off the pantry and charge accounts. Good thing we burn wood, and that the proprietors of the local store are neighborly. (I suspect some of the neighbors believe I'm a derelict; but hey, there's room for such in these woods.)

Our discouragement has been dark; this career of writing seems vain and stupid. Lord knows it's insecure. And we're both fighting nagging colds—all clogged up and snotty. There have been better times. I know it's going to be a long night of hacking, and there's no cough syrup. But there's a dusty bottle of brandy under the kitchen sink, and, as I splash three fingers into a glass, I catch a glint in the corner of my eye.

It's the fire in our woodstove, reflected from a pane in the living room window. Fire. I see the flames in the stove every day, but this nighttime reflection is chance, a different angle. I focus on it and think: fire, sweet fire—there *have* been better times. There were fires that bred comradeship and peak experiences; that generated paychecks—fat and well-earned. Fire, my enemy/friend. Perverse maybe, but this cold winter night I see only friend. And faces—the grins and grimaces of comrades from a hundred battles, our happy bands of brothers and sisters. I fervently wish we were all *out there* now.

I walk to the stove and stare at flames and embers. After a moment I spontaneously raise the brandy glass in a silent toast: to firefighters, to fire. And this before I take a single sip of alcohol. This mood is not the maudlin glow produced by a couple of shots. Where did it come from? My arm seems disembodied, the lifted glass distant and unreal. But I feel a smile spread my lips. Yes. This came from far inside, from the core of who I am. Here's to firefighters. And . . . what can I say? Here's to fire! I do love it so.

I downed the warm brandy and slept a lot better than I expected. But there have been better nights: I vividly recall a spike camp in Idaho, a clear black sky in the mountains, suffused with the glow of fire, and in that sky a blood-red curtain of aurora borealis. Have I told you that story? I remember it well. And on long winter nights you are what you remember.